From Open Secrets to Secret Voting
Democratic Electoral Reforms and Voter Autonomy

The expansion of suffrage and the introduction of elections after authoritarian interludes are momentous political changes that represent only the first steps in the process of democratization. In the absence of institutions and guarantees protecting the electoral autonomy of voters against a range of actors who seek to influence voting decisions, political rights can be just hollow promises. This book examines the adoption of electoral reforms that intended to protect the autonomy of voters during elections and sought to minimize undue electoral influences over decisions made at the ballot box. Empirically, it focuses on the adoption of reforms protecting electoral secrecy in Imperial Germany during the period between 1870 and 1912. The book shows that the political impetus for changes in electoral institutions originated with politicians who could not take advantage of opportunities for electoral intimidation under existing electoral rules, due to high costs of electoral repression. Empirically, the book provides a micro-historical analysis of the process of the democratization of electroral practices, by showing how changes in district-level economic conditions and partisan considerations contributed to the formation of an encompassing political coalition supporting the adoption of electoral reforms.

Isabela Mares is Professor of Political Science at Columbia University. She has conducted research on comparative democratization and electoral reform, comparative political economy, and comparative social policy. She is the author of *The Politics of Social Risk* (Cambridge University Press, 2003), which won the Gregory Luebbert Award from the American Political Science Association for best book in comparative politics, and of *Taxation, Wage Bargaining, and Unemployment* (Cambridge University Press, 2006).

Cambridge Studies in Comparative Politics

Other Books in the Series
Ben W. Ansell, *From the Ballot to the Blackboard: The Redistributive Political Economy of Education*
Leonardo R. Arriola, *Multi-Ethnic Coalitions in Africa, Business Financing of Opposition Election Campaigns*
David Austen-Smith, Jeffry A. Frieden, Miriam A. Golden, Karl Ove Moene, and Adam Przeworski, eds., *Selected Works of Michael Wallerstein: The Political Economy of Inequality, Unions, and Social Democracy*
Andy Baker, *The Market and the Masses in Latin America: Policy Reform and Consumption in Liberalizing Economies*
Lisa Baldez, *Why Women Protest: Women's Movements in Chile*
Stefano Bartolini, *The Political Mobilization of the European Left, 1860–1980: The Class Cleavage*
Robert Bates, *When Things Fell Apart: State Failure in Late-Century Africa*
Mark Beissinger, *Nationalist Mobilization and the Collapse of the Soviet State*
Nancy Bermeo, ed., *Unemployment in the New Europe*
Carles Boix, *Democracy and Redistribution*
Carles Boix, *Political Order and Inequality: Their Foundations and Their Consequences for Human Welfare*
Carles Boix, *Political Parties, Growth, and Equality: Conservative and Social Democratic Economic Strategies in the World Economy*
Catherine Boone, *Merchant Capital and the Roots of State Power in Senegal, 1930–1985*

(Continued after the Index)

From Open Secrets to Secret Voting

Democratic Electoral Reforms and Voter Autonomy

ISABELA MARES

Columbia University

CAMBRIDGE
UNIVERSITY PRESS

CAMBRIDGE
UNIVERSITY PRESS

32 Avenue of the Americas, New York, NY 10013-2473, USA

Cambridge University Press is part of the University of Cambridge.

It furthers the University's mission by disseminating knowledge in the pursuit of education, learning, and research at the highest international levels of excellence.

www.cambridge.org
Information on this title: www.cambridge.org/9781107495296

First published 2015

Printed in Great Britain by Clays Ltd, St Ives plc

A catalog record for this publication is available from the British Library.

ISBN 978-1-107-10021-3 Hardback
ISBN 978-1-107-49529-6 Paperback

Contents

Figures

Tables

Acknowledgments

The accumulation of several years of research also brings about the accumulation of enormous debts to many individuals and institutions. I began working on this book during a sabbatical year I spent in 2011–2012 at the Center for the Study of Democratic Politics (CSDP) at Princeton University. I am extremely grateful to Larry Bartels for extending me the invitation to spend a year at the CSDP and to Michele Epstein for making my stay at the Center so productive. I thank Monika Nalepa, Miriam Golden, Tom Romer, and participants in the CSDP seminar for their very helpful comments on early drafts.

To construct the dataset used in the empirical analysis, I worked closely with a number of outstanding students in the graduate program at Columbia University. I am extremely grateful to Martin Ardanaz, Lucas Leemann, and Boliang Zhu for their impeccable research assistance. Some of the chapters draw on earlier collaborative papers, which have been or will be published as: Leemann and Mares 2014; Ardanaz and Mares 2014; and Mares and Zhu forthcoming.

I have presented individual chapters in a number of seminars at several institutions and have benefited from feedback and suggestions that have significantly improved the presentation of my findings. I am grateful to participants in seminars at the Central European University, Florida State University, Indiana University, Juan March Institute Madrid, Princeton University, Stanford University, University of Washington and Yale University, and those in the All-UC Seminar on Economic History at Caltech. I thank John Ahlquist, Kate Baldwin, Aurelian Craiutu, Jim Fearon, Bela Greskovits, Tim Hellwig, Philip Hoffman, Armando Razo, Jean Laurent Rosenthal, and Susan Stokes for their comments. Other colleagues have read and commented on individual chapters of the manuscript: for this, I am grateful to Pablo Beramendi, Matthew Carnes, David Laitin, Victor Menaldo, Aurelian Muntean, Pierce

O'Reilly, Tsveta Petrova, Didac Queralt, David Rueda, Maria Paula Saffon, Fabio Wasserfallen, and Lauren Young.

I presented a preliminary version of the manuscript at the Seattle workshop in Comparative Politics organized by Margaret Levi in March 2014. I am extremely grateful to the participants in the workshop for a lively discussion. I would like to thank in particular Alberto Diaz-Cayeros, Aaron Ehrlich, Stephen Kosack, James Long, Beatriz Magaloni, and Erik Wibbels for their detailed and thoughtful comments on the manuscript during and after the workshop. A second workshop was held at Columbia University in April 2014, and I am grateful to Sheri Berman, Page Fortna, John Huber, Kimuli Kasara, Herbert Kitschelt, Victoria Murillo, Wolfgang Streeck, Pavithra Suriyanarayan, Nadia Urbinati, and Stephen Wilkinson for attending the workshop and for their extremely helpful feedback. Carles Boix, who could not attend the workshop, provided detailed comments on every chapter of the manuscript.

For a third (and hopefully not last) time, I benefited from the wonderful opportunity to work with Margaret Levi and Lewis Bateman at Cambridge University Press. Lewis Bateman, senior editor for political science and history at the Press, recognized the importance of the manuscript and provided guidance and support in preparing it for publication. Margaret Levi also provided guidance and advice on the manuscript on many occasions. Ann Loftin likewise supported me in preparing the manuscript for publication. I am grateful for her wonderful sense of humor and her editorial advice.

Finally, I want to express my deepest gratitude to my family. My husband and best friend, Radu Constantinescu, continually encouraged me to work on this study. Radu has listened to countless stories of electoral intimidation in contemporary and historical settings and has provided invaluable suggestions about the big picture of the project, as well as the minute details. My son, Andrew, watched me with surprise as I spent endless hours working on the database and rewriting various versions of the chapter. I hope that one day he will read and enjoy this book. I dedicate this book to Andrew and Radu, with love and apologies for the family events I missed on more than one occasion.

I

Introduction

1.1. FROM SUFFRAGE EXTENSION TO THE PROTECTION OF VOTERS' AUTONOMY

The process of democratization that unfolded in European countries during the nineteenth century involved multiple dilemmas of institutional design. The first question concerned the scope of political suffrage. The transition from restrictive to extended suffrage took place in different countries either through the adoption of piecemeal changes in the scope of the franchise or through dramatic extensions that enfranchised nearly all citizens. Reforms enacted in Britain exemplify the first approach. There, the expansion of suffrage proceeded gradually. The first Franchise Act, enacted in 1832, extended the scope of suffrage from 5 percent to 7 percent of the population. The second Franchise Act, enacted in 1867, extended the scope of suffrage to 16 percent of the population (Cook 2005: 68). By contrast, both France and Germany adopted electoral reforms expanding the share of the enfranchised population suddenly and dramatically. In Germany, the electoral law adopted in 1870 introduced universal suffrage for men. Similarly, France adopted universal male suffrage in 1799. Although France reverted to censitary voting during the Restoration, it restored full universal suffrage for all male voters in 1848.

A second question on the agenda of democratizing countries concerned the mode of voting. An important dilemma that underpinned electoral reforms throughout the nineteenth century was whether voting should be open or secret. Although secret voting triumphed – an outcome that from the perspective of the twentieth century appears to have been inevitable – its adoption was by no means unambiguous (Buchstein 2000). What is remarkable about nineteenth-century deliberations concerning the adoption of the secret ballot is that significant theoretical and practical ambiguity existed as to whether secret voting provided better protection for voters against intimidation than open voting would. Both methods of voting had prominent defenders at the time, and the political coalitions favoring either secret or open voting were extremely heterogeneous. Opponents of the secret ballot included successors of the Jacobins; conservatives, like Lord Russell and Otto von Bismarck; Catholics, such as Ludwig Windthorst; and liberals, such as John Stuart Mill (Buchstein 2000).

A third dimension of electoral reforms concerned the adoption of reforms protecting the autonomy of voters at the moment they cast their ballots: Should voters be protected against pressure or intimidation so their vote reflected their genuine preference? Or should the outcome of voting reflect the underlying economic realities of the time? In both theoretical and practical terms, this third dimension of electoral reforms, which concerned the protection of voters' electoral autonomy, was an extension of political debates about the adoption of the secret ballot. In political terms, those who supported both sets of reforms shared the belief that granting political rights was an empty and meaningless promise if sufficient electoral guarantees for the protection of voters were not in place. However, in many European countries, the question of the protection of voters' autonomy persisted as a salient issue of electoral reform even *after* the introduction of the secret ballot. The nominal protection of electoral secrecy remained insufficient in guaranteeing voters' autonomy unencumbered by external, illicit influences. Heinrich Rickert, a Free Liberal politician and tireless promoter of reforms protecting electoral secrecy, argued on the floor of the Reichstag in 1895, nearly three decades after the adoption of Germany's electoral law, that "the need to create a guarantee for the secrecy of the vote becomes more urgent with the passing of each year. Nothing is more contemptible and in conflict with the constitution than existing efforts to influence the dependent (*abhängige*) voters and to make it difficult for them to cast their free vote" (*Stenographische Berichte des Deutschen Reichstages* May 15, 1895). Similarly, a commission investigating electoral irregularities in the French Third Republic noted the regrettable persistence of voters intimidation as late as 1903. This commission stated: "One cannot say that the universal suffrage is free. Because voting is not entirely secret, it cannot be exercised with entire freedom. The voter, if he is employed, faces the pressure of employers, if he is a shopkeeper, he faces the pressure of customers, and if he is a state employee, he faces the pressure of the state" (*Journal Officiel de la République Française* October 27, 1904: 2197).

Undue electoral influences came in a variety of forms. One form of influence was the transfer of money and favors. Another was the production of a diffuse sense of fear of retribution in voters if they chose not to support a particular candidate. The persistence of such undue electoral influences in the aftermath of democratizing reforms was attributable to a wide range of factors. The first was institutional in nature. Electoral rules defined uneven levels of punishment for different electoral irregularities. This created incentives for political actors to use electoral strategies of undue influence that were punished with less intensity. In Britain, practices of "treating" voters at election times were not successfully regulated. Consequently, vote buying was the dominant type of electoral irregularity. The French electoral law imposed relatively stricter punishments for vote buying as compared to Britain's, but it punished electoral involvement of government officials more lightly. The *pression gouvernamentale* was therefore a pervasive electoral irregularity during both the Second Empire and the Third Republic. In Germany, the electoral law imposed relatively strong punishments for vote buying (which fell under the incidence of penal law). By contrast, electoral intimidation by private actors was one type of electoral offense that was unpunished.

Second, the autonomy of the vote was imperfectly protected even after the adoption of the secret ballot because of imperfections in voting technology. The two most prominent imperfections in voting technology concerned the design of the ballot and the design of the urn. Prior to the adoption of uniform standardized ballots – also known as Australian ballots – politicians manipulated the shape, color, and size of ballots to keep track of voters' electoral choices. Ballots with visible external differences were widely encountered in French and German elections. In France, the so-called *bulletins à clef* allowed electoral officials responsible for vote counting to identify voters' choices. In Germany, candidates competed using ballots of different shapes in an effort to observe the choices of voters. Imperfections in the designs of urns also created opportunities for the violation of voting secrecy. The use of small urns or urns of irregular shape enabled the stacking of ballots. If persons located in the polling stations maintained lists recording the order in which voters cast their ballots, it was relatively straightforward to identify the electoral choice made by every single voter.

After the adoption of electoral secrecy, economic inequalities continued to prevent the political autonomy of voters. One German politician summarized these political realities in a debate in the German Reichstag by observing that "the absence of economic freedom leads to the absence of political freedom" (*Stenographische Berichte des Deutschen Reichstages* May 15, 1895). Electoral autonomy and the freedom of voters to cast their votes for their preferred candidates were very distant political goals in elections where powerful rural and urban employers regimented their employees, marched them to the voting areas, and closely monitored their electoral choices. Economic intimidation of voters by powerful actors was a pervasive phenomenon in many European countries during the nineteenth century. Both rural and urban employers used their privileged labor market position to engage in such electoral intimidation. In Britain, large manufacturing firms in industrial constituencies used their economic position to influence the decisions of voters (Hanham 1959: 68–90; Nossiter 1974). In France, electoral reports of the Third Republic present ample evidence of electoral intimidation by rural employers. Finally, employer intimidation was also widely documented in German national elections.

Many nineteenth-century political reformers warned that the adoption of universal suffrage was only an illusion in environments characterized by pervasive economic inequality (Gagel 1958: 9; Anderson 2000: 153). Consider the worries voiced when universal suffrage was adopted in Germany in 1871.

At the time, politicians argued that "the person who has a significant social position, a great landowner or a great employer in the business world will exercise such an influence in every kind of election" (Meyer 1901: 240). In Britain, reformers also acknowledged the existence of electoral intimidation by private actors. There, we find both greater ambiguity about the normative implications of this private intimidation and an effort to distinguish between good and bad influences. For James Mill, for instance, legitimate influence prevailed where wealth was used benevolently, and it was a consequence of the "affection and reverence" of members of a community for their benefactor. The evil influence that had to be stopped prevailed where "wealth was used to control the will" (Mill 1963: 325–326).

To protect voters against these electoral influences and ensure their political autonomy, many first-wave democratizers adopted a range of additional political reforms. These reforms were adopted in two distinct stages. In the first stage, open voting was replaced by the secret ballot. Yet, in most countries, the adoption of the secret ballot did not guarantee the complete protection of voters against intimidation. In the second stage of reform of democratizing practices, many countries adopted further changes in electoral technology in an attempt to reduce the observability of the vote. This legislation mandated changes in ballot design or changes in the design of the urn. However, a significant temporal lag existed between the adoption of the secret ballot and the introduction of these additional reforms aiming to protect voters against intimidation. In France – where the secret ballot was adopted in 1795 – provisions mandating the introduction of a standardized urn were adopted only in 1914. Similarly, in Germany, legislation mandating ballot envelopes was adopted in 1903, more than three decades after the adoption of universal suffrage. Provisions for a standardized urn were introduced only in 1914.

All of these additional changes in electoral rules were important components of the process of democratization. Despite their importance, they have been insufficiently studied in the literature examining the determinants of democratization. With very few exceptions, the existing literature has examined either the decisions of incumbent elites to extend the scope of suffrage or the decisions of losers of democratic transitions to accept political defeat (Przeworski et al. 2000; Boix 2002). Regrettably, the study of electoral reforms reducing opportunities for electoral intimidation and protecting the political freedom of voters continues to be a blindspot in the literature on democratization. One possible explanation for this omission is that the substance of these reforms – which involves minute and technical details that concern the organization of the voting process – rarely makes the stuff of dramatic narratives. More dramatic changes in electoral institutions, such as those that expanded the scope of suffrage and granted lower-income citizens the right to vote, have overshadowed these subsequent reforms. One notable exception is Seymour and Frary's *How the World Votes*, a classic account of electoral reforms adopted during the nineteenth century (Seymour and Frary 1918). This study, which was published nearly a century ago, has not been followed by any other accounts of electoral reforms involving changes in the technology of voting.

The omission of these reforms by the literature on democratization has had stark consequences. Although we know a lot about the factors that have affected political decisions to expand the right to vote, we know remarkably little about the factors that have contributed to the further democratization of electoral practices following the adoption of nominally free elections. One consequence of this dearth of theoretical and empirical knowledge is that political science provides remarkably few insights that are relevant to new democracies that have adopted nominally free elections but still experience significant irregularities in their electoral practices. By examining the historical experiences of European countries and identifying the factors that accounted for the adoption of reforms that protected voter autonomy and, more generally, the integrity of the electoral process, this book opens up a new avenue of theoretical and empirical understanding that has implications for recent democracies.

This book presents an explanation for the adoption of electoral reforms aiming to protect voter autonomy. These reforms constitute a second stage of the process of democratization that has hitherto received insufficient attention. The central argument advanced in the book is that demand for these electoral reforms originated with politicians who encountered high costs of electoral intimidation and thus could not take advantage of the opportunities for electoral intimidation that were present under existing institutional rules. Politicians' calculations about the desirability of the political status quo were affected both by partisan factors and by economic conditions in electoral districts. With respect to partisanship, I argue that one finds a salient cleavage over the desirability of electoral reforms between politicians from parties with ties to actors who could engage in the intimidation of voters and politicians from parties that lacked such ties. Politicians from parties with ties to employees of the state and private actors opposed changes to electoral rules. By contrast, politicians who lacked these ties and who could not take advantage of the imperfections in the design of electoral rules supported changes to the political status quo. One important factor that contributed to the creation of an encompassing coalition favoring electoral reforms was the growth in political strength of these outsider parties, such as the Zentrum.

In addition to partisan variables, I show that support for changes in electoral rules was also affected by the economic and political conditions in a district. I show that politicians who encountered relatively higher costs of electoral intimidation – because of unfavorable economic and political conditions in a district – were also more likely to support changes in electoral rules. By contrast, politicians who encountered lower economic and political costs of intimidation supported the political status quo. In the empirical analysis presented in this book, I examine the relative importance of a large number of district-level economic and political factors influencing the costs of electoral repression. I show that economic heterogeneity was a strong and important predictor of political support for electoral reforms. Politicians from districts with high economic heterogeneity who were less likely to rely on economic intimidation by employers were more likely to support electoral reforms as compared to politicians from districts with high levels of economic concentration.

Empirically, this book analyzes electoral politics in Imperial Germany during the period from 1870 to 1912. In 1871, Germany took a significant democratic leap by adopting universal manhood suffrage for elections to the national parliament. The electoral law adopted at that time also introduced the principle of electoral secrecy for national elections. By contrast, open voting was still maintained in subnational elections in Prussia, the largest German state, as well as in several other principalities. Despite the adoption of the principle of electoral secrecy for national elections, imperfections in electoral technology contributed to frequent violations of electoral secrecy. Other imperfections in the design of the electoral code let private actors go unpunished for perpetrating electoral intimidation.

Germany's political experience confirmed the worries of nineteenth-century reformers. Imperfect electoral institutions and high levels of economic inequality led to the systematic and persistent violation of voters' autonomy. Electoral intimidation was, as Lavinia Anderson has argued, a pervasive, *taken-for-granted* feature of electoral politics (Anderson 2000: 29). Prominent politicians and constitutional experts at the time believed that the use of repression and intimidation were acceptable strategies during elections. Paul Laband, a leading constitutional scholar at the time and the author of *Das Staatsrecht des Deutschen Reiches* maintained that the right to influence elections was "an inalienable human right" (Anderson 2000: 29). Along similar lines, other conservative politicians suggested that the electoral law was specifically designed to encourage intimidation. Ludwig von Gehrlach, a conservative politician, claimed that election freedom was the freedom to influence elections (Anderson 2000: 29). Friedrich von Behr, a Free Conservative politician from Greifswald, argued that the goal of a campaign "is to exert yourself (*strenge dich an*), exercise your influence as well as you can so that the voters will elect the *Reichstag* of your choice" (Anderson 2000: 29). Despite these widely-shared beliefs, an encompassing coalition supporting electoral reforms came about during this period. This book presents an explanation of the economic and political factors that have contributed to the emergence of this coalition.

1.2. IMPERIAL GERMANY AS THE SITE FOR EMPIRICAL STUDY

This book develops and tests a number of arguments about the determinants of electoral reforms protecting the political freedom of voters by relying on historical evidence from Imperial Germany. Why Germany? And what insights can we learn from this case that also travel to other political contexts? For readers who are unfamiliar with the politics of the Second Empire, I begin by presenting some background information about Germany's constitutional arrangements and electoral institutions. Imperial Germany is an ideal case for examining these questions pertaining to the democratization of electoral practices because of the large variation in political and economic conditions within the Empire. With respect to its patterns of partisan competition, Germany is a microcosm of Europe. Different German regions resemble the different types of partisan competition one finds on the continent. Imperial Germany also displays remarkable variation in its economic conditions on account of the large internal heterogeneity in several economic variables that have been hypothesized to affect democratic outcomes. These include landholding inequality, vocational skills, economic concentration, and so on. This large variation in political and economic conditions within Germany mirrors the variation that one encounters in cross-national datasets. A study that leverages the large regional and temporal variation displayed in Germany compromises little in terms of external validity but brings a lot of advantages in internal validity. This within-country design allows us to address a range of questions that cannot be examined with cross-national datasets given the lack of information about many salient variables in cross-national datasets. In addition, this research design allows us to measure the political variables that might shape political incentives at the salient level: the electoral district. In doing so, we achieve greater precision when examining the relative importance of political, partisan, and economic factors as determinants of democratizing reforms.

1.2.1. Germany's Constitutional Rules

With respect to its constitutional rules, Imperial Germany was a semicompetitive authoritarian regime. Although the second chamber of Germany's parliament was elected through democratic elections based on universal manhood suffrage, the prerogatives of the parliament in setting policies were severely constrained by an unelected executive. A low parliamentary autonomy is a common characteristic of many historical and contemporary cases of competitive authoritarian regimes (Diamond 2002; Levitsky and Way 2002, 2010). The analysis of the democratization of electoral practices in the German case provides insights that are relevant to a large number of scholars interested in understanding electoral reforms in semicompetitive authoritarian regimes.

The constitution of the Second German Empire, which was adopted in 1871, introduced a complex division of political responsibilities between the executive and legislative branches of the government (*Gesetz betreffend die Verfassung des Deutschen Reichs* 1871). This division was further complicated by the federal nature of the German Empire and the delegation of significant veto power to Germany's upper chamber, the Bundesrat, which represented Germany's twenty-five principalities. The executive responsibilities in Germany's Second Empire were shared between the emperor, the chancellor of the Empire, and a cabinet of ministers. The chancellor was appointed by the emperor and was responsible to the latter. By contrast, the legislative responsibilities of the

Empire were shared between the Bundesrat, Germany's first chamber, and the Reichstag, Germany's second chamber, which was democratically elected. The Bundesrat consisted of fifty-eight representatives from the different princi-palities (*Gesetz betreffend die Verfassung des Deutschen Reichs* 1871: para. 6). The members of the Bundesrat were representatives of the individual states and, as such, were not elected. Prussia occupied a privileged position in the Bun-desrat because it held seventeen out of the fifty-eight votes. Bavaria, Germany's second largest state, had six votes; Sachsen and Württemberg had four votes each. These rules gave Prussia a comfortable majority but not an unrestricted veto right in the Bundesrat. The Bundesrat had to approve all legislation that was adopted by the parliament and had to issue administrative regulations that were necessary to implement federal legislation in each state.

The Reichstag, Germany's second chamber, occupied a special position in the complicated institutional landscape of the German Empire. The Reichstag was the only institution that was democratically elected. The Reichstag consisted of 397 deputies who were elected in single-member constituencies. Germany's second chamber had a wide range of prerogatives typical of parliaments at the time. First, all of the legislation falling within the competence of the Empire (as opposed to the competence of the individual states) needed the approval of both chambers of government, not only the approval of the upper house. Second, article 23 of the German constitution gave the Reichstag the right to initiate new legislation. Finally, the Reichstag exercised significant control over the finances of the Empire. According to articles 69 and 72 of the German constitution, the Reichstag had to approve the budget of the Empire.

Given this complicated institutional design, a large controversy exists among historians of the period about the relative importance of the Reichstag. A number of historians and constitutional experts of the German Empire have argued that the political power of the German Reichstag was severely limited (Berghahn 1985). Other constitutional experts have contradicted the notion of a German exceptionalism with respect to the absence of executive responsibil-ity toward the parliament. These scholars have noted that the failure of the Reichstag to elect a chancellor was the consequence of political fragmentation in this chamber rather than a result of legal provisions. The German consti-tutional definitions of the political responsibilities of the executive toward the parliament did not diverge significantly from those in other constitutions of the time (Laufs 2006: 308).

Other historians have presented additional challenges to the account of a powerless parliament in Imperial Germany. In one prominent study, Manfred Rauh argued that the "silent parlamentarization of the German Empire" was, in fact, underway prior to 1914 (Rauh 1977). In particular, Rauh argues that a long-term shift in political power away from the monarchy and executive and toward the parliament took place in Germany beginning in 1900. Other studies also pointed to the increase in the votes of non-confidence of the parliament over important decisions taken by the executive during the final years of the Empire.

Although this debate is still ongoing, it will hopefully be resolved through systematic analysis of the origins and the political trajectories of the most significant legislation of national scope and importance adopted in Imperial Germany. Both perspectives in this debate have made important contributions, but some uncertainty about the magnitude of the constraints posed by the Reichstag on the policies considered by the executive still exists. Like many developing countries today, Imperial Germany is an example of an electoral authoritarian regime with a mixture of democratic and authoritarian features. The implications of the analysis of the democratization of electoral practices in this political context are relevant to a large number of scholars interested in electoral reforms in similar types of regimes.

1.2.2. Germany's Partisan Landscape

Elections to the German Reichstag were vigorously contested during this period. As Lavinia Anderson reminds us, "the fact that this democratic national franchise existed in tandem with restrictive state franchises and within a whole nexus of authoritarian relationships only increased its power as a political symbol. Voters turned out in large numbers. The stakes in these elections were high: not the composition of the government but certainly its legislation – and its legitimacy" (Anderson 2002: 109). The partisan landscape varied significantly across Germany. More than thirty different parties competed electorally across the thirteen elections that took place during the period. The partisan competition varied tremendously across Germany's diverse regions. In itself, Germany can be regarded as a microcosm of the partisan landscape that one finds across Europe.

On the right end of the political spectrum, Germany had two parties representing the interests of rural elites, the German Conservative Party (Deutsche Konservative Partei) and the Free Conservatives (Deutsche Reichspartei), which was formed in the 1870s). The electoral strength of these two parties on the right slowly declined throughout the period. In 1871, the first election of the period, these two conservative parties won slightly more than 23 percent of the total votes, which sent eighty-four deputies representing landowners to the Reichstag. By 1912, the combined vote share of these two conservative parties declined to 11.6 percent of the votes, which translated into fifty-six seats.

The strength of conservative parties varied significantly between the different regions of the Empire. The political power base of the German Conservative Party was in East Prussia. Over the course of successive elections, the party lost some districts to Free Liberals and Social Democrats, but the conservatives succeeded in retaining political support in East Prussian districts. The main political base of the Free Conservatives was Silesia (Stalmann 2000; Thompson 2000: 322). In 1871, at the height of their political success, the

Free Conservatives won sixteen out of Silesia's thirty-five electoral districts (Ritter and Niehuss 1991). Silesian districts outside the city of Breslau and in the industrialized areas around Waldenberg continued to elect Free Conservative estate owners as their representatives even during the final elections of the period (Thompson 2000: 322). Outside of Prussia, Free Conservatives enjoyed initial support in Sachsen and Württemberg (Stalmann 2000), but they eventually lost these districts to Social Democratic or Free Liberal challengers.

By contrast, we find high political fragmentation among the parties that represented the interests of the rising urban sector in Germany. "Liberal parties," as many scholars of the period have noted, were fragmented and lacked organization (Nipperdey 1961; O'Donnell 1974; Sheehan 1978; Eley 1980). This observation goes back to the writings of contemporary politicians such as Friedrich Naumann and Max Weber. In 1906, Naumann published an article entitled "Can One Organize Liberals? (*Kann man Liberale organisieren?*)." The article concluded that "organization was a liberal idea, but not a liberal habit. There are thousands in the 'waiting room' of liberalism, willing to climb aboard if an imposing express train (*grosser D-Zug*) came along" (Naumann 1906: 22). Unfortunately, such an imposing express train never arrived.

On the right extreme of the liberal movement was the National Liberal Party. The political success of the National Liberals deteriorated dramatically over the course of the thirteen elections of the period. The National Liberal delegation in the first parliament of the period consisted of 125 deputies, but it had declined to 45 deputies by 1912. The initial regional strength of the National Liberal Party included northern regions of Prussia, Hannover, and Hessen. A variety of splinter liberal parties competed on the left of the National Liberal Party (Seeber 1965; Simon 1969). Across Germany, one finds a large number of parties belonging to the Free Liberal family. These include the German Freeliberal Party, the Democratic Association, the Free Liberal Association, the Democratic Association, the Free Liberal Association, the German People's Party, the Free Liberal Party, and the Liberal Association. Regions of Free Liberal political strength included large cities such as Berlin, Württemberg, and other southern German states.

The Zentrum, the party representing Germany's Catholic minority, consolidated its political position throughout the period. Its vote share remained relatively stable over time, hovering around 20 percent of the total vote. In 1871, the Zentrum won 18 percent of the votes. In 1912, the final election of the period, the Catholic vote share stood at 16.8 percent. The Zentrum reaped, however, significant advantages from the translation of votes to seats in Germany's majoritarian system, because many of its votes were concentrated in sparsely populated districts. During the thirteen elections of the period, the Zentrum sent between 61 and 106 deputies to the Reichstag. As such, during many parliamentary sessions, Zentrum politicians constituted the largest or second largest parliamentary fraction. With respect to the regional distribution of votes, the Zentrum was strong in areas with Catholic populations, including

Bavaria, the Rhine area, and some of the regions of East Prussia with large Polish minorities.

The Social Democratic Party (Sozialistische Partei Deutschlands, or SPD) was founded in 1876 as a national party, dissolved one year later, and founded again during the following year as the General Socialist Congress (Guttsman 1981: 149). During the period of the anti-socialist laws, rudimentary party organizations continued to exist. They worked in secret and were known as the *corpora*, or the core or heart, of the movement (Guttsman 1981: 316). After the abolition of the anti-socialist legislation, the party reconstituted itself and created a parallel body of men of trust who were veterans of the days of proscription (Nipperdey 1961: 316). The SPD took further advantage of legislation enacted in 1899 that granted the right of association to political organizations to strengthen the party organization. The party congresses of 1900 and 1905 revised the party statutes and established formal party organizations (*Wahlkreispartei*) in each district (Schorske 1955).

Chapter 8 examines at greater length the economic and political correlates of the rise in political strength of the Social Democratic Party within different German districts in an effort to provide an explanation for its remarkable political trajectory during the period. The examination of the aggregate temporal patterns of Social Democratic electoral support illustrates the extraordinary trajectory of this party. The Social Democratic vote share rose from 2.1 percent in the first elections of the period to 34.8 percent in 1912. As is discussed in Chapter 8, the adoption of ballot secrecy in 1903 marked an important turning point for the political strength of social democracy. Only two Social Democratic deputies were elected to the first German Reichstag of 1871. By contrast, in the thirteenth and final German Reichstag election in 1913, the Social Democratic Party had 110 deputies, the largest *Parteifraktion* in the Reichstag. The regional strength of the Social Democratic Party varied significantly across the Empire. The strongest political stronghold of the Social Democratic Party was "Red Saxony." Although the Social Democratic Party always contested vigorously in Saxony's election, it was able to solidify its control over the region only after 1903. Other regions of political strength for the SPD included Potsdam, Magdeburg and Merseburg, Schleswig-Hohlstein, and Hesse.

1.2.3. Diversity in Economic Conditions

Imperial Germany is a unique site for comparative research on democratization because of the wide heterogeneity in economic conditions across its provinces. No other case (except perhaps the United States) presents us with so much internal variation in its economic conditions. Many variables that are hypothesized to affect democratic transitions or democratic consolidation – such as socioeconomic development, landholding inequality, and the skill level of the labor force – vary dramatically across Germany. In addition to considering these factors, this study develops and tests a range of hypotheses about the importance of two additional variables for democratic outcomes: economic heterogeneity and labor scarcity.

In Chapter 2, I discuss at greater length the variation in economic conditions across German provinces. I also present the historical sources I have used to generate fine-grained measures of occupational heterogeneity, labor force skill level, and labor scarcity.

1.3. LOOKING AHEAD

The remainder of the book is organized as follows. Chapter 2 presents the theoretical argument and the empirical evidence that is used to test it. I begin by characterizing the political economy of voting under conditions in which electoral secrecy was imperfectly protected. I seek to characterize the factors affecting politicians' demand for electoral strategies that involved intimidation and also the factors influencing the decisions of different actors, such as employees of the state or private actors, to *supply* political support to politicians. Although these decisions of state employees were affected by political conditions, the calculations of private actors about the supply of electoral intimidation were influenced by economic conditions. I present a range of theoretical hypotheses about the relationships between a variety of district-level economic conditions and the production of electoral intimidation by private actors. The second section of the chapter formulates a number of hypotheses about the determinants of support for the electoral reforms aimed at ending electoral intimidation.

Chapters 3, 4, and 5 examine the political economy of voting in German national elections. In Chapters 3 and 4, I test a number of propositions that predict variation in the incidences of intimidation perpetrated by state employees and private actors by using qualitative evidence from the reports of electoral irregularities submitted to the Reichstag. Chapter 5 presents a quantitative test of these propositions using evidence of electoral irregularities in German elections during the period between 1870 and 1912.

In the second part of the book, I analyze the adoption of electoral reforms that protect voters' autonomy. As discussed in Section 1.1, my central hypothesis is that the demand for electoral reforms originated with politicians who faced relatively higher costs of electoral repression and thus could not take advantage of the opportunities for electoral intimidation in existence given Germany's electoral rules. Chapter 6 analyzes the economic and political factors that affected the decisions of politicians to cosponsor legislation designed to protect electoral secrecy in national elections. In Chapter 7, I explore the economic and political determinants of support for Prussian electoral reforms that attempted to introduce the secret ballot in Prussian subnational elections.

The third part of the book examines the political consequences of the 1903 legislation that adopted ballot envelopes and isolating spaces. The new electoral legislation, I argue, lowered voters' fear of economic reprisals for their electoral choices and diminished the economic risks voters faced when deciding whether to support opposition candidates. The immediate consequence of the adoption of ballot envelopes and isolating spaces was a dramatic increase in the level of political support for the main opposition party, the Social Democratic Party. Between 1898, when the final election before the adoption of the ballot envelopes was held, and 1903, when the first election under the new electoral rules was contested, the number of votes cast for Social Democratic candidates increased by 800,000 votes. During the 1903 elections, the number of ballots cast in favor of Social Democratic candidates exceeded 3 million. In Chapter 8, I examine the economic conditions within a district that affected variation in the political support for Social Democratic candidates. Chapter 9 explores the effects of changes in electoral secrecy on the electoral fates of parties on the right. The adoption of secret ballot reforms had varying political consequences for different parties on the right, and those consequences depended on the geographic distribution of their electoral support. The 1903 reforms had the most unfavorable consequences for the National Liberal Party. The ratio converting votes into seats deteriorated dramatically for this party during the final elections of the period. Because of the worsening of the translation of votes to seats, a number of parties on the right shifted their position on the question of electoral reform and supported the adoption of proportional representation. In Chapter 9, I argue that the 1903 reform contributed to a coalitional realignment among German parties, thereby facilitating the formation of an electoral coalition that supported changes in electoral rules. In that chapter, I analyze the district-level and partisan factors that accounted for the support of the adoption of proportional representation. Chapter 10 discusses comparative implications of the study for other instances of reforms ending electoral irregularities.

2

The Protection of Voters' Autonomy

During much of the nineteenth century, the electoral marketplace in many European countries exhibited ample imperfections. At the time, electoral politics was not significantly different from the politics one encounters today in many developing countries that have recently undergone democratic transitions. In their attempts to sway voters, parties and candidates combined promises of policy benefits with a variety of non-programmatic strategies. These non-programmatic strategies included a mix of positive and negative inducements. Candidates campaigned by offering money, food, or entertainment to voters. In addition to these positive inducements, electoral intimidation, pressure, and harassment were amply used during elections. Policemen, tax collectors, and other local notables were deployed to influence the decisions of voters to support particular candidates. Imperfections in voting technology allowed candidates and their agents to engage in intense monitoring of the political choices made by voters and to punish the latter for undesirable political choices. Such threats of post-electoral punishments were highly credible because of ample imperfections in voting technology.

In many countries, political dissatisfaction with these electoral practices gave rise to efforts to curb electoral irregularities and enhance the political freedom of voters. These reforms centered on the dimension of electoral rules exhibiting the most significant imperfections: the technology of voting. Improvements in the design of the ballot and the design of the urn were regarded as central elements in the broader agenda to complete the unfinished democratic project. Consider the statements of Paul Constans, a French deputy who supported a proposal to adopt electoral reforms protecting voter secrecy:

Through these legislative changes we will not be able to eliminate the force of money – namely, the influence of the capitalist plutocracy and of the employers. But what we ask is very modest and will not modify the essential laws – there will be a moment later when we will do this. Right now, we are asking you to support these measures to liberate the voter, who is subjected to many types of influences and to allow him to express his will freely, with more freedom than the current situation permits. (*Journal Officiel de la République Française* October 27, 1904: 2197)

These attempts to democratize electoral practices that had been underway in many European countries during the final decades of the 19th century focused on reforms in the technology of voting. One such type of reform brought about changes in the design of ballots. Improvements in the design of ballots – which came about mainly through the adoption of ballot envelopes – attempted to enhance the secrecy of the vote and protect voters from possible post-electoral retaliation. In 1894, for example, Belgium adopted legislation that introduced uniform ballot envelopes (Moniteur Belge 1894). Legislation adopted by Norway in 1900 introduced uniform ballot envelopes (Bundesarchiv Berlin Lichtenberg R1501/114470, Norwegisches Wahlgesetz vom 24. Februar 1900). France introduced legislation mandating ballot envelopes, and isolating spaces for voters were implemented after protracted political struggles in 1913 (Loi du 29 Juillet 1913).

A second change that contributed to significant improvements in voting technology concerned the design of electoral urns. In conditions where urns varied widely in their design, ballots could be easily stacked on each other and votes could therefore be identified. To prevent these practices, many countries introduced additional legislation that mandated the adoption of "standardized urns." The Ballot Act adopted in 1872 in Britain mandated that ballot boxes had to be locked to prevent the introduction or removal of ballots. Belgian legislation of 1894 also introduced complex regulations regarding the required size of the electoral urns, and these regulations varied across localities depending on the number of voters. Legislation adopted in Denmark in 1901 mandated that urns had to be locked to prevent the removal of ballots after they were cast. Similar legislation was introduced in Norway in 1909. Other countries, including Italy and Spain, took a different approach to the question of urn design by mandating transparent urns. This legislation was adopted in Spain in 1907 and in Italy in 1912 (Bundesarchiv Berlin Lichtenberg R 1501/114476).

This book provides an account of the origins and consequences of electoral reforms that protected the autonomy of voters from political influence by mandating changes in voting technology. It seeks to understand the sources of political cleavages about the desirability of reforms aimed at protecting the electoral autonomy of voters and the factors that contributed to an increase in the size of the political coalitions that were eventually successful in bringing about these electoral reforms. The starting hypothesis of my study is that politicians' preferences about the desirability of electoral reforms were affected by their ability to take advantage of opportunities for electoral malfeasance under existing electoral rules. Politicians who could take advantage of imperfections under existing electoral rules and engage in electoral influence (either through vote buying or intimidation) favored the status quo. By contrast, politicians who lacked the opportunity to carry out electoral irregularities favored the adoption of electoral reforms. Economic and political factors that increased a politician's costs to carry out electoral irregularities contributed to an increase in that politician's support for changing electoral rules. I present an explanation of electoral reform that highlights a distributional conflict between the winners and losers within the political status quo about the desirability of electoral reforms (cf. Knight 1992). This contrasts with functional explanations of electoral reforms, which attribute the choice of electoral rules to the functional needs of powerful economic actors.

This chapter presents an outline of the theoretical argument advanced in the book and a description of my empirical strategy I employ to test this argument. The first part of the chapter presents an account of voting under conditions in which electoral autonomy is imperfectly protected. In this section, I account for the mix in the types of electoral irregularities that can occur during elections and for the variation in their incidence. This variation, I argue, is affected by the punishment structure for different electoral rules and by differences in economic and political conditions in a district.

Building on this discussion of the variation in the incidence of electoral irregularities, Section 2.2 presents my main hypotheses about the factors affecting politicians' calculations about the desirability of electoral reforms. Their preferences were affected by a combination of partisan calculations and considerations about their own capacity to take advantage of electoral irregularities given the economic and political conditions in a district. I advance two conjectures about the determinants of political support of these electoral reforms. First, I hypothesize that politicians from parties that did not have opportunities to engage in electoral intimidation because of an absence of ties to powerful economic actors and to state employees means to engage in electoral intimidation were more likely to support the adoption of electoral reforms. In addition to these partisan considerations, I also argue that district-level conditions were likely to affect preferences toward electoral reforms. Politicians that encountered relatively high costs of electoral repression because of the economic and political conditions in their districts were also likely to support the adoption of electoral reforms protecting voter autonomy. In particular, economic conditions that increased the costs of the electoral intimidation of private actors – such as the economic heterogeneity of that district or the skill profile of the labor force – were also more likely to affect demand for electoral reforms. These district-specific variables help explain some of the intra-party conflict about the advantages and disadvantages of electoral reforms. Support for electoral reforms was unevenly distributed within each party and was higher for politicians from districts that faced relatively high costs of electoral intimidation.

In Section 2.3, I formulate a number of hypotheses about the consequences of reforms that enhanced the protection of voting secrecy for electoral competitions. I examine the consequences of these reforms for the political support of opposition candidates. I examine the calculations made by individual voters about supporting opposition candidates in conditions in which such electoral support could result in a loss of employment. This analysis shows that electoral reforms that protected voter secrecy also reduced the magnitude of such punishments and therefore increased the willingness of voters to support opposition candidates. I also examine the implications of these electoral reforms for parties on the right.

The final section of the chapter, Section 2.4, discusses the empirical strategy of my analysis. This study takes advantage of economic data of exceptional quality: the German Occupational Census. I employ historical information collected by German statistical authorities to compute extremely fine-grained measures of the key economic variables that are central to my analysis: the occupational heterogeneity of a district and the skill profile of its labor force. In that section, I discuss the sources, the construction of the variables, and the advantages of a micro-historical analysis over alternative modes of comparative research.

2.1. THE PRODUCTION OF ELECTORAL IRREGULARITIES IN CONDITIONS OF IMPERFECT ELECTORAL RULES

The goal of this book is to present an explanation for the adoption of electoral reforms that democratized electoral practices by protecting voters' political autonomy. Such reforms are a crucial yet underexplored dimension of democratization that mark the transition from an "electoral democracy" – which grants citizens the right to vote – to a "substantive democracy" – which ensures that votes reflect the genuine choices of voters who are free from coercion. The analysis presented in this book seeks to identify the economic and political factors that contributed to the formation of an encompassing political coalition in support of the adoption of these reforms in nineteenth-century Germany.

To understand the demand for electoral change and the distributional conflict over such change, we need to first understand the determinants of electoral irregularities prior to reform. The mix of different electoral irregularities varies significantly across countries and within countries across different electoral districts. Understanding this variation is important because it allows us to characterize the factors that affect the cost benefit calculations of different politicians about the attractiveness of the political status quo. As discussed in the introduction to this chapter, my working hypothesis is that politicians who had the resources to engage in different forms of irregularities without punishment were likely to support the political status quo. By contrast, politicians whose ability to use coercion or pressure was constrained by various economic or political conditions in a district were likely to embrace electoral reforms. We need to identify the factors affecting electoral corruption and the various constraints on its use in order to understand the calculations of individual politicians about the advantages of electoral reforms.

Electoral corruption is, in itself, a multidimensional phenomenon. A first distinction that can be made between the different forms of irregularities is that of "positive" and "negative" inducements for voters. Positive inducements include efforts to sway the political decisions of voters through various transfers that bring about an increase in the overall utility of those voters. By contrast, negative inducements are strategies that bring about a reduction in the overall utility of voters. They include harassments, threats, and a variety of post-electoral punishments that reduce future income streams for voters. One also finds significant variation in the types of agents deployed by politicians in the latter's efforts to influence the decisions of voters by using non-programmatic appeals. I consider two types of actors: employees of the state, and private actors.

The mix among these different irregularities varied significantly across countries. The historical landscape of nineteenth-century elections amply illustrates the variation in this mix. Patronage, or the use of positive inducements by employees of the state, was a pervasive electoral irregularity in nineteenth-century France (Charnay 1964). Such strategies were almost absent in Britain and German national elections. The practice of "bribing," or "treating," voters was a pervasive electoral irregularity in British elections. Vote buying and treating were relatively rare in German elections. Finally, German elections were characterized by unprecedented levels of political intervention by employers as compared to other countries.

Electoral laws played an important, yet insufficiently understood, role in cross-national variation in electoral irregularities. Electoral rules did not punish electoral irregularities uniformly. In most countries, electoral laws singled out particular irregularities as extremely problematic while treating other irregularities more leniently. This differential punishment structure created incentives for politicians and for the agents operating on their behalf to avoid irregularities that were sanctioned with high levels of stringency and to turn instead to electoral strategies that were punished less stringently or were not punished at all. This differential punishment of electoral laws helps us account for some of the cross-national variation in electoral irregularities.

To illustrate this proposition, consider the punishment structure for electoral irregularities established by the German electoral law for national elections to the Reichstag. German lawmakers singled out "vote buying" as a particularly severe electoral irregularity and placed this offense under the jurisdiction of the penal code (Freudenthal 1895; Arsenschek 2003: 245). According to article 109 of the German penal code, "the person who buys or sells votes will be punished with imprisonment between a month and two years" (Freudenthal 1895: 38). These provisions of the electoral law created strong incentives for German politicians to avoid strategies premised on vote buying. Freudenthal (1895) compiled aggregate statistical data on violations of these provisions of the

German penal code. Unfortunately, German statistical authorities aggregated violations of paragraph 109 of the German penal code along with violations of four other paragraphs (paras. 105–108). As such, these statistics are likely to overestimate the incidence of vote buying. During the period between 1880 and 1892, we find on average eleven convictions per year of violations of these sections of the penal code (Freudenthal 1895: 38). Other historical studies assessing the mix of different irregularities in German elections reach similar conclusions with respect to the absence of vote buying in German elections (Klein 2003). Consider Lavinia Anderson's characterization of the importance of bribery in German national elections:

Germany presented a very different picture from England. Cotters in the east Elbian Herrschaft Pnuwno were given a half bushel or dried peas for voting Conservative. Voters in the Rheinisch village of Rodenkirchen who accepted "loyal" ballots were handed a sausage from a large hamper at the door of the polls. A dram of schnapps at the beginning of our period and much larger quantities of *Freibier* at the end were common, although not always considered respectable features of German elections. Nevertheless, I know of only three contests in the entire Imperial Period in which corruption in the form of treating or bribery was even rumored to have affected the outcome of the election – and in two of them the rumors seem untrustworthy, given that the losing party did not bother to file a complaint. Whatever the incidence of these little reciprocities, it is clear that German voters were not considered venal even by parties hoping to overturn an election, nor did enough money change hands to give Reichstag deputies, unlike their British counterparts, any stake in regulating it. *Bribery simply did not play a role in what Germans thought was wrong in their political process.* (Anderson 2000: 26–27, emphasis added)

Whereas vote buying was punished extremely harshly, the German electoral law lacked any punishment for electoral intimidation perpetrated by employers. Electoral intimidation by private actors was an offense that remained unpunished during the entire Imperial Period. On one occasion, in 1886, German politicians proposed an amendment of the electoral law that recommended including employer pressure in the list of irregularities punishable under article 109 of the penal code. This proposal met, however, with defeat. An important objection raised by liberal politicians was that the punishment of electoral intimidation by employers "intervened too strongly in contractual relations between employers and employees." As liberal politicians argued at the time, "one cannot draw a boundary in electoral intimidation. This would imply that *any* layoff could be branded as electoral layoff" (*Stenographische Berichte des Deutschen Reichstags* February 13, 1886).

German politicians competing in national elections enlisted two types of agents: state employees and employers. Both actors engaged in repressive electoral strategies. State employees attempted to sway voters not through promises of future largesse but rather through repressive strategies, which included threats of post-electoral punishment for dissenting voters. German employers engaged in the systematic control of the voting choices of voters and threatened post-electoral punishments that included wage cuts, reductions in benefits provided by the company, such as housing or pensions, and electoral layoffs – that is, the loss of employment because of political decisions made at the ballot box.

These strategies of economic intimidation were credible because of imperfections in voting technology. Voters knew that their ballots were observable and that they could be punished for their choices at the ballot box. The German electoral law allowed two such imperfections of voting technology: the design of the ballot and the design of the urn. Imperfections in the design of the urn led to the stacking of ballots. Both employees of the state and private actors took advantage of these imperfections of the voting technology and located representatives in the voting areas to monitor the types of ballots cast by every voter. Representatives of firms also maintained counter-lists (*Gegenlisten*) that monitored the votes cast by each and every voter. This close monitoring of voting decisions enhanced the precision and accuracy of the post-electoral punishments that could be targeted against dissenting voters.

The first part of this book provides an analysis of the variation in the different electoral irregularities across Germany's electoral districts. I distinguish between "demand-side" and "supply-side" considerations of the production of electoral irregularities. I begin with an analysis of the factors that affect the decisions of individual candidates to *demand* political support from a variety of actors – such as employees of the state or employers – during elections. Next, I discuss the calculations of both private actors and employees of the state to *supply* this political support to candidates. Different variables affect the considerations of these different actors about the supply of electoral support. Although political factors act as important constraints on the activities of employees of the state, the considerations of employers about their production of electoral irregularities (and about the intensity of those irregularities) are affected by economic conditions in the district.

2.1.1. The Demand Made by Candidates

The production of electoral irregularities was a byproduct of the decisions made by individual candidates in the conduct of their electoral campaigns. These included decisions about announcing their candidacy to voters, holding electoral rallies, mobilizing voters during elections, and monitoring ballots being cast. Because of the weak development of party organizations at the time, individual candidates bore most of the responsibility for financing their own campaigns, for the amount and types of resources deployed during elections, and for deciding whether to form electoral coalitions with other candidates in the district. I hypothesize that the demand made by candidates for political support that could result in the production of electoral irregularities was shaped by two factors: the competitiveness of a race and the candidate's hostility toward political opponents advocating political changes that were subversive to the economic and political order.

The first factor likely to affect the demand made by candidates for additional support from employees of the state – such as policemen or tax collectors – or from private actors was the tightness of the race. I hypothesize that demand for political support was higher in tighter races. This hypothesis builds on a large comparative literature on the incidence of electoral corruption that argues that "political competition fuels ballot rigging" (Lehoucq 2003: 56; see also Lehoucq and Molina 2002). The tightness of the race was likely to enhance the perception of political urgency by candidates and increase their willingness to engage in more risky behavior, which could trespass on some of the provisions of the electoral law.

Not all candidates, however, posed similar levels of threat. As such, candidates calibrated the intensity of their electoral intervention depending on the type of their political opponent. Social Democratic candidates challenged both the existing economic and political order and were seen as the primary political enemies of the *Reich*. One crucial political motivation for the deployment of the bureaucratic apparatus during elections and for the reliance on the coercive power of German employers was the desire to curtail the growth in strength of this subversive political movement. As such, one expects that an increase in the political strength of Social Democratic candidates in a district was likely to increase the demand on candidates on the right to deploy additional administrative and economic resources to tilt the outcome of the race in their favor.

I hypothesize, however, that the relationship between the strength of Social Democratic candidates in a district and the demand made by their opponents for electoral support from employees of the state and private actors was likely nonlinear. An increase in the political strength of a Social Democratic opponent in a district was likely to increase the demand made by a candidate for political support from employees of the state or private actors. However, at very strong levels of Social Democratic support, the marginal political returns from electoral intimidation were likely to be low. In those cases, intimidation was unlikely to modify the outcome of a race. All things equal, I expect that the political demand made by candidates for electoral support from employees of the state and private actors was highest in districts where Social Democratic candidates exhibited intermediate levels of electoral strength.

Other dimensions of electoral competition were likely to lower candidates' demand for electoral irregularities. I conjecture that candidates were likely to refrain from electoral intimidation or other possible irregularities if such strategies could affect their ability to form political coalitions with other candidates on the right. Given the electoral rules that were in place in German national elections, such electoral coalitions were necessary during runoffs (which occurred when a candidate did not win an absolute majority during the first electoral round). Such coalitions were also more likely in districts characterized by high levels of fragmentation on the political right prior to runoffs. I hypothesize that the demand made by right-wing candidates for electoral support from employees of the state or private actors was lower in districts with high levels of fragmentation on the right and whose outcomes were determined in runoffs. Heavy-handed intervention by state employees on behalf of particular candidates could become a liability during runoffs and hamper the ability of those candidates to form electoral coalitions with other candidates on the right. These considerations about future political coalitions were thus likely to constrain candidates' demand for electoral irregularities.

2.1.2. State Employees and Their Decision to Lend Electoral Support to Candidates

In the previous section, I discussed the determinants of the candidates' demand for electoral support that could violate the provisions of the electoral law. In this section, I examine the most salient factors likely to affect the cost-benefit calculations of employees of the state and their decisions to supply electoral intimidation. Employees of the state were pervasive electoral agents in German elections. However, their intervention in elections varied significantly across German provinces. Different political conditions affected not only variation in the political demand made by candidates for electoral support but also the decisions of state employees to supply such political services to candidates. I propose a few hypotheses that may have affected the variation in these supply-side considerations by state employees.

Let us first consider how the tightness of a race affects the incentive of employees of the state to provide political support to candidates. From the perspective of employees of the state, narrow political races are associated with higher uncertainty about the identity of the future political incumbent. This implies that the willingness of employees of the state to provide political support to candidates will be lower in tighter races than it will be in less competitive ones. The tightness of a race thus has offsetting effects for the demand and supply of electoral irregularities. Although tighter races increase the demand made by candidates, they reduce the willingness of political agents to engage in activities trespassing the boundaries of the electoral law. This implies that the overarching theoretical prediction about the relationship between the tightness of a race and the incidence of electoral irregularities is indeterminate.

Finally, one also expects to find a nonlinear relationship between the electoral strength of Social Democratic candidates in a district and the decision of employees of the state to provide electoral support during elections. Policemen and tax collectors shared with right-wing candidates a preoccupation with mounting a strong defense against Social Democratic political mobilization. This political variable exerted reinforcing incentives for the demands made by candidates and the supply-side calculations of employees of the state. In aggregate, I expect to find a nonlinear relationship between the political strength of Social Democracy in a district and the incidence of irregularities during elections.

2.1.3. Employers and the Supply of Electoral Intimidation

In addition to enlisting policemen, teachers, and tax collectors as their agents, political candidates competing in elections to the German Reichstag could also rely on electoral support from private actors. I document the political strategies of intimidation used by German employers in elections in Chapter 4.

What factors explain the decisions of employers to intervene during elections? In deciding whether to provide political support to candidates during elections, employers were likely to weigh the advantages and disadvantages of their actions. Firms' gains from electoral intervention were political in nature. Through their political activities, firms hoped to curtail the growth in electoral strength of candidates who challenged the existing political and economic order, such as Social Democratic candidates. However, political intervention was not entirely costless to firms. Electoral repression could be costly if it resulted in the loss of valuable employees. To understand the decisions of firms to use electoral intimidation, we need to specify how economic conditions in a district affected the costs of electoral repression. I hypothesize that three different variables affected the magnitude of the costs of repression: the economic heterogeneity of a district, the skill profile of its labor force, and the level of labor scarcity. Let us consider each variable in turn.

I advance the hypothesis that the occupational heterogeneity of a district affected firms' costs of electoral repression. To illustrate this argument, let us consider two hypothetical districts that differ in their number of firms (I) and in the number of occupations (J). One extreme case is a district in which both the output and employment levels are controlled by a small number of economic actors; in other words, both $I \rightarrow 1$ and $J \rightarrow 1$. I refer to this type of district in the remainder of this chapter and throughout this book as a district with high economic concentration or low occupational heterogeneity. The opposite case is a district where both I and J are very large. I refer to this second type of district as a district with a high level of occupational heterogeneity or a low level of economic concentration.

I hypothesize that the costs of electoral intimidation are lower in districts characterized by high levels of economic concentration. Three factors lower the costs of electoral intimidation for employers in these districts as compared to districts with high occupational heterogeneity. First, in the short run, workers have fewer employment opportunities outside the firm, because there are fewer competing firms to rehire them in the event of electoral layoffs. Second, the concentration of employment in the hands of a small number of actors also reduces the coordination problems faced by employers who decide to punish workers with "dangerous" political views by denying them employment opportunities. Finally, because of their large scale, dominant firms face lower costs when carrying out political activities such as distributing voting material and controlling turnout. These three considerations reinforce each other, making the economic heterogeneity of a district an important predictor of the costs of electoral repression of employers. All other factors being equal, we expect to find a higher willingness of firms in more concentrated regions to engage in electoral intimidation.

The costs of electoral intimidation for private actors increase as the economic heterogeneity of a district increases. Both an increase in the number of occupations and an increase in the number of firms contribute to an increase in the costs of electoral intimidation. First, an increase in the number of occupations in a district is likely to increase the employment opportunities available to workers, with low or no costs of economic relocation. In districts with high occupational heterogeneity, the costs for employers of other repressive strategies that fall short of layoffs – such as on-the-job harassment of workers for their perceived political loyalties – are also higher. Given that workers have more employment opportunities in districts with high levels of economic heterogeneity, they may respond to on-the-job harassment by moving to another employer. As such, these potential economic losses to firms may outweigh any potential gains from intimidation. Coordination among employers to punish disloyal workers is also more difficult in a district characterized by high levels of occupational fragmentation.

The second economic variable that may affect the costs of electoral intimidation for private actors is the skill profile of the labor force. The levels of vocational skills were already high during this period of industrial takeoff for the German economy, but we find significant variation across industries in their skill profile (*Statistisches Jahrbuch des Deutschen Reiches* 1914; Thelen 2004). The costs of electoral intimidation for firms that made higher investments in the skill of their workforce were likely to be higher than the costs of electoral layoffs for firms that did not make these investments. This second hypothesis tests a crucial prediction of the Varieties of Capitalism literature, which attributes a significant importance to vocational skills in explaining economic and political outcomes in nineteenth-century Europe (Hall and Soskice 2001; Cusack et al. 2010).

In addition to economic heterogeneity and the skill level of the labor force, I hypothesize that the costs of electoral repression for employers are affected by the immediate labor market conditions in a district. All other things being equal, I hypothesize that the costs of electoral repression for employers are higher in districts with higher levels of labor scarcity. Electoral intimidation carries higher economic costs for firms in labor-scarce areas because employees have better employment opportunities. As such, I conjecture that firms' willingness to engage in the harassment of their employees is lower in districts that experience higher levels of labor scarcity and higher in conditions of labor market surplus. In Chapter 7, I test a number of the observable implications of this proposition by examining the political consequences of the labor shortage of agricultural workers in Prussia's districts.

Table 2.1 summarizes my hypotheses about the economic and political factors that affect the probability of electoral irregularities. The theoretical predictions concerning the overall effect of the tightness of a race on the incidence of electoral irregularities are ambiguous. Although a close race is likely to increase

TABLE 2.1. *The Demand and Supply of Electoral Irregularities during Elections*

		Demand made by candidates for electoral irregularities	Supply of electoral irregularities by employees of the state or private actors	Effect on probability of electoral irregularities
Political variables	Electoral margin	+	–	Ambiguous
	Strength of Social Democracy (SD)	Nonlinear; highest at medium levels of strength of SD	Nonlinear; highest at medium levels of strength of SD	Nonlinear; highest at medium levels of strength of SD
	Electoral fragmentation among right-wing parties and runoffs	–		–
Economic variables	Economic concentration		⏐	⏐

politicians' demand for electoral irregularities, it is also likely to limit the willingness of employees of the state to supply electoral intimidation. As such, the relationship between the competitiveness of a race and the production of electoral irregularities is, from a theoretical point of view, ambiguous. I also conjecture that a combination of runoffs and high levels of political fragmentation on the right is likely to limit the production of electoral irregularities. Finally, I suggest that a range of economic variables affect the costs of electoral intimidation by private actors. These include the occupational heterogeneity of a district, the skill profile of its labor force, and the relative labor scarcity in that district.

I use two distinct empirical strategies to test these propositions. In Chapters 3 and 4, I draw on the historical evidence from the reports of the commission that investigated electoral irregularities in national elections to map out the variation in the incidences of electoral irregularities perpetrated by employees of the state and private actors. This qualitative analysis allows me to document both the specific strategies of electoral intimidation used by public officials and private actors and the variation in the voters' political vulnerability to electoral intimidation at different stages of the electoral process. In Chapter 5, I present a quantitative analysis of a dataset on the production of electoral irregularities in German elections.

2.2. THE DEMAND FOR ELECTORAL REFORMS: ECONOMIC AND POLITICAL DETERMINANTS

The second part of this book examines the adoption of reforms that provided voters with greater protection against political pressure. Proposals to reform the electoral system and protect voters against electoral intimidation were on the agenda of the German parliament in nearly every legislature of the period. The first bill recommending an amendment to the law to improve electoral secrecy was submitted in 1875. Nevertheless, it took nearly thirty years before the German parliament adopted legislation improving voting secrecy. The most important turning point in the democratization of electoral practices in national elections occurred as a result of the adoption of electoral reforms in 1903. These reforms mandated the introduction of ballot envelopes and isolating spaces (*Isolierzelle*) and improved the protection of voters' autonomy when casting their ballots.

Who were the politicians that supported reforms of electoral practices and the protection of voters against electoral intimidation? What factors had the most important effect on their decision to support changes in electoral rules? The second part of the book seeks to characterize the economic and political factors that accounted for legislators' demand for electoral institutions enhancing electoral secrecy. The starting point of my analysis is that the advantages of the imperfect protection of electoral secrecy were distributed unequally across districts. Some politicians could easily benefit from imperfections in electoral design and faced very low costs of electoral intimidation. By contrast, other politicians were much more constrained by the underlying economic and political conditions in their districts from engaging in the electoral intimidation of voters and from perpetuating other forms of electoral irregularities. The severity of these constraints was the basis for the political cleavage over the desirability of electoral reforms.

Demand for electoral reforms, I conjecture, was affected by a combination of partisan considerations and district-specific conditions that affected the ability of different candidates to take advantage of the loopholes of the electoral system and engage in the production of electoral irregularities. Consider first the partisan variables. Politicians' ties and access to different actors who could engage in the electoral intimidation of voters varied significantly across the parties competing in German elections. Parties on the right – including the German Conservative Party, Free Conservatives, and National Liberals – also had close ties with private actors who fulfilled important roles as electoral agents. In Prussia and many other small principalities located in the heartland of the Empire, conservatives also had significant control over the appointment of local bureaucrats such as policemen and tax collectors, and bureaucrats whose conservative political sympathies had been previously established were favored in these appointments. Other parties, such as the Zentrum, Free Liberals, and Social Democrats, lacked this political access. As a result, I expect one dimension of political cleavage over the desirability of electoral reforms protecting voter secrecy to fall along partisan lines. More specifically, I hypothesize that politicians from parties lacking ties to state and private actors and the opportunity to engage in electoral intimidation favored the adoption of electoral reforms. By contrast, politicians from parties who did have ties to private actors and employees of the state were more likely to oppose electoral reforms and support the political status quo.

In addition to partisan variables, I hypothesize that politicians' considerations about the advantages of electoral reforms were affected by district-specific conditions. These district-specific conditions explain within-party variation in support for electoral reforms. Both economic and political conditions in a district affected the opportunities for electoral intimidation by politicians and thus their calculations about the desirability of electoral reforms. My overarching hypothesis is that politicians who encountered relatively higher costs of electoral repression because of the specific economic and political conditions in their districts were likely to find the political status quo more unattractive and to support the adoption of electoral reforms. Because of its high costs, electoral intimidation was an unattractive and unusable strategy for these politicians. Political support for electoral reforms likely reflects a desire to establish an even playing field for all candidates competing for seats in the Reichstag.

The implication of this hypothesis is that the economic variables in a district accounting for variation in the electoral costs of electoral repression also predict political support for electoral reforms. Building on the hypotheses formulated in Section 2.1, I conjecture that politicians from districts with high levels of occupational heterogeneity are likely to support the adoption of electoral reforms. As discussed in Section 2.1.3, the costs of electoral repression for politicians are higher in districts with higher levels of occupational heterogeneity because of the relatively higher costs of electoral intimidation encountered by private actors in these districts. By contrast, I expect politicians from districts with lower levels of occupational heterogeneity to support the political status quo and oppose electoral reforms.

The presence of vocational skills in a district is also likely to increase the costs of political repression for employers. Employers that have made investments in the skill level of their employees are likely to face higher costs when they economically harass workers with undesirable political views than do employers that have not made similar investments in the training and skill level of their workforce. This implies that politicians from districts with high levels of vocational skills are more likely to support the adoption of electoral reforms.

In Chapter 6, I test these propositions in a quantitative analysis of the cosponsorship of all legislative bills supporting increased protection of electoral secrecy that were submitted to the Reichstag from 1870 to 1912. Questions of electoral reforms were on the agenda of the Reichstag in seven out of the thirteen parliaments of the period. In examining the determinants of electoral reform, I also control for a range of variables that have been considered salient in existing theoretical approaches to democratization, including rural inequality and economic development. The empirical results confirm both the partisan and the district-specific hypotheses about the determinants of electoral reforms.

I find support for both the partisan hypotheses and the economic hypotheses about the determinants of support for electoral reforms.

In Chapter 7, I examine one additional hypothesis of the determinants of support for electoral reforms. There, I explore whether labor scarcity affects politicians' preferences for electoral reforms. As discussed in Section 2.1.3, I expect that politicians in labor-scarce areas encounter higher costs of electoral repression as compared to politicians in labor-abundant areas. As such, I expect labor scarcity to predict political support for electoral secrecy.

I lack data that measures labor scarcity for all provinces of the German Empire, but I was able to find such data for Prussia, the largest region of the Empire. Using information about rural agricultural wages in all Prussian localities, I have constructed a new dataset on the relative shortage of agricultural workers across Prussian districts from 1870 to 1912. Using this Prussian dataset, I examine the economic determinants of support for electoral reforms that attempted to introduce voting secrecy. The findings lend support for my hypothesis: labor scarcity is an important predictor of support for electoral reforms, even after controlling for partisanship and all of the other relevant economic and political factors in a district.

Although it resonates with leading accounts of democratization, my explanation of the determinants of support for electoral reforms protecting voter secrecy identifies a new mechanism to account for the source of political cleavages over electoral reforms: this book points to the importance of occupational heterogeneity as a determinant of support for electoral reforms. Economic heterogeneity both restrains private actors from using economic intimidation against their employees and simultaneously becomes an important predictor of support for political reform. Because reforms protecting electoral secrecy were the result of a distributive conflict between those politicians who had opportunities for electoral intimidation and those who lacked such opportunities, economic heterogeneity becomes an important predictor of this political conflict.

2.3. THE CONSEQUENCES OF ELECTORAL REFORMS

The third part of this book examines the political consequences of the 1903 legislation known as the "Rickert law," which introduced two improvements in voting technology: changes to the ballot envelope and isolating spaces. These reforms were implemented relatively smoothly and uneventfully. Several reports by the Ministry of the Interior noted only minimal disruptions in the implementation of the new regulations (Bundesarchiv Berlin Lichtenberg R1501/114475, Aufzeichnung über die am 27. Juni 1910 stattgehabte kommissarische Beratung betreffend Abänderungen des Wahlreglements; Bundesarchiv Berlin Lichtenberg R1501/114475, Äußerung des Ministers des Innern zu der Frage der Beschaffung einheitlicher Wahlurnen für die Reichstagswahl). In Chapters 8 and 9, I examine two consequences of these electoral reforms.

First, I consider their implications for the political strength of the main opposition party, the Social Democratic Party. Did the reforms change voters' decisions to take electoral risks and support opposition candidates? In Chapter 9, I examine the consequences of these electoral reforms for political parties on the right. I show that the increase in electoral competition from the Social Democratic Party, coupled with the reduction in the ability of candidates to monitor the choices of voters, had varied implications for different parties on the right, which depended on the geographic distribution of their supporters prior to the adoption of reforms. A number of parties on the right (such as the National Liberals and Free Liberals) experienced a worsening of the ratio translating votes into seats during the final elections of the period. In the new political environment of the post-Rickert legislation, these parties understood that their political survival was exceedingly difficult in a majoritarian electoral system. As a result of such calculations, these parties on the right endorsed a reform of electoral system and the adoption of proportional representation.

In Chapter 8, I examine regional variation in the political support for Germany's main opposition party, the Social Democratic Party, and changes in the political strength of this party following the adoption of the Rickert law. Voting for opposition candidates carried immense risks for voters when voting secrecy was insufficiently protected. Representatives of firms manned polling stations and closely monitored electoral choices by using counter-lists (*Gegenlisten*). Following the vote, employers could enact a range of punishments for voters who had supported undesirable candidates. Voters who had made the incorrect political choice could lose access to company housing or other social benefits provided by the company. They could also face a reduction in their wages for protracted or indefinite periods of time. Finally, these voters could experience a loss of employment if the employer decided to use layoffs as a strategy for post-electoral punishment. The duration and severity of this loss in income could be magnified if particular employers in a region colluded and decided to deny employment to workers who had been dismissed because of political reasons. Such decisions to collude to punish rebel voters were common at the time and were reported in several industries, including forestry and mining.

To understand the variation in political support for opposition candidates, we need to understand how voters balanced gains in political utility – which were derived by supporting a candidate whose policy position was closest to their own – against the potential economic losses that could be incurred if employers identified how they voted and punished them for their choice. One simple way to analyze the calculations made by voters is to consider their expected utility after they cast their ballots for opposition candidates. First, voters assessed the possible ideological and policy gains they could derive from their political choices. Some of these gains in utility were ideological in nature, whereas others were associated with expectations of an increased future income and benefits that could result from policies adopted by a new parliamentary majority. Voters weighed these considerations against the possible economic losses that they could face if their employers or other political agents identified the nature of their votes.

This starting premise of my analysis contrasts with more standard models of vote choice because it considers the potential economic costs incurred by voters if their political choices at the ballot box were identified. These additional factors are critical for unpacking the choices made by voters because of the importance of employer intimidation in German elections. I conjecture that these considerations about the magnitude of economic losses are likely to have varied systematically across districts and that they account for the variation in political support for the Social Democratic Party.

Let us further unpack these calculations and consider some the factors that affected voters' expected economic loss. The probability of punishment for their political choices was affected by voting technology, on the one hand, and by the efforts deployed by various political agents operating on behalf of candidates to detect opposition votes, on the other hand. It follows that the likelihood of economic retribution was higher if ballot secrecy was insufficiently protected. The probability of detecting voters' choices approaches zero in conditions where voter secrecy was fully protected. In such cases, the fear of economic punishment is likely to be low.

In addition to voting technology, the magnitude of economic punishment was also affected by the efforts of state employees and employers, the two main types of political agents present in German elections, to monitor voters' political choices. As discussed in Section 2.1, the considerations of state employees to support a candidate were influenced by political competition in a district. This effort was likely to be highest in districts with a unified right and lowest in districts with a fragmented right and runoffs. By affecting the efforts of state employees, these patterns of electoral competition also affected voters' fear that their political choices would be detected. Because this fear was likely to be lower in districts with a fragmented right and runoffs, I expect that support for Social Democracy was highest in these districts. Finally, the willingness of private actors to monitor the choices of voters was also likely to vary across districts. As conjectured at numerous points in this chapter, I expect employers in concentrated districts to face lower costs of electoral involvement.

Social Democratic voters were likely to face important economic repercussions for their political choices if their vote choices were detected. The magnitude of these economic losses was also likely to vary systematically across districts. As discussed in Section 2.1, the decision of a firm to lay off voters who had Social Democratic political sympathies was not entirely costless to employers. Firms were likely to weigh the advantages of a political environment free from subversive Social Democratic mobilization against the potential economic costs associated with the loss of valuable employees. The factors affecting the calculations of firms are discussed in the analysis of the determinants of the costs of economic intimidation presented in Section 2.1.

TABLE 2.2. *Taking Risks: Explaining Political Support for Opposition Candidates*

	Probability That Vote is Detected	Likelihood That Firms Will Punish Voters Who Supported Opposition Candidates	Likelihood That Voters Will Find Reemployment	Predicted Effecton Support for Opposition Candidates
Secrecy of Ballot	−			+
Employment Concentration	+	+	+ (small effect that can be offset if costs of mobility are low)	−
High Vocational Skills	−	?		+
Labor Scarcity	−	+		+
Fragmented Right and Runoffs	−			+

By affecting costs, these economic factors also affected voters' calculations about supporting Social Democracy. Labor scarcity, economic heterogeneity, and vocational skills were likely to increase the costs of economic intimidation for employers and to reduce the likelihood of economic losses for voters because of their political choices. As such, I expect to find a positive relationship between labor scarcity, vocational skills, and economic heterogeneity and support for Social Democracy prior to the adoption of electoral reforms promoting voting secrecy.

Voters' calculations about the magnitude of their economic losses also included considerations about their ability to find alternative employment. I conjecture that workers who had better opportunities for reemployment were more likely to take electoral risks and support opposition candidates. Several factors are likely to affect opportunities for reemployment. First, opportunities for reemployment are higher in conditions of labor scarcity. Second, workers have better opportunities for reemployment in districts with high levels of occupational heterogeneity because of the presence of multiple firms with similar production profiles in the same district. The relationship between vocational skills and the likelihood of reemployment is ambiguous. The reemployment opportunities for high-skill and low-skill workers are likely to vary across industries depending on the technology of firms, and it is ex ante unclear whether high-skilled workers have better opportunities for reemployment than low-skilled workers do.

Table 2.2 summarizes this discussion about the factors that affect the willingness of voters who face economic repercussions for their political choices to take risks and support opposition candidates. The main conjecture is that voters assessed the magnitude of the potential economic losses associated with the political choice to support Social Democratic candidates. These losses were affected by the probability that their votes would be identified, by the political efforts of state employees to monitor voters' choices, by firms' willingness to impose economic punishments on voters, and by the available reemployment opportunities.

This discussion yields a number of observable implications about cross-sectional and temporal variation in the level of support for Social Democracy. Consider first the implications of the adoption of legislation promoting electoral secrecy on Social Democratic support. Because this legislation reduced the probability that opposition votes would be detected, the magnitude of the economic losses incurred by voters for their political choices was likely to decline after its adoption. The new legislation likely had two consequences on the political support for opposition candidates. First, I expect that political support for Social Democracy increased following the adoption of electoral secrecy legislation. Second, I expect that the economic conditions in a district – such as labor scarcity or economic heterogeneity – became less important determinants of variation in the political strength of opposition candidates following the adoption of this legislation. As the economic costs incurred by voters for their political choices became negligible, the relationship between various economic conditions in a district and support for Social Democracy that had been present prior to the adoption of legislation that protected electoral secrecy should have attenuated after the passage of legislation.

By contrast, in conditions where voter secrecy was imperfectly protected, support for Social Democracy was likely to be highest in districts where political and economic actors faced high constraints in monitoring the choices of voters. Thus, the same variables that are expected to predict the costs of economic and political repression are also likely to explain support for Social Democracy. All other factors being equal, I hypothesize that prior to the adoption of the Rickert law, support for Social Democracy was higher in districts with high occupational heterogeneity, a high concentration of vocational skills, and a fragmented and divided right whose elections were determined in runoffs. I also expect to find high levels of Social Democratic support in districts that experienced labor scarcity. To my knowledge, this is the first study to examine the relationship between economic factors, such as heterogeneity and labor scarcity, and the political strength of Social Democracy at this critical political juncture in the development of the labor movement.

The magnitude of electoral intimidation directed against workers affected not just the strength of Social Democratic support in a district. It also affected the *types* of Social Democratic politicians that were likely to be elected. Despite the strong organizational unity of the Social Democratic Party, scholars of German Social Democracy have noted the existence of significant variation in the willingness of Social Democratic candidates to engage in electoral cooperation with candidates on the right. My analysis formulates a number of novel propositions about the factors that were likely to contribute to the election of different types of Social Democratic candidates. I hypothesize that the Social Democratic politicians elected in districts characterized by high levels of economic concentration were likely to be more radical and to exhibit less willingness to engage in cooperation with candidates on the right. By contrast, candidates elected in districts where voters were subjected to lower levels of electoral intimidation were likely to show a higher willingness to cooperate with candidates on the right during elections. Thus, the history of electoral intimidation in a district, which was itself influenced by its own economic heterogeneity, was a predictor of the type of Social Democratic candidate. I test my argument using a dataset that codes the existence of electoral alliances during runoffs between a Social Democratic candidate and a candidate on the right.

The existence of these electoral coalitions testifies to an important division within the Social Democratic Party between accommodationist and non-accommodationist candidates. In a prominent study of electoral alliances, Gregory Luebbert hypothesized that Lib-Lab alliances were absent in Germany (Luebbert 1991). Luebbert's hypothesis proves correct with regard to political and electoral outcomes for a large majority of German districts. Contra Luebbert, however, I show that Lib-Lab alliances were formed in districts characterized by a prior history of low electoral intimidation, as proxied by their own economic heterogeneity.

2.3.1. The Consequences of Electoral Reforms for Parties on the Right

The final part of this book examines the consequences of the adoption of electoral secrecy legislation on the electoral fate of parties on the right. Although the 1903 law increased the costs of electoral intimidation for all candidates on the right, it had different political consequences on the vote share of different right-wing parties, depending on the geographic concentration of their votes. The adoption of the 1903 law had no significant effect on the ability of candidates to hold on to their seats for parties whose voters were concentrated geographically. An example of one such party with a concentrated distribution of votes was the Conservative Party. The electoral strength of the Conservatives was only weakly affected by the legislation. The situation was different for parties whose votes were diffused across multiple districts. By raising the costs of electoral intimation, the Rickert law weakened the ability of candidates from these parties to hold on to their seats and to convert votes into seats. One example of a party with a very diffuse geographic base was the National Liberal Party. The ability of the National Liberal Party to convert votes to seats deteriorated beginning with the 1903 election. Although National Liberals had experienced a positive vote-seat ratio prior to that time, the party experienced a negative vote-seat disproportionality after the adoption of the Rickert law.

These calculations about the translation of votes into seats had particularly strong consequences for the final electoral reform adopted in the Reichstag – namely, the adoption of proportional representation. In the aftermath of the

1903 election, National Liberal politicians who experienced a worsening vote-seat ratio shifted their position on questions of electoral reform and joined Social Democratic politicians in advocating the adoption of proportional representation. By contrast, two other large parties on the political right, the Zentrum and the Conservative Party, benefited from the vote-to-seat ratio and continued to support the political status quo. In Chapter 9, I reconstruct parliamentary and extra-parliamentary deliberations about the final question of electoral reform that confronted members of the German Reichstag before and during World War I. This shift in the position of the National Liberal Party facilitated the creation of an electoral coalition supporting the reform of electoral institutions and the adoption of proportional representation. I conclude this chapter by examining the political determinants of the vote leading to the adoption of proportional representation in 1914. The analysis presented in this chapter tests a variety of different explanations for the adoption of proportional representation that have been proposed in other studies, including anti-Rokkanian hypotheses about the economic determinants of support for these reforms.

2.4. THE EMPIRICAL STRATEGY

Recent comparative research on democratization has relied on cross-national analysis as its preferred empirical strategy for testing hypotheses about regime transitions. The groundbreaking contribution by Adam Przeworski and his collaborators illustrates both the strengths and also the most significant methodological limitations of this approach (Przeworski et al. 2000). Boix (2003) advances a simple model of regime choice that stresses the opposition of landholding elites to the extension of franchise and regime transitions in countries with high levels of unequal landholding. Similarly to Przeworski, Boix also chooses a cross-national design and tests his parsimonious argument using a panel of cross-national data for the period between 1800 and 1950.

   Although cross-national analysis helps us identify broad empirical regularities present in the data, it has significant limitations as an empirical strategy. In this section, I consider several such limitations and illustrate how a within-country research design can overcome such shortcomings. First, cross-national studies seek to examine a range of hypotheses linking highly aggregated concepts – such as economic development – to political outcomes. In addition to this theoretical shortcoming, an empirical limitation of this mode of analysis is that the measures used to test these concepts are only weakly linked to their underlying theoretical constructs. Measurement errors are an endemic problem of cross-national research. More problematically, the variables employed in such cross-national analyses only tenuously measure the theoretical mechanism hypothesized to produce the outcome of interest. This gap reduces significantly our confidence in the empirical tests used in cross-national studies. Finally, cross-national studies rarely include political or electoral variables in their analyses. As such, cross-national studies seldom examine how political and economic variables interact to affect democratic outcomes. Because of these omissions, the main findings reported in these studies are likely to be biased.

For an illustration of these propositions, consider the use of highly aggregated theoretical concepts in existing cross-national research. There is a vibrant literature that examines the consequences of economic development for regime outcomes (Przeworski et al. 2000; Boix and Stokes 2003). Economic development, or modernization, is a highly aggregated concept that includes components such as urbanization, industrialization, and higher levels of wealth. Each of these different components of modernization may affect political outcomes through a variety of mechanisms. The discussion of the multiple pathways through which economic concentration affects the adoption of democratic reforms presented in this chapter illustrates the importance of utilizing a more careful specification of the mechanisms linking various components of economic development with electoral reforms. Such discussion is often absent in much of the existing research.

Because of their high levels of aggregation, the theoretical concepts at the center of the literature on democratization are often measured imprecisely. For an illustration of one shortcoming resulting from the poor measurement of key explanatory variables, consider the analysis of the role played by rural inequality in regime transitions in existing comparative research. Rural inequality is a multidimensional concept involving inequalities in the distribution of land, labor, and wages. Each of these separate dimensions of rural inequality affects the preferences of key actors and the resulting distributional conflicts over political regimes through different political mechanisms. The available historical datasets claiming to contain measures of rural inequality for a large number of countries, such as the Vanhannen or Bourguignon datasets, which are widely used in cross-national research, use different dimensions of rural inequality for different countries interchangeably (Vanhannen) or, even more problematically, impute missing values for several countries by using observations from neighboring countries (Bourguignon). These large imprecisions in empirical measurement limit the inferences one can make from these studies. Because of their blunt instruments, none of the existing studies adequately addresses questions about the mechanisms through which landholding inequality affects political outcomes.

An additional limitation of a large number of empirical studies premised on cross-national analysis is the absence of political variables from the analysis. Cross-national studies do not examine the importance of variables such as the partisan composition of the government or the political fragmentation of the government or legislature on regime outcomes because of the absence of these measures in cross-national datasets. This is a severe limitation for cross-national studies, and it leaves some of the most salient questions of political inquiry still unexplored.

A within-country research design makes it possible to circumvent these short-comings of cross-national analyses. First, this research design allows me to rely on precise measures of the central explanatory variables. Because of the higher precision in these measurements, I can distinguish between and test a variety of mechanisms through which explanatory variables (such as rural inequality and economic development) affect political outcomes. The empirical design allows me to include both economic and political variables in the analysis and to examine the relative influence of these factors on politicians' calculations about electoral reform. As such, I examine the interplay of economic factors, such as landholding inequality and labor scarcity, and political factors, such as partisanship and electoral competition, on the probability of electoral reforms. The remaining chapters in the book illustrate at greater length the relative strength of this method of empirical analysis.

2.4.1. Occupational Heterogeneity

One of the central theoretical hypotheses of this study is that the occupational heterogeneity of a district affects both the willingness of private actors to engage in electoral intimidation and the costs of electoral repression for politicians who deploy private actors as their electoral agents. I further hypothesize that support for electoral reforms protecting voter autonomy originates with politicians from districts with high levels of occupational heterogeneity. To test these hypotheses, I digitize and make use of extremely fine-grained information collected by the German Statistical Office on the occupational conditions present in more than 1,000 different communes. The study of the occupational landscape during Germany's industrial takeoff occupied a central place in the data collection efforts of this statistical agency. The Census of Occupation and Statistics (*Berufszählung*) was the centerpiece of Wilhelmine statistics and the crown jewel of European historical statistics. The census, which was a hugely expensive enterprise, "was conceived as an integrated system for registering the nation's social and economic structure" (Tooze 2001: 52). The German Statistical Office collected this detailed information at two points in time, in 1895 and 1903. Tooze describes the two censuses further:

They were enormous projects, involving millions of households and firms, armies of census takers, hundreds of temporary staff hired by the statistical bureau to mark up and count the millions of returns and the entire resources of the statistical profession. They were hugely expensive. Even the German system of using "volunteer" civil servants as census takers could not keep the costs below many millions of marks. They were accomplished through a collective effort involving the *Reich* in collaboration with the statistical bureaus of all the member states in the federation.... They were divorced from all other branches of state administration. Above all, they were carefully preserved from any entanglement with the fiscal authorities. Respondents were assured that the census returns would be used exclusively for "statistical purposes." The censuses were under the sole control of professional statisticians and they reveal most clearly the profession's understanding of German economic and social life. (Tooze 2001: 51)

The occupational census includes disaggregated information about employment in 220 occupations across more than 1,000 localities (communes) in the German Empire. A great deal of empirical heavy lifting was necessary to make this information available and to use it in the quantitative analysis for this book. I digitized both waves of the occupational census, an effort that generated nearly 1 million lines of digital information. I then aggregated all of the information to the level of the German electoral districts using the mapping of localities to districts provided by Reibel (2007). This detailed occupational information allowed me to compute a range of indicators measuring the variation in occupational heterogeneity across German regions at an extremely disaggregated level of analysis.

Economic concentration is a concept that has occupied a central role in existing research on Germany's economic development during the nineteenth century. Considerable disagreement exists about the relationship between economic concentration and economic development. Gerschenkron's classic study *Bread and Democracy in Germany* (1946) hypothesized that the engine of Germany's economic development was located in regions characterized by high levels of economic concentration, such as the Ruhr region. During the early 1990s, scholars such as Charles Sabel, Jonathan Zeitlin, and Gary Herrigel challenged this Gerschenkronian perspective of economic development. Sabel and Zeitlin (1996) argued that economically heterogeneous regions experienced a takeoff in nineteenth-century Germany that was comparable to the development in economically concentrated areas. Herrigel (1996) argued that the organization of production differed across "concentrated" and "diversified" regions and that these differences in the organization of production persisted well into the twentieth century.

This study builds on these contributions in two respects. The first extension is empirical. Both Herrigel (1996) and Jürgen Kocka worked with aggregated measures of occupational heterogeneity across German regions. Here, by contrast, I use for the first time the wealth of economic information available in the German census to measure systematic differences in Germany's occupational landscape at a much lower level of aggregation. Second, whereas existing studies have explored the economic consequences of differences in heterogeneity, I provide an empirical examination of their political consequences by considering the effects of those differences on the costs of electoral intimidation. This book documents a strong and robust relationship between occupational heterogeneity and the incidence of electoral intimidation, the preferences of politicians toward electoral reforms, and also the variation in the vote share of Social Democratic candidates.

2.4.2. Vocational Skills

Vocational skills (or co-specific assets) constitute a central variable for comparative politics research because of the theoretical importance of this variable in the literature on varieties of capitalism (Hall and Soskice 2001). The presence (or absence) of vocational skills distinguishes coordinated market economies from uncoordinated ones and is hypothesized to explain a range of political outcomes, including different levels of social protection, labor peace, and industrial relations. In recent years, a number of studies have advanced a range of bold conjectures linking the variation in vocational skills during the nineteenth century with a range of salient political variables, such as democratic outcomes during the interwar period, choices in electoral rules, and the adoption of proportional representation (Cusack et al. 2010; Iversen 2010).

Despite the theoretical importance of vocational skills for a wide range of scholarship, existing studies lack measures of differences in human capital at this critical turning point in European political development. The numerous conjectures formulated by these studies have therefore remained, as yet, untested. My study seeks to address this empirical deficit in our understanding of the political implications of vocational skills by developing measures of the skill profiles of the labor force that are extremely disaggregated geographically and also extremely fine-grained in their occupational coverage.

German statistical authorities collected information about the ratio between skilled and unskilled workers for 180 occupations as part of the 1895 occupational census. I use this information in conjunction with the occupational information to compute very precise measures of the skill profile in every German locality. I aggregate these measures at the district level to compute measures of the skill distribution that can then be then used in conjunction with other explanatory variables.

2.4.3. Rural Inequality

Landholding inequality occupies a central role in theories of regime transitions. Despite the importance of this variable, considerable uncertainty exists about the mechanisms through which it affects political outcomes and about the robustness of the relationship between landholding inequality and political regimes (Ansell and Samuels 2014; Ardanaz and Mares 2014). Two issues are at the center of this disagreement. Some of the ongoing disagreement about the consequences of rural inequality goes back to questions about model specifications. Disagreement also exists about the mechanisms through which different dimensions of inequality affect political outcomes. The study of the political consequences of landholding inequality in Imperial Germany provides us with the opportunity to address some of these outstanding theoretical and empirical controversies.

Landholding inequality is a multidimensional concept. It comprises numerous dimensions, including inequalities in the distribution of land and employment conditions in the countryside (Ardanaz and Mares 2014). The study of Imperial Germany provides us with an ideal opportunity to examine which of these dimensions of inequality are more consequential politically. We find significant internal variation among both dimensions of inequality in Imperial

Germany. The magnitude of the variation in inequality one finds within Germany is comparable to the variation one finds in cross-national contexts.

This study examines the political consequences of two dimensions of inequality: inequality in the distribution of land and inequality in employment conditions. The first dimension is inequality in landholding. I assess the consequences of rural inequality by using a standard measure – a Gini coefficient of landholding inequality. This measure calculates the magnitude of the deviation from a perfectly equal distribution of land among landholders. To ensure comparability with earlier studies, I use a measure of landholding inequality computed by Dan Ziblatt (2009) based on information collected by the German statistical authorities (Statistisches Reichsamt 1895). The measure for a second dimension of rural inequality is a Gini coefficient of inequality in agricultural employment. The main input for this measure is the number of workers employed on farms of different sizes, rather than the physical area of those farms. The source for this second variable is information collected by Prussian statistical authorities as part of the Prussian agricultural census (Königliches Preussisches Statistisches Landesamt 1895, 1907).

To conclude, Imperial Germany is a unique laboratory that allows us to subject a wide range of hypotheses about the determinants for the adoption of democratic reforms in competitive authoritarian contexts to more rigorous testing. We find significant variation among all economic variables that are hypothesized to affect demand for electoral reforms within Germany. These include occupational heterogeneity, vocational skills, and landholding inequality. Germany also exhibits large subnational variation in its partisan landscape, which allows us to examine the relative importance of political and economic factors in accounting for the adoption of electoral reforms. At the same time, a better empirical measure of the central explanatory variables from this literature allows us to investigate the wide range of mechanisms through which these variables affect political outcomes.

3

Electoral Intimidation by State Employees

> The authority of the state is powerful in the hands of each person, also in the hands of the last night watchman and policeman.
> (Eduard Lasker, *Stenographische Berichte des Reichstages* April 17, 1871)

This chapter begins the empirical investigation of the production of electoral irregularities in German elections by analyzing the variation in electoral irregularities perpetrated by employees of the state. Electoral intimidation by state employees was pervasive in German national elections. The majority of the petitions submitted to the electoral commission of the Reichstag invoked electoral irregularities committed by employees of the state (Klein 2003). The ubiquitous presence of state employees as well as the brutal nature of their harassment and intimidation of voters added an unusually harsh character to nineteenth-century German elections. The identities of the employees of the state that supplied electoral services to politicians varied significantly across German regions. In Prussia, *Landräte* and policemen played a pervasive role in elections. The former cumulated important political responsibilities, serving as both the collectors of taxes (and assessors of tax liabilities) and making decisions on who was conscripted into the Prussian army. In Saxony, a region that experienced very high levels of electoral irregularities, policemen were ubiquitous in elections. By contrast, in southern German states such as Baden or Württemberg, where the electoral intervention by public employees was lower, mayors were the actors who occasionally trespassed against the provisions of the electoral law and engaged in the electoral intimidation of voters.

I begin this chapter by developing a number of hypotheses about the political considerations of politicians and employees of the state, and the incentives for the former to demand and the latter to supply electoral services conflicting with the provisions of the electoral code. In particular, I examine the relationship between political competition and the production of intimidation in

German national elections. Chapter 4 then examines the political strategies used by private actors during elections. As discussed in Chapter 1, a unique characteristic of German national elections is the pervasive presence of private actors who were deployed by candidates as agents of electoral intimidation. I develop a range of hypotheses about the economic and political factors affecting the variation in the intensity of private electoral intimidation. In Chapter 5, I present a quantitative test of these hypotheses. A reader eager to see these results might consider skipping ahead to that chapter.

The empirical analysis in this chapter draws on the qualitative evidence collected by the commission that examined irregularities in elections to the Reichstag. By relying on the parliamentary petitions documenting electoral irregularities, a variety of secondary sources, and unpublished documents located in the archives of the German Ministry of the Interior, I seek to reconstruct the variation in the strategies of electoral intimidation used by employees of the state during national elections. In addition to these primary sources, my analysis draws on a range of historical studies published in recent years that examine "everyday" electoral practices in Imperial Germany during the first decades following the adoption of mass suffrage (Kühne 1994; Anderson 2000; Klein 2003; Arsenschek 2003).

I draw on the evidence available in these different sources to explore a number of questions about the strategies of electoral intimidation used by employees of the state. The first question pertains to the calculations made by bureaucratic officials about the optimal level of electoral pressure that could be exerted at a particular time and the political constraints that these officials considered salient. To this end, I draw on publications and internal documents found in a variety of Prussian ministries and a wealth of secondary sources. This evidence also allows me to analyze variation in the intensity with which employees of the state deployed their subordinates during elections. Within Prussia, I demonstrate the existence of significant temporal variation in the intensity of the political pressure exerted by bureaucrats of the central ministries on lower-level officials to deliver electoral services to the desirable candidates, which is consistent with the theoretical hypotheses outlined in the previous chapter. The intensity of political pressure was highest during moments when parties on the political right were coordinated electorally. The use of political pressure declined, however, as the fragmentation among parties on the political right and the share of elections whose outcomes were determined during runoffs increased. These changes in the patterns of political competition contributed to a change in the electoral strategies of bureaucratic officials of the Ministry of the Interior. In this new political environment, officials in the center used a "noiseless" strategy of electoral intervention, one that attempted to minimize the traces of political intervention from the center.

This chapter also presents descriptive evidence about the strategies of electoral intimidation used by employees of the state. Which specific actions of policemen, tax collectors, mayors, and election officials led to the production of electoral irregularities? Which stage of the electoral process was most vulnerable to the production of electoral irregularities? To answer these questions, I disaggregate elections into their separate components – the campaign, the act of voting, the emptying of urns, and the tallying of results. I analyze the types of electoral irregularities present at each of these different stages. In doing so, I examine where and at what point in elections the political pressure exerted by employees of the state on voters was highest. I employ a similar analysis in the Chapter 4, which analyzes the electoral strategies used by private actors. To anticipate the results, I find that officials of the state exerted the highest amount of political effort when attempting to deter the mobilization of candidates representing opposition parties and when attempting to influence the choices made at the moment of voting. Election officials and employees of the state that were stationed in a precinct took advantage of imperfections in voting technology by trying to identify the choices made by individual voters. By contrast, we find remarkably few irregularities committed during the final stages of an election, that is, during the process of tallying the electoral results. The "rigging of urns" – a common electoral experience in many European and Latin American countries at the time – was an uncommon practice in German elections.

This chapter tests the political explanation for the determinants of electoral intervention by employees of the state by examining variation in the political strategies used by employees of the state in four regions of the Reich: Prussia, Saxony, Baden, and Württemberg. These regions exhibit significant variation in the crucial political variables that are hypothesized to affect the electoral incentives for employees of the state: the number of parties and candidates competing on the political right, the presence or absence of runoffs, and the political strength of Social Democratic candidates. These regions were among the five largest and most populous regions of the German Empire. Therefore, the detailed account of political practices in these regions can be seen as a representative pattern of electoral competition for the entire Empire.

This test of the hypotheses formulated in Chapter 2 using regional-level data provides preliminary support for the main theoretical hypotheses. Electoral intimidation perpetrated by employees of the state was highest in Prussia and Saxony, two regions characterized by low levels of fragmentation among parties on the political right. This form of electoral intimidation was lower in the two southern German states exhibiting higher levels of electoral fragmentation among parties on the right and a higher incidence of runoffs. Also, the temporal variation in the evolution of electoral intimidation is consistent with the theoretical predictions formulated in Chapter 2: an increase in the electoral strength of opposition parties (especially during the final elections of the period) increased the political costs of the reliance on employees of the state and contributed to a decline in the incidence of electoral intimidation.

3.1. STATE EMPLOYEES IN GERMAN ELECTIONS

Electoral interventions by employees of the state were illegal according to German electoral law (Hatschek 1920: 551–554). As Julius Hatschek, a leading legal scholar of electoral law, demonstrated in his evaluation of the changing German jurisprudence, the definition of "public employee" and the specific actions that were considered illegal evolved over time. The initial conception of electoral irregularities committed by officials of the state defined them as instances "when the electoral call was announced by an official person with an indication of the administrative responsibilities of the latter" (Hatschek 1920: 531). Over time, however, the list of illegal electoral irregularities committed by employees of the state expanded. These included:

A generally strong partiality of the government for a particular candidacy, the so-called "official candidacy," the calling of a meeting of voters by an official person, the publication of an electoral call in an official publication, even if the latter was only an indirect announcement of a candidacy, the sending of ballots by official persons, the distribution of ballots by employees of the state, the illegal bans of electoral meetings, the illegal confiscation of ballots and the illegal pressuring of the owners of certain public spaces not to make the space available to particular parties (Hatschek 1920: 552).

Beginning with the first elections of the Empire, prominent German politicians, such as Otto von Bismarck, challenged the principle of the political neutrality of state employees during elections. In an intervention to the Reichstag in 1881, Bismarck argued that "employees of the state could not be entirely non-partisan. The position of the latter in the administration *presupposes* a certain level of partisanship on behalf of the government" (*Stenographische Berichte des Deutschen Reichstages* March 3, 1881: 136, emphasis added). Robert von Puttkammer, Prussia's Minister of the Interior at the time, expressed a similar view. In his own political intervention on the floor of the Reichstag in 1881, Puttkammer summarized the political strategy used by his ministry. "The government," he asserted, "expected and supported an open intervention of government officials during elections. The absence of their support, he argued, would impede the ability of the government to carry out its desired policies." Puttkammer ended his intervention by reassuring the employees of the state who had provided electoral support to governmental candidates during elections of the "gratitude and appreciation of the government" (*Stenographische Berichte des Deutschen Reichstages* 1881: vol. 66, 373).

In January 1882, German Emperor Wilhelm I issued a decree that attempted to clarify the political responsibilities of civil servants (*Beamte*) of the Prussian state. The decree mandated that "every Prussian minister and all employees that had provided an official oath (*Amtseid*) have the duty to represent the prerogative rights of the monarchy and are bound by the obligation to represent the prerogatives of the crown in protesting against doubts and defamation of the latter" (Rejewski 1973: 175, Arsenschek 2003: 193). The German *Kaiser* also expressed his expectation that government officials "will refrain from any agitation against the government during elections." The 1882 decree codified the political expectations vis-à-vis the activities of the Prussian bureaucracy until 1918.

The decree did not *require* the active involvement of Prussian employees of the state on behalf of particular candidates. But its provision was unambiguous in its explicit prohibition of electoral support for opposition candidates. As such, the "negative expectations" of the Prussian *Beamtenerlass* conflicted with a central principle of the national electoral law: the principle of the strict neutrality of employees of the state. The tension between these two laws created an opening for officials of the Prussian Ministry of the Interior to push for an activist involvement of employees of the state, with the explicit aim of limiting political opportunities for parties that were considered official "enemies" of the *Reich*. This more activist understanding of the proper electoral responsibilities of employees of the state, which was shared by officials of the Prussian Ministry of the Interior, conflicted with the provisions of the national electoral law. Other regions of the Empire lacked similar legislation detailing expectations for the political responsibilities of state employees. These differences in the legal framework that outlined the expectations for the political behavior of state employees suggest that the costs encountered by those employees of intervening politically in elections on behalf of particular candidates were significantly lower in Prussia than they were in other German provinces.

This variation in the legal provisions outlining the expectations about the political involvement of public employees is one factor in the explanation of the variation in the incentives for the electoral engagement of state employees. One implication of this discussion is that the level of electoral intervention by state employees during elections was much higher in Prussia than in other German regions of the *Reich*. However, within each region we find both significant temporal and geographical variation in the incidence of electoral irregularities. To account for this variation, we need to complement the initial institutional explanation – which highlights cross-regional variation in the permissiveness of legislation in each province toward the political activities of state employees – with additional political factors.

As hypothesized in Chapter 2, to understand the electoral involvement of employees of the state, we need to examine both the factors that affected the variation in the demand made by politicians for electoral support from employees of the state and the decisions of employees of the state to supply electoral services. The first factor affecting the intensity of the demand made by candidates is the level of electoral competition. Politicians' demand for electoral support from employees of the state is likely to increase as the tightness of a race increases. Yet, a tighter race might also constrain the willingness of state employees to supply electoral services during elections, given that the uncertainty about the political identity of the future principal is higher. This suggests that the tightness of a race creates offsetting incentives for politicians and state employees. Which effect prevails is an empirically open question. I postpone a systematic empirical analysis of the relationship between the margin of victory and the incidence of electoral fraud until Chapter 5.

A second political variable that may account for the variation in electoral intimidation perpetrated by state employees is the political fragmentation among candidates on the right, especially in races that are determined by runoffs. This hypothesized relationship between right-wing fragmentation, runoffs, and electoral intimidation is a consequence of the incentive structure of the German electoral system. Consider first the demand and supply for electoral irregularities in districts where the right is fragmented and where the outcome is likely to be determined in a runoff. In these districts, both candidates and state employees are likely to exercise restraint in using electoral intimidation, as opponents during the first round are likely to support each other in runoffs. The heavy-handed use of the state apparatus by a particular candidate could alienate potential coalition partners during runoffs and make the latter less willing to support the candidate who had received official backing during the first electoral round. In addition, higher fragmentation among right-wing candidates is also likely to diminish the incentives of employees of the state to supply electoral support for candidates. Here, competition among multiple possible principals may inhibit the incentives of employees of the state to intervene politically in elections. In districts where right-wing fragmentation is low (i.e., one political candidate from the right dominates) and the outcome will be decided during the first round, both candidates and state employees are unrestrained from using electoral coercion.

Finally, as hypothesized in Chapter 2, the political strength of Social Democracy was likely to affect candidates' reliance on state employees as agents of intimidation during elections. Candidates on the right that faced intense political competition from Social Democratic candidates were more likely to demand electoral support from employees of the state. Thus, an increase in the electoral strength of Social Democratic candidates was likely to lead to an increase in the demand for support by employees of the state during elections. However, I hypothesize that the relationship between the strength of opposition candidates and the production of electoral intimidation is nonlinear. With very strong Social Democratic candidates, the marginal costs of electoral intimidation were also very high. The likelihood that intimidation – no matter how strongly it is applied – could affect the outcome of a race was low in districts where Social Democratic candidates were expected to win by large majorities. This suggests that both candidates and employees of the state could refrain from using electoral intimidation in districts where the political support for Social Democratic candidates was very high and also implies that the production of electoral irregularities was highest when Social Democrats exhibited intermediate levels of strength.

We find significant variation across Germany's regions in the political variables that affected the incentives of employees of the state to produce electoral

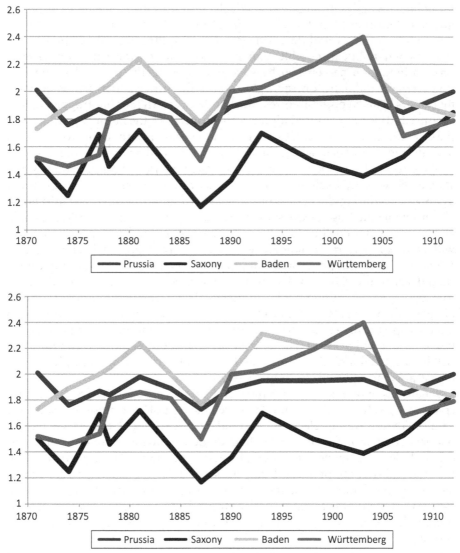

FIGURE 3.1. Temporal and regional variation in the effective number of right-wing parties across four provinces. *Source*: ICPSR 1984.

irregularities. Let us consider first the variation in the political fragmentation on the right. Figure 3.1 presents descriptive information about the temporal and regional variation in the political fragmentation among right-wing parties across four German regions: Prussia, Saxony, Baden, and Württemberg. Here, I use the standard measure of right-wing political fragmentation: the effective number of right-wing parties. For each election, I compute the measure of the

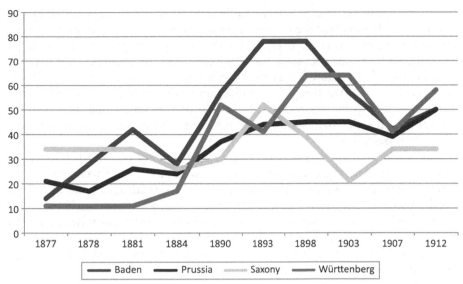

FIGURE 3.2. Share of districts whose outcomes were determined in runoffs in four German provinces.

effective number of right-wing parties in a district and aggregate that measure to the level of the region. The graph reveals the existence of significant regional and temporal variation in the political fragmentation among right-wing parties. Out of the four regions, Saxony exhibits the lowest level of right-wing political fragmentation. With the exception of the 1877 election, Saxony's political fragmentation was significantly lower than that of the other three regions. By contrast, Baden had the highest level of political fragmentation among these states. Right-wing political fragmentation in Prussia was also low and comparable to that of Saxony during the earliest elections of the period. Over time, however, its political fragmentation increased sharply because of the dissolution of the electoral cartel among the Conservative Party and the National Liberal Party, as well as the increase in rival parties to the Conservatives (such as the Bund der Landwirte).

As hypothesized in Chapter 2, right-wing political fragmentation was likely to lower the production of electoral irregularities primarily in races that were determined during runoffs. One of the most remarkable developments in electoral politics in Germany during the period was the increase in the number of races whose outcomes were decided during runoffs. Consider the trends for the entire German Empire. In 1877, the share of races that were decided in runoffs was 17 percent, but this share increased to 48 percent by 1912 in the final election of the Empire. We find significant variation across the four different regions in the number of races that were determined during runoffs. In Figure 3.2, I present descriptive information about the share of elections that were decided in runoffs across the four provinces. In Prussia, the share of races determined in runoffs closely mirrored the German average. In Saxony, the share of elections decided in runoffs was relatively stable throughout the period, at around 35 percent, with the exception of the 1893 elections. By contrast, the share of elections decided in runoffs was much higher in the two southern principalities of Baden and Württemberg. In conjunction with the high levels of political fragmentation on the right, the high number of runoffs created incentives for restraint in the deployment of state employees during elections in southern German provinces.

The third political factor that affects the incentives of state employees to engage in electoral repression – the political strength of the Social Democratic Party – also varies significantly across these four German states and over time. As discussed in Chapter 2, I expect to find a nonlinear relationship between the strength of opposition candidates and the supply of electoral intimidation by candidates on the right. The Social Democratic vote share experienced a steady rise across all provinces. It was highest in Saxony as compared to Prussia and the southern German principalities. This suggests that the incentive to engage in electoral intimidation rose at a higher rate in Saxony than it did in Prussia and the two southern principalities. A second implication is that the incentive to use the resources of the state eroded first in Saxony.

The combination of these variables, I argue, affected politicians' reliance on voter intimidation during elections. These incentives should be highest in districts with low levels of fragmentation among right-wing parties, no runoffs, and intermediate levels of strength of opposition candidates. These conditions were in place in many Prussian districts at a time when the two largest parties on the right – the National Liberals and the Conservatives – formed electoral cartels and when the electoral strength of the Social Democratic candidates was low. In Saxony, the percentage of elections decided in runoffs was higher (which lowered the incentive to turn to electoral intimidation), but at the same time, the political strength of Social Democracy was considerably higher than it was in Prussia. This combination of political variables also created strong preconditions for the use of intimidation in Saxony. Compared to these cases, one expects to find lower levels of electoral intimidation in regions with high political fragmentation and a high number of runoffs, as was the case for the two southern German provinces of Baden and Württemberg.

I provide a quantitative test of these hypotheses in Chapter 5. In the current chapter, however, I draw on the qualitative evidence found in the electoral petitions to the Reichstag to document the irregularities that were committed by employees of the state during elections. The qualitative evidence is invaluable because it allows us to disaggregate among multiple types of irregularities perpetrated by employees of the state and investigate which stages of the electoral process were most vulnerable to various forms of electoral malfeasance.

3.2. PRUSSIA

Electoral conditions in Prussian districts during the first nine elections of the period provided an auspicious terrain for the use of electoral intimidation. During these initial elections, an electoral alliance between the Conservatives and National Liberals – the *Kartellbündnis* – extended across many provinces in Prussia. This cartel effectively limited competition among parties on the right and lowered the political costs of intimidation. The rise of Social Democracy from low to intermediate levels of strength created additional incentives to turn to electoral intimidation. Over time, the electoral alliance among parties on the right fragmented because of increasing political disagreements between the main parties on the right (the Conservatives, Free Conservatives, and National Liberals) about the salient policy questions that were on the agenda of the Reichstag. In particular, questions of trade protection and taxation turned out to be particularly divisive during this period. I hypothesize that this increase in right-wing fragmentation increases the political costs of electoral intimidation.

I start by exploring the considerations of actors located in the bureaucracy of the Prussian Ministry of the Interior about the advantages and disadvantages of a heavier involvement of the apparatus of the state in elections. When bureaucratic officials perceived the costs of electoral intervention to be low, they pushed for an ample deployment of the bureaucratic apparatus. At other times, bureaucrats located in this central node of the German administration advocated a more restrained approach to the deployment of policemen, tax collectors, and teachers as electoral agents in support of particular candidates. At such times, the Prussian Ministry of the Interior used a more subdued set of electoral strategies. When the costs of electoral repression were perceived to be high, officials of the Ministry of the Interior attempted to reduce the visibility of their relationship to employees of the state operating in different districts.

The intensity of the pressure imposed by high-level officials of the Prussian Ministry of the Interior on mid- and low-level bureaucrats to display political "engagement" varied significantly between the different elections of the period. The earliest elections of the period mark the high point of political activism on the part of officials from the center. Political activities displayed by employees at the center of the administration declined after the 1890 election. Beginning with this election, one finds a more subdued and restrained political approach to the question of whether or not to deploy public employees as electoral agents. This temporal pattern is consistent with my hypothesis that a decline in electoral coordination among parties on the right constrains the deployment of public employees as agents of electoral intimidation. The increase in the electoral strength of opposition candidates – most notably, the increase in the strength of Social Democracy during the final elections of the period – created additional political dilemmas for Prussian officials. In districts with extremely high levels of Social Democratic political strength, electoral intimidation was unlikely to change the outcome of the race. In these races, the costs of electoral intimidation were likely to outweigh its potential electoral benefits.

The Prussian Ministry of the Interior developed and perfected an elaborate system for deploying bureaucratic officials as agents during the first elections of the period. The architect and chief designer of this system was Robert von Puttkammer, who served as Prussia's Minister of the Interior during the period between 1881 and 1888 (Kehr 1965). Puttkammer's political strategy as Prussian Minister of the Interior relied on a sophisticated system of punishing officials who supported opposition candidates and rewarding those who intervened on behalf of candidates on the right. The right was unified during Puttkammer's tenure and included candidates from the Conservative, Free Conservative, and National Liberal parties. As Arsenschek summarized Puttkammer's approach: "[T]he spectrum of sanctions included the threat to withhold promotions, awards and gratifications and threats of transfers or disciplinary measures" (Arsenschek 2003: 194). Puttkammer enforced these rewards and punishments primarily on mid-level bureaucratic officials. "In particular, the mid-level officials that displayed indolence during the elections were under regular attack from above. After all, these employees played a critical role in affecting whether the armies of low-level employees could be set in motion as multiplicators or as voters in a district" (Kühne 1994: 61). Such strategy met with support from Bismarck, who was chancellor at the time. Bismarck argued that "employees of the state need to serve a particular administration and have to carry out the directives of the latter" (*Stenographische Berichte des Deutschen Reichstages* 1881: 135).

However, beginning in the 1890s, Puttkammer's electoral strategy came under strong attack. The political impetus for this policy reversal was the breakdown of the electoral cartel among parties on the right. The formidable and seemingly undefeatable electoral cartel among Conservatives and National Liberals fragmented because of increasing disagreement between these parties about questions of trade. From the perspective of the local-level bureaucratic officials who were willing to supply support during elections, this political division between parties that had been previously aligned created significant uncertainty. The likelihood of runoffs and the anticipated need for electoral coordination during a second round between candidates who had opposed each other during the first round further limited the incentive for public officials to supply electoral intimidation.

In a harsh critique of the practices that had been condoned under Puttkammer's tenure as Minister of the Interior, Emperor Friedrich III vowed to "clean the administration of the suspicion of having condoned these abuses" (cited in Arsenschek 2003: 196). Following Puttkammer's resignation, "the Prussian administration employed a policy attempting to limit the involvement of employees of the state." During the 1890s, Prussian officials in the central ministry refrained from using the ample rewards and punishments that had been in place under Puttkammer. Even employees of the state who reportedly supported candidates' critical position on the government's new trade policy remained unpunished. This represented an extraordinary change in policy from that of the previous decade (Arsenschek 2003: 197).

The final elections of the Imperial Period were characterized by an increase in the electoral strength of the Social Democratic Party and by changing coalitional alignments among parties on the right. These electoral conditions created a distinct set of challenges for officials of the Prussian Ministry of the Interior and led to further changes in their electoral strategy. For the first time, ministry officials published "guidelines" that identified candidates who deserved electoral support and singled out undesirable ones. Arsenschek characterized this change in political strategy as follows:

[I]n cases when this decision was difficult to make, the government recommended which parties were to be favored. During the first round, the government recommended taking particular precautions against all candidates that could become potential coalition partners during runoffs. In concrete terms, in 1898 and 1903, the government predominantly urged officials to support Conservatives, Free Conservatives, and National Liberals, but it added Free Liberals during the 1907 elections. Opposing Social Democratic candidates was viewed as a "self-evident" goal during all of the elections. Likewise, candidates fielded by the Polish, Danish, and Guelph parties were to be opposed. The Zentrum was classified as a political adversary, but the government recommended supporting it rather than Social Democrats and, during the 1898 elections, rather than the radical Anti-Semites and the "Party Richter." (Arsenschek 2003: 198)

The deployment of the bureaucracy in the later elections was "noiseless" in comparison to those from earlier periods (Müller 1963). Successive governments took all possible steps to conceal the traces of their political intervention from the public. Consider the measures taken by the Caprivi government during the 1903 elections. The government relied on the extensive dissemination of leaflets and other electoral materials attempting to justify its position on issues of taxation and reassure low-income voters (*kleiner Mann*) that they would not disproportionately bear the new tax increases. The government established a special office in Berlin led by a military official whose goal was to disseminate electoral material to voters. In a secret memorandum, the Ministry of the Interior instructed local government officials to oppose the policy positions advocated by critics of the government while simultaneously taking unprecedented levels of precaution to hide any trace of its intervention. To avoid exposing officials' participation, the *Landräte* had to provide the addresses of contact persons (*Vertrauensmänner*) whom the central office in Berlin could contact (Müller 1963). This noiseless strategy contrasts the heavy-handed intervention of earlier elections.

Thus, the broad patterns of the temporal variation in the strategies used by central officials of the Prussian administration are consistent with the main political hypotheses outlined earlier in this chapter. In political contexts characterized by high levels of electoral coordination among parties on the right and by relatively weak opposition candidates, Prussian bureaucrats used a heavy-handed policy characterized by the aggressive deployment of state officials during elections. Changes in electoral competition at the beginning of the 1890s modified, however, the calculations made by government officials and reduced their reliance on employees of the state as electoral agents. The disintegration of the electoral cartel of parties on the right constrained the use of electoral intervention. The policy used by the Ministry of the Interior tried to respond to these conflicting imperatives: the government continued to rely on employees of the state, but it did so in a more subdued and noiseless manner. During the final elections of the Imperial Period, both the electoral fragmentation among right-wing parties and the electoral strength of opposition parties increased. Officials located at the center of the Prussian bureaucracy tried to adjust to these new political realities by issuing district-specific guidelines for recommending "desirable" political candidates they deemed worthy of political support. As in the 1890s, however, the high level of electoral fragmentation among candidates on the right constrained the heavy-handed deployment of state employees as agents of electoral repression.

   This discussion illustrates the fact that the decisions made by the officials of the Prussian Ministry of the Interior about the deployment of employees of the state during elections and the amount of effort demanded from them varied significantly during the thirteen elections that were held in Imperial Germany. This temporal variation disconfirms the theoretical hypothesis of a "capture of state officials by powerful rural elites" (Ziblatt 2009). The argument invoking "state capture" fails to unpack the motivations of bureaucratic officials and the political constraints they faced in elections. Empirically, this explanation also fails to account for the significant temporal variation in the incentives of public officials to perpetrate electoral irregularities. The empirical evidence presented in this section suggests that the calculations of officials located at the center of the Prussian bureaucracy varied significantly over time and were affected by shifting levels of electoral competition.

3.2.1. The View from Prussian Districts

High-ranking officials in the Ministry of the Interior used the administrative tools available to them to incentivize state employees to participate during elections. But what strategies did local-level officials use in their efforts to support particular candidates on the political right? In this section, I reconstruct the electoral strategies of local-level officials in Prussian districts, by drawing on the rich evidence presented in reports of complaints about electoral irregularities. To analyze the variety of electoral strategies used by these actors, I disaggregate elections into different stages and examine the strategies used by employees of the state at each different stage. These stages include the campaign, the act of voting, the tallying of results, and the determination of a winner in each district. This disaggregation has two advantages. On the one hand, it allows me to identify more precisely the actual strategies used by employees of the state. On the other hand, it allows me to examine which of the different stages of the electoral process were most vulnerable to electoral irregularities.

Who were the employees of the state that supplied electoral support to candidates in Prussian districts? One surprising aspect of German electoral practices is the wide heterogeneity in the socioeconomic backgrounds of state employees of the German state who were willing to intervene during elections. In Prussia, the most visible representatives of the state were policemen and *Landräte*. The latter were officials whose administrative responsibilities included tax collection (and the assessment of tax liabilities) and conscription into the military. The list of officials who were engaged in the electoral intimidation of voters also included postal workers, school inspectors, department heads, heads of localities and communes, village mayors, patrolmen, and, yes, night watchmen (*Stenographische Berichte des Deutschen Reichstages* 1878: encl. 16). Eugen Richter, a prominent Free Liberal politician and a member of the electoral commission of the Reichstag, compared the Prussian bureaucratic apparatus at election time to a hydra: new heads sprang up even after the old heads were chopped off.

The starting point of a political campaign was the announcement of candidacy, the *Wahlaufruf*. This announcement created the opportunity for candidates to display their political connections with the powerful political actors in a locality. The publication of *Wahlaufrufe* by candidates in official government publications was illegal under German electoral law. In a review of the electoral irregularities that occurred during the 1878 election, the electoral commission reiterated this principle forcefully: "[T]he intervention of a public official on behalf of a candidate transforms the electoral competition from a competition among the different parties to a competition between the government and one of the parties" (*Stenographische Berichte des Deutschen Reichstages* April 2, 1879).

Numerous electoral protests testify to the pervasive violation of this interdiction. They display an overall picture of excessively zealous mayors who were eager to display their support for particular candidates. Consider one such example of the interdiction of this violation from the 1878 election in Frankfurt Sorau. At the time, two official local publications – the *Sorau Kreisblatt* and the *Provinzial-Korrespondenz* – published a number of articles in which prominent state employees of the district, such as the *Königlicher Landrat* and the *Geheimer Regierungskandidat*, recommended the conservative candidate Schon as the candidate who represented "the intentions and desires of the government in the best way" (*Stenographische Berichte des Deutschen Reichstages* 1878: encl. 167). In their efforts to sway voters to support particular candidates, state employees often invoked the symbols of the monarchy. This was the case during the 1878 election in Danzig. At the time, the *Landrat* Dippe wrote a number of articles for official government publications in which he praised the conservative candidate and asserted that by showing support for him, voters would follow the "orders of his majesty" (*Stenographische Berichte des Deutschen Reichstages* 1878: encl. 180).

On other occasions, state officials used military symbols together with the *Wahlaufrufe*. This was the case in the East Prussian district of Labiau Wehlau during the 1878 election (*Stenographische Berichte des Deutschen Reichstages* 1878: encl. 123). Von Knobloch, the conservative candidate, distributed electoral materials that included a variety of military symbols, such as the Imperial Cross, and demanded that voters be present for the "call" (*Appell*). Officials distributed electoral information to voters in which they addressed formerly demobilized soldiers using their military titles. This created considerable uncertainty among voters, who interpreted the electoral announcement as a military order. Numerous voters in the district "demanded immediate release from their work," arguing that "they knew what they had to do as soldiers." Others asserted that voting for the candidate von Knobloch was a military order and that they would be punished if they did not vote. This extreme form of irregularity led to the invalidation of von Knobloch's election.

Employees of the state played a particularly important role in distributing electoral materials on behalf of particular candidates, a practice that, again, violated the electoral law (Hatschek 1920). The electoral commission referred to employees of the state as the "multiplicators" of candidates of the *Kartellparteien* in each district (*Stenographische Berichte des Deutschen Reichstages* 1890: encl. 296). In the East Prussian district of Osterode, the mayor distributed ballots for the conservative candidate and asked, at the same time, voters to burn the ballots distributed by the challenger (*Stenographische Berichte des Deutschen Reichstages* 1878: encl. 16). In Kassel Hersfeld, patrolmen in uniform reportedly went from house to house distributing election ballots. In Königsberg's tenth district, the electoral commission found evidence of the "undisputed dissemination of electoral calls" by *Landräte* during the 1898 election.

This illegal distribution of electoral material on behalf of particular candidates gave state employees opportunities to subject voters to additional political pressures. For example, the deputy of the mayor (*stellvertretende Amtsvorsteher*) in one village threatened voters that he would "turn them into serfs" if they did not vote for the conservative candidate (*Stenographische Berichte des Deutschen Reichstages* 1878: encl. 67). In Harburg, an electoral district in the province of Hannover, the heads of one commune threatened voters who mustered the courage to vote against the conservative candidate, Graf Gorte, with forced labor in the construction of the roads of the commune (*Stenographische Berichte des Deutschen Reichstages* 1878: encl. 67). In Osterode-Neidenburg, a district in East Prussia, Szygan, the school inspector of the district, was reported to have traveled to more than sixty schools in different villages to recommend that teachers vote for the conservative candidate, Becker. Szygan threatened the teachers, suggesting that "an improvement in their wages could be approved only by conservatives and not by liberals. Teachers, thus, had an obligation to vote for Becker" (*Stenographische Berichte des Deutschen Reichstages* 1878: encl. 16).

In 1884, the election in Elbing, Danzig, was contested between the conservative candidate, von Puttkamer-Plauth (the brother of the Prussian Minister of the Interior), and a Free Liberal challenger. Nearly every state official in Elbing supported Puttkammer's candidacy. Members of the electoral commission characterized this election as the clearest example of

[an] official candidacy similar to those encountered in neighboring France. The *Landräte* in Elbing und Marienburg have provided massive support to Puttkammer. They have recommended his candidacy in public meetings, have accompanied Puttkammer on trips in the district, and have participated in his electoral meetings. With a handshake, they obtained the commitment of agricultural workers to support his candidacy. Even electoral officers have distributed ballots with Puttkammer's name and have acted in similar ways as the *Landräte*. (*Stenographische Berichte des Deutschen Reichstages* 1884: encl. 180)

One of the most important electoral functions performed by employees of the state was that of deterring opposition candidates from reaching voters. Prussian elections were characterized by particularly harsh interventions directed against Social Democratic candidates. Policemen routinely arrested and harassed people who distributed electoral ballots on behalf of those candidates. Consider the 1890 election in Blankenberg Ziegenrück. There, policemen arrested people who distributed Social Democratic ballots and retained them for hours. After a long interrogation, the police deported the ballot conveyors across Prussia's border. In 1881, in Ottweiler, Trier, police officers searched the houses of voters suspected of supporting Virchow, the opposition candidate, and confiscated any electoral material or ballots found in the houses (*Stenographische Berichte des Deutschen Reichstages* 1881: encl. 323). Likewise, during the 1884 elections in Kassel, policemen in Rossdorf arrested people who distributed Social Democratic ballots. The mayor of the village threatened to "beat them up with clubs to make them leave the village" (*Stenographische Berichte des Deutschen Reichstages* 1884: encl. 179).

The arrests of people who distributed Social Democratic ballots sometimes escalated into political violence. Consider the incidents that occurred during the 1891 election in Potsdam's tenth district (*Stenographische Berichte des Deutschen Reichstages* 1892: encl. 165). In Neuhoff bei Zossen, one of the localities in the district, policemen on horseback reportedly recklessly attacked Social Democratic ballot conveyors. After the latter hid in a guesthouse, the policemen followed them inside and used weapons to chase them away from the village. In Klein Roris, another village in the district, the mayor encountered conveyors of Social Democratic ballots at the entrance of the village and asked them to show identification papers. After the ballot conveyors identified themselves, the mayor engaged in a series of acts of violence. A witness reported:

The mayor forcefully ripped the ballots and copies of the *Berliner Volksblatt* from the hands of Kaiser, the Social Democratic ballot conveyor. The latter protested and showed the mayor a copy of the electoral law, but the mayor ripped the document to pieces. Then, he stuck his hand in Kaiser's pocket, removed the ballots, and also ripped those to pieces. He threw Kaiser to the ground and then threw him onto the street on the staircase. In the end, he shouted: "Let the dogs loose. Somebody released two dogs, and they attacked Kaiser." (*Stenographische Berichte des Deutschen Reichstages* 1892: encl. 165)

Officials of the Prussian state also sought to weaken opponents by preventing opposition candidates from holding electoral meetings. Complaints about the unlawful cancellation of election meetings by Social Democratic candidates are abundant throughout the period. During the 1884 election in Eltiville-Langenschwalbach, a district in Wiesbaden, one finds six distinct reports that include complaints about the decisions by mayors to cancel electoral meetings of Social Democratic candidates without a clear statement of their reasons. The 1881 elections in Kassel's second district were also characterized by an unprecedented effort of public election officials to prevent the Social Democratic candidate from campaigning. One strategy through which state employees tried to prevent candidates from holding meetings was threatening not to renew the licenses of restaurant owners who opened their doors to the opposition groups. During the 1891 election in Ringleben, near Erfurt, policemen prevented Social Democratic candidates from holding electoral meetings by invoking a "special local law" that did not allow the presence of "foreigners" during elections (*Stenographische Berichte des Deutschen Reichstages* 1891: encl. 296).

Under German electoral law, representatives of parties were responsible for the distribution of ballots. Thus, a recurrent electoral strategy of officials was to prevent representatives of opposition parties from distributing their ballots to voters. During the 1890 election, the entire apparatus of the state in each respective locality was used for this purpose. The bureaucratic apparatus included policemen, tax collectors, and the night watchmen to which Lasker referred in the quote at the start of this chapter (*Stenographische Berichte des Deutschen Reichstages* 1891: encl. 296). In Allach, a small village near Erfurt, ballot conveyors were locked in stables (*Stenographische Berichte des Deutschen Reichstages* 1891: encl. 296). And on numerous occasions, policemen were reported to have ripped ballots from the hands of voters (*Stenographische Berichte des Deutschen Reichstages* 1878: encl. 16). The incidents reported in Oschersleben-Halberstadt-Wernigerode during the 1881 election are representative of the overall tenor of electoral intimidation in Prussian elections (*Stenographische Berichte des Deutschen Reichstages* 1881: encl. 91). In this district, the mayor of Giesecke was reported to have instructed policemen to remove people who were distributing ballots on behalf of Social Democratic candidates from the precinct and "lock them up." Following this order, policemen pushed a person who had been distributing ballots for the Social Democratic candidate down the staircase. They then used force to push him away from the area in front of the voting precinct (*Stenographische Berichte des Deutschen Reichstages* 1881: encl. 91). In Osterwieck, a neighboring locality, the mayor threatened to arrest Wilhelm Kamm, a worker in a cigarette factory, who distributed ballots on behalf of the candidate Heine "because [Kamm] created a great amount of mischief with these ballots" (*Stenographische Berichte des Deutschen Reichstages* 1881: encl. 81). In Redderer, another locality in the district, a policeman threatened to arrest a person who was distributing electoral material. This threat was effective: the ballot distributor fled the locality "without having been able to distribute either pamphlets (*Flugblätter*) or ballots" (*Stenographische Berichte des Deutschen Reichstages* 1881: encl. 81).

On other occasions, the passivity of local officials was as costly for the Social Democratic organizers as these officials' interventions had been. Consider incidents that occurred on election day in Potsdam's tenth district during the 1890 election (*Stenographische Berichte des Deutschen Reichstages* 1891: encl. 165). As one witness reports:

On March 1, 1890, Friedrich Krüger was driven out of the voting precinct in Zossen. He had tried to station himself in front of the precinct to distribute ballots, but he was surrounded by a group of people, punched, thrown to the ground, stomped upon, and slandered. All of this happened in front of the eyes of the mayor, other members of the election board, two policemen, several employees of the railway company, and other "order-loving" citizens of Zosse. When Krüger turned to a policeman and asked the latter for protection, the policeman told him: "Get out of here." (*Stenographische Berichte des Deutschen Reichstages* 1891: encl. 165)

Electoral intervention by employees of the state was common at the moment of voting, as well. State employees took advantage of two imperfections in the technology of voting to pierce the veil of electoral secrecy and observe the electoral choices made by voters. Consider first imperfections in the design of the ballot. Different candidates used ballots that varied widely in color and shape. As such, it was relatively easy for policemen or *Landräte* stationed at the voting place to identify both the electoral intention of voters and also how individual voters cast their ballots. After observing the ballot held by each voter, election officials could deploy threats to convince him to change his vote. In Namslau-Brieg, an electoral district in Breslau, electoral officials were reported to have dismissed voters who did not have square-shaped ballots (*Stenographische Berichte des Deutschen Reichstages* 1878: encl. 286). Other strategies of electoral influence included exchanging the ballots held by the voters as they entered the voting space. In Staakow, a village near Teltow, Potsdam, policemen were reported to have confiscated the Social Democratic ballots held by voters and placed conservative ballots in their hands. This was followed with the threat: "I will find out who votes for the opposition" (*Stenographische Berichte des Deutschen Reichstages* 1891: encl. 165).

Policemen and other employees of the state positioned themselves in voting stations to monitor the choices of voters by using information about the ballots the voters held. A widely used tactic was to make up counter-lists (*Gegenlisten*) that tracked how each individual voted. To illustrate this practice, consider incidents reported in Tost Gleiwitz during the 1874 election. This election was contested between a conservative candidate, Prince von Hohenlohe Ingelfingen, and a contender representing the Catholic Zentrum, Alexander von Schalscha. Prince von Hohenlohe Ingelfingen won by a narrow margin of 691 votes. In this election, both candidates tried to take advantage of imperfections in the design of the ballot. In some of the precincts, von Hohenlohe Ingelfingen used square-shaped ballots and von Schalscha used ballots that had a longer shape. In addition to their unusual shape, von Hohenlohe Ingelfingen's ballots were printed on thicker and sturdier paper. In several of the polling stations, employees of von Hohenlohe Ingelfingen were present in the proximity of the voting place and "distributed ballots of the prince, while also issuing threats to voters." Another employee noted the names of those who supported the opposition candidate, von Schalscha. As one witness declared, "this was an easy thing to do because the ballots for prince von Hohenlohe were folded in a square, whereas the ballots for von Schalscha had a long and 'broken' shape" (*Stenographische Berichte des Deutschen Reichstages* 1874: encl. 159).

Imperfections in the design of the urn gave election officials additional opportunities to violate electoral secrecy. The absence of seals on urns tempted election officials to open the urns and pull out "suspicious" ballots. Such incidents were widely reported at the time. During the 1884 election in Königsberg, election officials would open the urn and return the ballot to the voter, reprimanding him for an irregularity in his ballot (*Stenographische Berichte des Deutschen Reichstages* 1884: encl. 232). During the 1877 election in Boichow, a village in Oppeln, a voter who initially chose the Catholic candidate returned to the voting precinct and demanded to exchange his ballot. The election official obliged by opening the urn and returning the voters' ballot to him (*Stenographische Berichte des Deutschen Reichstages* 1877: encl. 387).

Using the pretext of ensuring that each voter cast only a single ballot, election officials took great latitude in inspecting individual ballots. Many electoral officials reportedly displayed an excess of administrative zeal by opening up ballots to be sure that additional ballots were not hidden inside. The imperfection in the design of the urn also led to the practice of stacking votes on top of each other. This allowed officials to identify the electoral choices made by voters. As one voter in the ninth district of Schleswig-Holstein reported on the practice of stacking of ballots during the 1893 election:

In yesterday's election, I voted second to last and remained in the voting district to participate in the determination of the results of the vote. At 7 o'clock, the polling officer Tietgen grabbed the urn – which was a soup tureen (*Suppengefäss*) with a wooden lid that had an opening of the size of a ballot. He took the ballots from the urn and gave them to his deputy who turned them around so that my ballot was the second from the top of the pile. Given that under these conditions, one can no longer speak of secret elections, I demanded the return of my ballot, but the election officials refused to return it to me. (*Stenographische Berichte des Deutschen Reichstages* 1893: encl. 373)

The final stage of an election was the emptying of the urn and the tallying of the results. An important legal principle of German electoral law was the "publicity of voting." Article 9 of the German electoral code stated that the determination of the results of voting should be a public event (Hatschek 1920). This provision implied that the opening and emptying of urns had to be done in public. A number of decisions made by the commission of the Reichstag established the additional legal precedent that representatives of parties could remain in the voting precinct during the opening of the urns (*Stenographische Berichte des Deutschen Reichstages* 1896: encl. 286). Compared to other moments in the electoral process, one finds remarkably fewer irregularities at this stage. In my own reading of the electoral documents of the period, I have found only occasional reports of violations of the publicity of voting. On one such occasion, representatives of the Social Democratic Party complained that they were not allowed in the voting precinct at the opening of the urn. On another occasion, election officials excluded an entire group of voters – teachers – from the process of determining the electoral results. The electoral commission considered this a violation of the "publicity of voting" (article 9 of the electoral code), but it was not grave enough to justify voiding that particular election (*Stenographische Berichte des Deutschen Reichstages* 1904: encl. 301). Instances where election officials opened the urns behind closed doors or filled them with an entirely different set of ballots were types of electoral irregularities that were common to France, Spain, and other European countries at the time, but they were remarkably rare in German elections. This final stage of the electoral process, the emptying of urns, thus enjoyed the highest levels of protection.

3.3. BADEN AND WÜRTTEMBERG

> The electoral influence of the *Landrat* is a north German peculiarity. My colleagues from the south will agree with me that such influences are much less frequent in the German south than they are in the north, and I believe that nothing hurts the authority of the state, the government, and its organization more than illegal efforts to influence voters by using state officials do. (*Stenographische Berichte des Deutschen Reichstages* February 2, 1874: 564)

As discussed in Section 3.1, Baden and Württemberg displayed much higher levels of electoral fragmentation among right-wing parties than Prussia. One significant factor accounting for this high level of electoral fragmentation among parties on the right was division in the liberal block. A wide array of parties competed under the liberal label. Strong competition from Free Liberal parties also pulled National Liberal candidates toward the left, which increased the ideological distance between National Liberal and Conservative candidates. As a result, National Liberal and Conservative candidates were much less likely to form pre-electoral cartels in these two southern states than those in Prussia were. This electoral fragmentation of the right increased the need for electoral coordination during runoffs. These considerations about future electoral coordination, I hypothesize, restricted the incentives of candidates to rely too forcefully on employees of the state as electoral agents during individual races. Opponents during the first round could become coalition partners during runoffs. These considerations lowered the incentives for various candidates on the right to activate their connections to the bureaucratic apparatus and encourage those bureaucrats to act as agents of electoral intimidation.

In aggregate terms, the number of electoral irregularities in these two *Länder* is significantly lower than that of other provinces in the Empire. The average percentage of contested elections in Baden throughout the period stands at 11 percent. Andreas Gawatz noted that Württemberg, with its aggregate rate of contestation of 6.8 percent, had the lowest rate of contested elections among the larger German states. In his discussion of the use of the bureaucratic apparatus of the states in elections in southern German states, Arsenschek also noted a more restrained use of the power of the state in the latter: "For election to the regional parliament before and after 1871 and for elections to the Reichstag, the government made important efforts not to be exposed as the source of the administrative intervention. Due these considerations, the government activated the subordinate bureaucratic apparatus in a noiseless fashion" (Arsenschek 2003: 178).

The open-handed electoral intervention that was perpetrated by Prussian state employees was less common in southern German states such as Baden and Württemberg. Consider the following incident that triggered, at the time, widespread discussion in Württemberg's lower chamber and in the press (Gawatz 1983: 14). In 1893, the Minister of Finance distributed a secret memorandum requiring employees of his ministry "to get in touch with the superiors in their respective administrative districts and to support the efforts of the latter in the upcoming elections." Moreover, these employees were urged to "steer the rest of the employees toward candidates that support the welfare of the King and the country and who are committed to supporting the government" (documented cited in Gawatz 2001: 74). When this memorandum was leaked to the public, it was heavily criticized by several newspapers of the period. This form of electoral intervention was decried as an "importation of abominable habits," presumably from Prussia (Gawatz 2001: 75). In response to this outcry, Württemberg's Minister of the State distanced his administration from the statements, arguing that they were a private and not an official communication and that such practice was not to be encouraged.

The electoral deployment of employees of the state was not entirely absent in these two southern German states, however. Although it occurred less frequently than it did in Prussia, one can find in both Baden and Württemberg examples of pressure exerted by higher-level bureaucrats on their subordinates to provide electoral support for particular candidates or to prevent the election of less desirable politicians. As Arsenschek demonstrates, "the government in Stuttgart went beyond the circle of its internal administration to mobilize public sector employees when that government absolutely wanted to limit the election of a candidate that was hostile to it. On those occasions, the government secretly conveyed its preferences to employees in the postal services and railroad but also to clerics and tax administrators" (Arsenschek 2003: 178). Other means of electoral involvement consisted of the "use of finances of the state and the involvement of the bureaucratic apparatus for electoral agitation on behalf of particular candidates" (Gawatz 2001: 199). State employees could exert influence at elections either through intimidation or threats of monetary sanctions. On several occasions, these threats were directed against small firms. For example, one finds reports of electoral irregularities in which officials of the state threatened to withhold business to inns that permitted undesirable candidates to host electoral meetings and in which officials issued interdictions to soldiers to visit taverns where Social Democratic candidates appeared (Gawatz 1983: 199ff).

We also find reports of candidates using policemen during elections. During the 1884 election in Baden's thirteenth district, policemen in uniform reportedly stood on the stairs leading to the voting place and distributed ballots on behalf of certain candidates (*Stenographische Berichte des Deutschen Reichstages* 1884: encl. 104). Similar reports were made in Württemberg's first district. There, policemen were reported to have distributed electoral material on behalf of a candidate, von Hoelder, while simultaneously discouraging Social Democratic ballot conveyors from distributing their electoral material. In Leinfelden, policemen reportedly seized Social Democratic election materials, arguing that "we already have ballots in the city hall; we don't need ballots from you rags (*Lumpen*) anymore" (*Stenographische Berichte des Deutschen Reichstages* 1884: encl. 74).

The descriptive evidence of electoral irregularities in southern German states supports this characterization of noiseless interventions. The irregularities committed by employees of the state do not exhibit the same level of political intensity as that of the irregularities committed in Prussian elections. Consider just a few additional examples of reported irregularities. During the 1874 election in Baden's tenth electoral district, the mayor convened a public electoral meeting in support of a candidate. Such intervention violated the principles of the electoral law – which prohibited any intervention by state officials. The mayor also violated the law by threatening to fine citizens who did not attend this meeting. Some members of the commission that investigated electoral irregularities argued that the actions of the mayor did not come into conflict with the electoral law because of the status of mayors in Baden. Mayors were elected by the community and as such were not an extension of the government.

The 1881 election in Württemberg's fourth district – Ulm-Geisslingen-Heidenheim – provides additional evidence of the noiseless electoral intimidation committed by employees of the state in southern German states (*Stenographische Berichte des Deutschen Reichstages* 1882: encl. 113). On this occasion, citizens who disputed the fairness of the election cited a secret memorandum by a senior civil servant (*Regierungsrat*) in Ulm to his subordinates. The *Regierungsrat* informed the subordinates about the candidacy of a conservative named Rieker and urged them "to exert efforts to ensure that voters support this candidate" (*Stenographische Berichte des Deutschen Reichstages* 1882: encl. 113). Some members of the parliamentary commission agreed that this memo constituted an instance of official pressure, because the government employee used symbols of his official power when making the request. By contrast, other members of the commission argued that the exchange was private and that no irregularity occurred.

The noiseless electoral intervention of state officials in the two southern German states was even recognized by members of the Social Democratic Party, the political opposition group that was the target of electoral intimidation. At the 1908 Social Democratic Party congress, Hildebrand, a Social Democratic politician, argued that "there is no case that has become known in the past ten years where the government or a governmental representative has attempted to rely on either employees of the state or private actors to influence electoral outcomes" (*Protokoll über die Verhandlungen des Parteitages der SPD* 1908: 329).

To sum up, the patterns of electoral intervention by officials of the state in Baden and Württemberg differed significantly from the political intervention by state employees in Prussian elections. First, we find considerable differences in the level of electoral irregularities across these regions. The share of contested elections in Baden and Württemberg was significantly below the average for the Empire. Second, we find considerable differences in the intensity of political intervention by state employees in elections. In the two southern German states, we find instead much more subdued and noiseless efforts to deploy the bureaucratic apparatus, which contrasts with the brutal intervention that was present in Prussian elections.

3.4. SAXONY

Saxony was the problem child of the electoral commission. (Klein 2003: 418)

Electoral competition in Saxony contrasted with political competition in the southwestern German states (Baden and Württemberg) along two dimensions. The first was the level of strength of Social Democracy. The level of electoral strength of the Social Democratic Party in Saxony exceeded the national average in each election to the Reichstag. As early as 1874, the Social Democratic Party obtained 35 percent of the total number of votes, which translated into six mandates. In 1903, Saxony elected Social Democratic deputies to the Reichstag in twenty-two out of a total of twenty-three electoral districts. The second important difference was the level of electoral coordination among the parties on the right. The two largest parties on the right that dominated politics in both state-level and national-level elections were the National Liberals and the Conservatives. Beginning with the 1874 election, these parties formed an electoral cartel that sought to limit competition between candidates from parties on the right across Saxony's districts. In contrast to southern German states, the Zentrum and the Free Liberals were a much smaller political force in Saxony. In several elections during the period, Free Liberals were included in the electoral cartel that had been formed by other parties on the right.

In the case of Saxony, both electoral variables – the level of electoral strength of Social Democracy and the level of electoral coordination among political parties on the right – created reinforcing incentives for state employees to engage in voter intimidation. The high levels of electoral strength exhibited by Social Democratic candidates increased the incentives of political candidates on the right to demand electoral help from state employees in deterring voters from supporting opposition candidates. The preexisting electoral coordination between Conservatives and National Liberals removed possible concerns that heavy-handed electoral intervention on behalf of one candidate could affect the willingness of other candidates to enter electoral coalitions during runoffs. This suggests that political factors created strong incentives for a consistently high level of electoral involvement on the part of state employees. Patterns of electoral competition changed during the final three elections of the period, when the electoral coordination among right-wing parties weakened. Furthermore, as in other German regions, the electoral strength of the Social Democrats increased dramatically in Saxony after the 1903 election. As hypothesized, these changes likely increased the marginal costs of electoral involvement for public officials and decreased their incentives to intervene in elections.

Saxony's elections were characterized by an unusually high level of electoral intimidation. Contemporary politicians, such as August Bebel, commented on the floor of the Reichstag that "Saxony has the sad honor of enjoying the highest number of electoral protests" (*Stenographische Berichte des Deutschen Reichstages* 1893, page 2233). Other historians of the period, such as Thomas Klein and Robert Arsenschek, argue that during the early elections of the Second Empire – at a time when candidates on the right were coordinated electorally and also faced increasing electoral competition from the Social Democratic Party – the harshness of the intervention by state employees during Saxon elections exceeded that of their Prussian counterparts (Klein 2003; Arsenschek 2003: 180). The percentage of contested elections as a share of the total number of elections in Saxony stood at 20 percent, a number that was slightly higher than the average rate of contested elections in the German Empire. We find, nevertheless, significant temporal variation in the number of contested elections across Saxony. The "peak" of electoral contestation was reached during the 1881, 1890, and 1893 elections, when the contestation rate stood at 34 percent (1881) and 31 percent (1890 and 1893). By contrast, the contestation rate was significantly lower during the final elections of the period. During the 1903 election, the contestation rate stood at 17 percent, and it declined to 13 percent during the 1907 and 1912 elections. These temporal patterns support the predictions about the political determinants of electoral intimidation presented in Section 3.1.

In Saxony, electoral intimidation by state employees outweighed by a significant margin electoral intimidation by private actors. As in Prussia, candidates competing in Saxony relied greatly on policemen as agents of electoral intervention, which was in stark contrast to patterns of electoral intervention in southern German states. The ubiquity of policemen in Saxony's elections imparted to its elections a character of stark brutality and harshness.

A common goal of the interventions by local election officials was to limit opportunities for opposition parties – most notably Social Democrats – to reach voters. This was achieved by closing off electoral meetings or by refusing to grant opposition candidates the right to organize electoral events. During the 1893 election in Pirna, policemen prohibited a Social Democratic meeting that had attracted voters from miles away (*Stenographische Berichte des Deutschen Reichstages* 1894: encl. 114). Numerous other electoral reports complained of meetings being banned by local officials. This was the case during the 1884 election in Wolkenstein, the 1887 election in Chemnitz, and the 1893 election in Auerbach (*Stenographische Berichte des Deutschen Reichstages* 1884: encl. 247; *Stenographische Berichte des Deutschen Reichstages* 1887: encl. 56, encl. 155). Another way local election officials attempted to limit the ability of opposition candidates to reach voters was by hindering the distribution of election materials. During the 1881 election in Glauchau, which was contested between the National Liberal candidate Leuschner and the Social Democratic candidate Auer, policemen were deployed to confiscate Auer's *Wahlaufruf* (*Stenographische Berichte des Deutschen Reichstages* 1882/2: 1457, *Stenographische Berichte des Deutschen Reichstages* 1883: encl. 154). A protest submitted to the Reichstag argued that this strategy imposed a very high cost on the Social Democratic Party, because the party lacked newspapers that could reach Saxony's voters.

A related strategy of the electoral demobilization of opposition candidates used by electoral officials involved limiting the ability of Social Democratic candidates to distribute ballots to their voters. Numerous electoral petitions present vivid descriptions of the brutal methods deployed by lower-level bureaucratic officials to limit the ability of Social Democratic electoral agents to distribute ballots. During the 1881 election, police officers confiscated between 4,000 and 5,000 Social Democratic ballots in the first electoral district of Dresden (Dresden Rechts der Elbe) (*Stenographische Berichte des Deutschen Reichstages* 1882/1883: encl. 174). During the same election, policemen arrested agents that were distributing Social Democratic ballots in three other districts: Glauchau, Meerane, and Wolkenau (*Stenographische Berichte des Deutschen Reichstages* 1885: encl. 174, encl. 327; *Stenographische Berichte des Deutschen Reichstages* 1886: encl. 108). In 1884 in Stolberg, we find reports of electoral threats directed against conveyors of Social Democratic ballots. During the 1887 election in Chemnitz, policemen confiscated electoral material from the Social Democratic Party, while at the same time distributing electoral materials that supported the conservative candidate in the district (*Stenographische Berichte des Deutschen Reichstages* 1887: encl. 56, encl. 155).

Finally, we find ample reports of electoral intimidation at the voting place in Saxony. There, state employees and election officials used a variety of tactics to discourage voters from supporting opposition candidates. In an incident reported in the second Dresden district in 1884, people who were suspected of supporting the opposition candidate were "chased away" from the voting precinct (*Stenographische Berichte des Deutschen Reichstages* 1884: encl. 173). On other occasions, election officials took advantage of imperfections in the design of the ballot to closely monitor the electoral choices made by voters. This was the case in the 1874 election in Borna, a district contested between von Konneritz, a Free Conservative candidate, and Fink, a Social Democratic candidate. Local election officials present in the polling place monitored votes cast in support of the Social Democratic candidate, whose ballot was significantly smaller than that of his opponent (*Stenographische Berichte des Deutschen Reichstages* 1874: vol. II.1, 283–285). In Freiberg during the 1884 election, local officials placed ballots for the conservative candidate on the voting table, while also maintaining a parallel list of the individual choices made by voters.

The patterns of electoral intervention by employees of the state in Saxony's elections lend support to the theoretical predictions outlined in Section 3.1. Saxony was the "problem child of the electoral commission" because political conditions created reinforcing incentives for candidates to demand political support from state employees and for the latter to supply political support during elections. The level of the electoral strength of Social Democratic candidates during the final elections of the Empire increased the cost of electoral intimidation for politicians, and that lowered both the demand for and the supply of electoral services by employees of the state.

3.5. CONCLUSION

In this chapter, I began to investigate the variation in irregularities in German national elections. I examined the electoral strategies used by employees of the state and the variety of approaches they used to sidestep the provisions of the national election law, which mandated the absolute neutrality of the state during elections. Using qualitative evidence from reports of irregularities in elections to the Reichstag, I investigated the variety of strategies used by state employees at various stages of the electoral process. This analysis illustrates that state employees devoted the highest amount of political effort preventing opposition candidates from reaching voters and monitoring the choices of voters at the moment of voting. By contrast, one finds very few irregularities during the tallying of the urns.

Chapter 2 presented my main hypotheses about the factors affecting the demand made by candidates for support from employees of the state and the willingness of policemen and tax collectors to supply political services to candidates. I hypothesize that candidates' demand for electoral services from state employees is highest when electoral fragmentation among parties on the right is low. Political unity on the right is also likely to mitigate the concerns of state employees about possible post-electoral reprisals. One expects to find a high incidence of electoral irregularities committed by employees of the state in districts where candidates on the right are coordinated, either formally (through cartels) or informally. By contrast, an increase in political fragmentation on the right is likely to lower the demand made by candidates for electoral support from employees of the state.

In this chapter, I presented a first empirical test of these hypotheses and explored regional variation in the electoral irregularities perpetrated by employees of the state across different regions of the German Empire. A more precise quantitative test of these propositions at the level of the electoral district will be presented in Chapter 5. The variation in the electoral involvement of employees of the state across Prussian regions is in agreement with the theoretical hypotheses outlined at the beginning of this chapter. Both the involvement of employees of the state during elections and the intensity of the strategies of electoral intimidation are highest in Prussia and Saxony, two regions characterized by high levels of coordination among parties on the right. By contrast, electoral irregularities committed by employees of the state are much lower in the two southern German provinces, which are characterized by higher levels of political fragmentation among parties on the right. An analysis of the temporal variation in the strategies of electoral intimidation used by employees of the state also supports these hypotheses. Within Prussia, the dissolution of the electoral cartel among parties on the right contributed to a change in the strategies of electoral intimidation used by officials in the Prussian Ministry of the Interior and to the adoption of a strategy of noiseless electoral intervention. Finally, the temporal patterns of electoral intimidation across these regions lend support to the hypothesis that the political strength of the Social Democratic Party affects the perpetration of electoral intimidation by officials of the state. The intensity of the electoral pressure by employees of the states during elections was lowest during the final elections of the period, at a time when the political strength of the Social Democratic Party has dramatically increased.

4

Electoral Intimidation by Employers

> The absence of economic freedom leads to the absence of political freedom.
> (Dr. Förster, Neustettin, *Stenographische Berichte des*
> *Deutschen Reichstages* May 15, 1895: 2290)

Chapter 3 documented the existence of a wide variety of strategies of electoral intimidation carried out by employees of the state. In addition to policemen and tax collectors, private economic actors also played a dominant role as agents of electoral intimidation. During elections, companies turned into political battlegrounds. Private actors mobilized voters at the workplace, regimented them in columns, and marched them to the polls. Supervisory personnel of these companies ensured that voters entered the precinct equipped with the "correct" ballots. Employer representatives located in close proximity to the voting place maintained voting counter-lists (*Gegenlisten*) that recorded the electoral choices made by each and every employee. Using this information, employers engaged in post-electoral reprisals by punishing voters who had made incorrect electoral choices. Among the strategies of post-electoral punishments used by employers, the strategy that imposed the highest costs on voters involved being laid off for having made the wrong electoral choice.

In this chapter, I draw on the historical evidence presented in the electoral reports of the parliamentary commission charged with examining electoral irregularities to document pre- and post-electoral strategies used by private economic actors and the regional and temporal variation in these strategies. The main source of my analysis is a subset of reports on electoral fraud, which comprises 15 percent of the contested elections of the period. Using this subset of the total number of electoral reports, I code in greater detail whether instances of electoral intimidation by employers were present and the types of strategies used by private actors in elections. This qualitative evidence allows me to disaggregate the incidences of intimidation across different stages of the electoral process and examine *when* voters were most vulnerable to pressure from employers. I also take advantage of this qualitative evidence on private intimidation during elections to map out the variation across different German regions and elections.

The chapter is organized as follows. I begin in Section 4.1 with a discussion and critique of several competing hypotheses that have been proposed by prominent social scientists, beginning with Max Weber, to account for the unusually high levels of electoral intimidation utilized by German employers during the elections to the Reichstag in the period between 1870 and 1912. Next, I develop a number of hypotheses to account for the variation in electoral intimidation by employers. I then draw on the qualitative evidence presented in electoral reports to provide a preliminary test of these hypotheses. I examine the geographic and temporal variation in the strategies of electoral intimidation used by rural and industrial employers. Chapter 5 provides a systematic analysis of the relationship between economic conditions in a district – such as occupational heterogeneity and the skill profile of the labor force – and the incidence of electoral fraud.

This chapter takes advantage of the wealth of qualitative information available in the reports submitted to the Reichstag to also explore a range of questions pertaining to the intensity of the effort and pressure exerted by employers at various stages of the electoral process. As with the analysis presented in Chapter 3, I seek to identify the stage of the voting process in which voters were most vulnerable to electoral intimidation. I also intend to examine whether the toolkit of strategies available to employers and the intensity of the intimidation varied systematically across German regions. The final section of the chapter, Section 4.4, turns to the question of the temporal variation in private electoral intimidation across German elections during the period between 1890 and 1912. I note a decline in the instances of private electoral intimidation over time and formulate a number of hypotheses to account for this evolution.

4.1. PRIVATE INTIMIDATION IN GERMAN NATIONAL ELECTIONS

Contemporary observers of elections to the German parliament noted the pervasive influence exerted by German employers in elections. In a debate in the German parliament, Heinrich Rickert described how employers would "lead the voters to the voting place like animals to slaughter. In front of the door of the voting precinct some supervisor or inspector pushes a ballot in the hands of the worker. As [the worker] does not want to lose his job, he is in no position to vote according to his conviction" (*Stenographische Berichte des Deutschen Reichstages* May 15, 1895: 2285). And as a deputy from the Polish party noted in his intervention to the Reichstag, "[t]he commission investigating electoral irregularities has presented in recent years a large amount of materials concerning electoral influence, redundancies, obstructions at the workplace, [and] threats of layoffs" (*Stenographische Berichte des Deutschen Reichstages* January 29, 1902: 3727).

Electoral intimidation by private actors was not a uniquely German phenomenon. Similar instances are reported in other European countries, as well. In Britain, large employers in industrial constituencies reportedly made "party allegiance one of their hiring terms." As Harold Hanham argues, "particularly in districts where solitary big firms dominated the local economy, the owners had a powerful hand in assuring that labor voted liberal" (Hanham 1959: 68–90). In France, reports show that private electoral intimidation was one of several types of electoral irregularities during the nineteenth century. As late as 1914, one finds French employers trying to control the votes of their employees by using ballots of different shapes, a practice that was also encountered in German elections:

They handed over to workers who were dependent on them ballots that were folded in different ways. Some were folded in the shape of a triangle, others in the shape of a diamond, a hat, or an accordion. Naturally, they did not hesitate to inform these voters that they would keep an eye on them when the votes were counted and that it was imperative to find these particular ballots. (*Journal Officiel de la République Française, Débats Chambre* 1914: 2639)

Nevertheless, the intervention of German employers in elections appears to be more pronounced than that of employers in neighboring countries. Lavinia Anderson's study of electoral politics in Imperial Germany speaks to this variation:

[T]he intervention of German employers in national elections seems of a different order of magnitude than any encountered elsewhere. In every German parliamentary election, but especially from 1881, the evidence of massive employer intimidation is overwhelming. In no other country – at least among the "civilized lands" to which Germans liked to compare themselves – was the practice of election intimidation by bread lords felt to be so universal, so unvarnished and so enduring. (Anderson 2000: 227)

What explains this particular dimension of "German exceptionalism"? Scholars of electoral practices in German national elections during the period preceding World War I have proposed two explanations for the high levels of electoral involvement by employers. These explanations stress the role played by culture and institutions, respectively. The first hypothesis, which was advanced by Max Weber, stresses cultural factors. In an intervention to the Social Policy Association (*Verein für Sozialpolitik*) in 1905, Max Weber noted the unusually high level of electoral involvement by private actors in elections and attributed this behavior to the concern of German employers with the "appearance of power" and their desire to project this appearance beyond the confines of their company (Weber 1958: 395–397; cf. Anderson 2000: 227). Weber argues that "something like this just sticks in the blood of our employers, they cannot get away from the itch to control, they want not simply the power alone, the powerful, factual responsibility, and the power that lies in the management of every great firm, no, they must be also able to document outwardly the subordination of others" (Weber 1958: 395).

However, this cultural explanation cannot account for the wide regional and temporal variation in the electoral involvement of German employers. Even if German employers manifested a desire to project power beyond the confines of their company, this theory fails to account for the divergence in the political practices of German employers across regions and over time. To understand this variation, we need to understand how other political and economic variables mediated employers' concerns with the outward projection of power. Also, we need to understand the factors that *constrained* the electoral involvement of German employers.

A second explanation for the unusually high electoral involvement of employers is institutional in nature, and it stresses the uneven punishment structure established by Germany's electoral law for different types of electoral irregularities. Electoral misconduct, such as vote buying, fell under the jurisdiction of the German penal code and was punished with relatively high levels of stringency. By contrast, German electoral law imposed no punishment on employers for their involvement in elections. This uneven punishment structure created clear incentives for politicians to enlist private actors as agents of electoral mobilization in their districts.

However, this institutional explanation cannot account for the variation in the willingness of private actors to supply political support to candidates or for the variation in the incidence of electoral intimidation by private actors. As with the explanation invoking the importance of cultural attributes, the institutionalist explanation also over-predicts the occurrence of electoral intimidation by private actors. Given that private electoral intimidation went unpunished under German electoral law, the question is not why private electoral intimidation was so pervasive but why it was not ubiquitous.

In Chapter 2, I have developed a number of hypotheses about the demand made by politicians for electoral activities trespassing the boundaries of the electoral law and the willingness of private actors to supply political support to candidates. As discussed in that chapter, the demand made by candidates for electoral irregularities is affected by several political variables: the strength of opposition candidates, the political fragmentation among candidates on the right, the existence of runoffs, and the tightness of a race.

By contrast, I hypothesize that the willingness of private actors to provide electoral support to political candidates is affected by the economic conditions in a district. These economic conditions affect the costs of electoral repression encountered by firms. Firms, I hypothesize, intervene electorally only if the expected future benefits of their political participation exceed their potential economic costs. Three economic variables are likely to affect the costs of electoral repression for firms. First, the economic heterogeneity of a district is likely to increase the costs of intimidation. The costs of electoral intimidation are higher for firms in districts with higher economic heterogeneity. There firms experience competition from firms with similar production profiles for a similar pool of workers. Secondly, firms that hire a higher number of skilled workers are likely to face higher costs of electoral intimidation than do firms that have not made similar investments in skills. Finally, labor scarcity is hypothesized to increase the costs of electoral intimidation.

The remainder of this chapter provides evidence of regional and temporal variation in private intimidation in German elections. I use evidence from the petitions submitted to the Reichstag to document the political strategies deployed by German employers. This qualitative evidence allows me to assess the variation in the *incidence* of electoral intimidation as well as variation in its *intensity*. I provide a preliminary investigation of the hypotheses linking economic heterogeneity and the skill level of the labor force by examining the variation in electoral intimidation across regions of Germany that differed in their economic endowments and in their levels of vocational skills.

4.1.1. Geographic Variation in Electoral Intimidation

How pervasive was intimidation by private actors during elections? When and where were employers more likely to engage in the intimidation of workers? To obtain descriptive information about the pervasiveness of private intimidation during elections, I have coded the variation in the instances of electoral intimidation for 15 percent of the electoral fraud reports of the period. Because the electoral commission that investigated reports of electoral violations was only established in 1874, the first election of the period is excluded from the analysis. For this subset of electoral reports, I have coded not only whether allegations of electoral intimidation by private actors were present but also the types of pressures and irregularities carried out by employers in those elections.

In geographic terms, the variation in these incidents of electoral intimidation by private actors is largely consistent with the theoretical hypotheses. The most numerous cases of private electoral intimidation were found in the Ruhr and Saar regions. Both areas are located in Germany's industrial center. With respect to their underlying economic structure, these are areas in which output and employment were dominated by a small number of firms. They included some of Germany's industrial giants, such as Krupp AG, Gelsenkirchner Bergwerke, Hösch, Hörder, and Gutehoffnungshütte. In contrast to these areas, which are characterized by high levels of industrial concentration, other German regions witnessed much less private electoral intimidation. In Württemberg, an example of a region with decentralized economic production, only sporadic cases of private intimidation occurred. Saxony, another region characterized by high levels of occupational heterogeneity, experienced some electoral intimidation during the early elections, but the electoral intimidation of employers became rare in subsequent elections. This contrasts the high instances of electoral intimidation perpetrated by state employees in Saxony's elections and supports the idea that private and state actors were not equally able to influence electoral outcomes within one region. Finally, we also find reports of private electoral intimidation in Prussia's rural districts, most notably Silesia. Nevertheless, instances of private electoral intimidation in Germany's rural districts are not as pervasive as they are in the regions with high levels of economic concentration. The remainder this chapter draws on the qualitative information presented in the electoral reports to assess the variation in the types of strategies used by German employers during elections.

4.2. PRIVATE ELECTORAL INTIMIDATION IN REGIONS WITH HIGH ECONOMIC CONCENTRATION

Section 4.1.1 identified a distinct regional cluster characterized by high and repeated occurrences of private electoral intimidation. Several historians of the period referred to this region as the "corridor of electoral terror" (Klein 2003; Arsenschek 2003). This corridor of terror is located in the western part of Germany and stretches from the Saar region to the Ruhr region in the north. The high incidence of private intimidation in this area was widely noted at the time. Contemporaries referred to the Saar region, an area known for its extensive occurrence of private electoral intimidation, as *Saarabien* (Bellot 1954; Spencer 1984).

Most of the electoral districts located in this corridor of electoral terror have higher than average values of the economic variable hypothesized to predict the incidence of private electoral intimidation: economic heterogeneity. To use Gary Herrigel's term, these districts are located in Germany's "autarkic" economic regions (Herrigel 1996: 72). Economic output and employment opportunities in many localities were controlled by a limited number of producers. High levels of economic concentration, I hypothesize, lowered the costs of electoral intimidation for private actors through a number of related mechanisms. First, high economies of scale reduced the costs for employers to mobilize workers. Secondly, in areas of high economic concentration, workers had fewer opportunities for outside employment, unless they incurred some costs of relocation to other districts. From firms' perspective, repressing workers with fewer alternative economic options was relatively less costly than was repressing voters with a higher number of employment opportunities. Finally, the costs of punishing workers who made undesired political choices by refusing employment were also lower for employers in areas with high economic concentration.

Several of the reports contesting electoral results noted that in districts dominated by one large firm, the entire locality, not just the firm's employees, was dependent on that particular employer. Consider the report from Ottweiler-St. Wendel, Trier's sixth electoral district, after the 1890 election. A complaint against the electoral practices used by the local employer noted the unusual dependence of the entire community on Stumm's commercial enterprises: "Even a minority of voters in the district," the report noted, "is indirectly dependent on Stumm, because they are customers of the manufacturer. There are only a few isolated voters in the district that are independent of Stumm" (*Stenographische Berichte des Deutschen Reichstages* 1890: encl. 346).

In districts characterized by high levels of economic concentration, employers perfected electoral strategies that allowed them to extract electoral advantages from their privileged labor market position. These strategies relied on three interrelated elements. First, employers exploited their control over labor supply to micromanage electoral turnout. Secondly, employers took advantage of the imperfections in voting technology to monitor the electoral choices of voters. Nearly all election reports of the period document the presence of representatives of the dominant employer at the voting place. Imperfections in the design of the ballot opened up opportunities for identifying the vote choice made by each and every employee. Finally, reports note extensive postelectoral retaliation by employers. The reports note that the same electoral strategies were used by firms in concentrated areas again and again.

I structure the discussion of the electoral strategies of employers by disaggregating an election into its different stages. This allows me to investigate at which stages of the electoral process employers exerted the highest amount of pressure and when voters were most vulnerable.

In a meeting convened in July 1878, a group of notables in Essen announced their support for Alfred Krupp as the candidate of the district. The proposal was accepted "unanimously" by participants in a broader meeting of "voters loyal to the Reich" that was held during the following days. The recommendations of this meeting were reported in the *Essener Zeitung*: "[Krupp] is Europe's first industrialist and the first worker of our district. Nobody is in a better position to represent our district. Nobody has more empathy for the workers. Nobody has done more than him. Let us unite around the name Alfred Krupp and stay loyal to his name for Kaiser and the Reich" (*Essener Zeitung*, no. 1157, July 8, 1878). Krupp initially refused this endorsement and announced in a letter to the managers of his firm that others should step up and take on this responsibility, but he eventually agreed to compete as a candidate and to represent multiple right-wing political parties that united to endorse his candidacy (Paul 1987).

After Krupp accepted the candidacy, the company turned into a political battleground. A large number of the resources of the company were deployed for electoral purposes. The massive deployment of economic resources was intended to help avoid the outcome of the previous electoral contest in the district, when the race had been narrowly lost by the National Liberal candidate to a representative of the Zentrum. The *Essener Zeitung* reported that fifty-eight workers in the Krupp factory were appointed as electoral agents of the company (*Essener Zeitung*, no. 162, July 15, 1878). In an electoral meeting held in the beer hall of the Scherdorf colony, these representatives "educated" other factory workers about the importance of the upcoming race (*Essener Zeitung*, no. 162, July 15, 1878). Then they waged an aggressive campaign in the housing quarters of the company. During the final days of the campaign, more than 339 voters were reported to have campaigned on behalf of Krupp's candidacy there (Paul 1987). The *Essener Zeitung* warned, however, of possible complacency. The victory could be ensured only if these electoral agents took their electoral responsibility seriously and drove all loyal voters to the voting precinct (*Essener Zeitung*, July 27, 1878).

Employers often attempted to influence the electoral choices of their employees by threatening them with layoffs and other economic sanctions for supporting an "undesirable" candidate. During the 1887 election in Breslau Waldenburg, Egmont Tielsch, the owner of a local porcelain factory, convened a number of porcelain painters in his factory and asked if they were members of the Social Democratic Party. The painters confessed to being members of the choral society Frohsinn in Neu-Weissstein, which pursued Social Democratic goals. The employer asked his workers to leave the society or promise not to vote on election day. A witness to this meeting testified that the employer stated: "Either each of you will promise not to vote during the elections or I will lay you off" (*Stenographische Berichte des Deutschen Reichstages* 1888: encl. 105). During the 1903 election, a local employer in Malstatt Burbach threatened workers in his company with layoffs if they did not support the National Liberal candidate in the race. As one witness reported, the employer threatened: "If you do not elect Volz, working conditions will deteriorate and workers will be laid off." To signal his resoluteness, the employer laid off three workers who were known to be members of the Zentrum party on the day of the election (*Stenographische Berichte des Deutschen Reichstages* 1888: encl. 300).

Employers also threatened future reductions in wages. In Schlesingen Ziegenrück, a district in Erfurt, the employers in a mining company threatened to lower workers' pay by 25 percent if they supported the Social Democratic candidate (*Stenographische Berichte des Deutschen Reichstages* 1890: encl. 1896). Another type of threat reported at the time was that of a reduction in the benefits provided by the company. German employers could use this threat effectively, given the large number of company-level social policy benefits they provided. These included housing, sickness, and disability benefits, among others (Mares 2003). During the 1912 election, the owner of the Burbacher Hütte, a mine located in Trier's fifth district, convened all of the members of the miners guild (*Knappschaftsverein*). The employer announced that disability pensions would be cut if workers chose not to vote for the National Liberal candidate, Ernst Bassermann (*Stenographische Berichte des Deutschen Reichstages* 1912: encl. 1639).

Employers in districts with high economic concentration controlled sizeable blocs of voters and developed sophisticated strategies to manipulate electoral turnout by either boosting or reducing it. Consider first examples of turnout reduction strategies. During the 1878 election in Oppeln's fifth district, employers of the Florentinen mine in Beuthen were reported to have removed the stairs to the mine. The miners were thus trapped underground and were unable to vote. Employers replaced the stairs and allowed miners to leave the mine only after the voting place had closed (*Stenographische Berichte des Deutschen Reichstages* 1878: encl. 105).

In other cases, employers used a strategy of maximizing their employees' electoral participation. Consider an incident reported in Bochum during the 1884 election. On this occasion, Röber, a foreman of the coal factory Ostermann made the following announcement to the employees of his company the day before the election: "Tomorrow morning, I will convene my entire staff and take them to the voting place. Whoever comes too late will be punished, whoever doesn't come at all will be laid off" (*Stenographische Berichte des Deutschen Reichstages* 1884: encl. 181). Employers used lists to monitor the turnout of voters and to bring laggards to the polls. This was the case in Trier during the 1881 election, when a local mining employer used lists to monitor the "missing voters and bring them, like sheep, to the urns" (*Stenographische Berichte des Deutschen Reichstages* 1881: encl. 104).

German employers perfected a sophisticated system of bringing voters to the polls in columns. In the words of one contemporary, the long columns of workers being marched to the polls resembled more a "transport of prisoners rather than free voters" (*Stenographische Berichte des Deutschen Reichstages* 1881: encl. 292). Company personnel were used to supervise voters during these marches. In Ludwigshafen, masters of the Badische Anilinie company were reported to have taken groups of workers to the polls. In Arnsberg's sixth district, owners of the local steel company and owners of mines were reported to have ordered workers to gather in front of particular locations and then to have sent these "regiments" of workers, which were led by foremen, to the polling places. During these marches, employers dispersed loyal supervisory personnel among the voters and ensured that they were equipped with the right ballots (*Stenographische Berichte des Deutschen Reichstages* 1881: encl. 292).

At the entrances to the polling places, employers also positioned employees whose job it was to ensure that voters entered the polling area equipped with the correct ballots. In 1894, an employer in the company von Kohler-zu-Rauxel, which was located in the vicinity of Dortmund (sixth district of Arnsberg), removed the ballots for the opposition candidates from the hands of workers and tore them to pieces. Then the employer distributed ballots for Möller, the "correct" candidate in the district, and asked the workers to hold these ballots over their heads when entering the voting area (*Stenographische Berichte des Deutschen Reichstages* 1893: encl. 354).

Employers in the Ruhr and Saar made great efforts to control workers at the time of voting. No detail about the organization of the polling place was left to chance alone. What is striking about the electoral reports from districts characterized by high levels of economic concentration is the remarkable similarity in the strategies used by employers in election after election. There was a common repertoire of strategies consisting of a finite number of modules that together ensured tight control by representatives of the firm over nearly every activity taking place at the moment of voting. The common elements of this repertoire of electoral repression included the presence of employer representatives in the voting area and the existence of counter-lists, which allowed representatives of the firm to record the vote of every single worker.

Firms that dominated the local economic landscape of a district took advantage of their economic power to ensure that their representatives were members, or even presidents, of the electoral boards in each precinct. The report of electoral irregularities in Arnsberg's fifth district after the 1884 election illustrates the way in which local employers were disproportionately represented in these institutions. This report noted that a disproportionate number of the electoral boards members and their deputies were either employers or persons employed by the large companies or mines: "Whoever knows about the state of economic dependence in which workers in these companies find themselves, whoever knows about the high economic pressure (*Hochdruck*) that the superiors can exert on the workers, that person will have no doubt that the presence of these [employers] at the voting place will unfavorably affect the electoral freedom of voters" (*Stenographische Berichte des Deutschen Reichstages* 1884: encl. 320). In their position as presidents of the polling stations, employers had ample opportunities to monitor voters' choices. A report of electoral irregularities that occurred in Breslau Waldenburg during the 1887 election documents the way in which local employers used their positions as members of the electoral commissions to influence the choices made in the voting area (*Stenographische Berichte des Deutschen Reichstages* 1887: encl. 105). In that district, the owner of a local company that produced mirrors served as the chair of the election board in a precinct located next to an area of dense company housing, the Sandberg colony. One voter recalled that on election day:

The election took place in a room located in the basement of a restaurant. Director Monting was the chairman of the polling station. The voting table was located in front of a door that was kept open, thus giving Monting the opportunity to observe all activity in the voting area. A table with electoral ballots for Dr. Websky was located behind the open door. A foreman named Leon from the mirror factory was found at this table and distributed these ballots. During the period between noon and one, when foreman Leon was at lunch, he was replaced by Gunke, a different supervisor from the mirror factory. Each worker from the mirror factory received from Leon a ballot for Dr. Websky, even if they stated that they already had a ballot. Leon offered the ballots in a way that could be observed by Monting. There were only four steps between Leon's table and the voting table, so that the ballots could not be exchanged. (*Stenographische Berichte des Deutschen Reichstages* 1887: encl. 105)

One element common to this strategy of voter monitoring across all districts of the region was the so-called "agitation table" – a table with electoral ballots for the candidate favored by the local employer. This table stood in the immediate vicinity of the voting area and was manned by representatives of the firm. This placement allowed the employer representatives to exert influence on voters at the most critical point in the act of voting by pressuring them to "exchange" the ballots with which they had entered the voting area for a ballot from the table. In Hattingen, a locality in Arnsberg's fifth district, a representative of the firm asked voters their names and tried to ensure that they carried a "Haarmann ballot" for the National Liberal candidate in the district (*Stenographische Berichte des Deutschen Reichstages* 1890: encl. 181). In Wilhelmsgarten, a neighboring locality, the miner Heinrich Eschenroder, who had been posted by the National Liberal Party to supervise the elections, "ripped the ballots away from voters for Schorlemer, put those ballots in their pockets, and gave them a ballot for Dr. Haarman, urging them to vote for Haarman." Because this political exchange took place in close proximity to the urn, "voters had no choice but to cast a ballot for Dr. Haarman" (*Stenographische Berichte des Deutschen Reichstages* 1890: encl. 181). In Arnsberg's fifth district, during the 1884 election, the agitation table was located roughly six feet from the voting table. There, representatives of the firm distributed ballots for the liberal candidate and urged voters who had entered the voting area with different ballots to "exchange" them (*Stenographische Berichte des Deutschen Reichstages* 1884: encl. 57). During the same election, in another precinct of the same district, an engineer from Hörsterwerken confiscated the ballots for the opposition candidate Fusangel and then commanded the workers to go to the urn while keeping their right hands raised in the air (*Stenographische Berichte des Deutschen Reichstages* 1884: encl. 57).

Another example, this time from Dortfeld, a locality in Arnsberg's sixth district, also illustrates the use of the agitation table. Nearly half of the voters in Dortfeld's first precinct were employed by a mining company (*Stenographische Berichte des Deutschen Reichstages* 1903: encl. 1488). Figure 4.1, which was submitted as part of an electoral report, depicts the organization of the electoral space in Dortfeld during the 1903 election. The perimeter of the voting area is marked ABCD. K and L show where the election board and the voting urn (K) and the president of the election board (L) were located. The agitation table – which was manned continuously by employees of the Dortfeld mine – was located in area I. This location allowed representatives of the firm to observe with relative ease the activities of each voter in the precinct and made it very difficult for voters to exchange the National Liberal ballot that had been handed to them with another ballot (*Stenographische Berichte des Deutschen Reichstages* 1903: encl. 1488). One witness of the voting in this precinct describes the scene thus:

Supervisors from the mine stood at the entrance to the room and distributed ballots for Möller. If a person who had received a ballot for Möller took another ballot out of his pocket, then Schmidtmann pointed to his own bag, which gave the supervisors from the mine a clear signal that the voter had not voted for Möller. (*Stenographische Berichte des Deutschen Reichstages* 1893: encl. 1488)

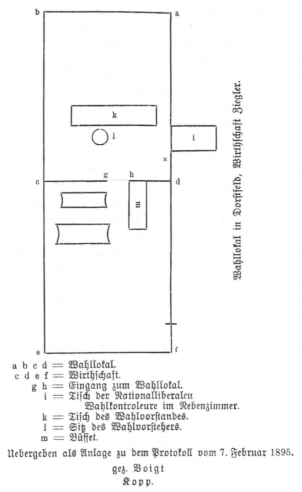

FIGURE 4.1. The organization of the voting precinct in Arnsberg's sixth district during the 1893 election.

To monitor the electoral choices made by voters, company representatives posted at these agitation tables used counter-lists to record the voting decisions made by each and every voter. In Trier's sixth district during the 1881 election, officials from the large mine of the locality, the Königliche Steinkohlenwerke, were reported to have observed and recorded voting decisions in these counter-lists (*Stenographische Berichte des Deutschen Reichstages* 1881: encl. 103).

  Employers also monitored the electoral choices of voters by introducing ballots that were easily distinguishable. As members of the electoral verification commission recognized, ballots of irregular shapes, colors, and weight made it possible for any person present in the voting station to pierce the veil of voting secrecy. Let us consider a number of examples of irregular ballot design by candidates in areas with high levels of economic concentration. During the 1893 election in Dortmund, the candidate Möller, representing the National Liberal Party, attempted to differentiate his ballot from those of his opponents by folding it multiple times (*Stenographische Berichte des Deutschen Reichstages* 1893: encl. 354). Whenever election officials received a ballot that was folded only once, they held it up in the air for a long time, so the director of the local company, who was seated in the vicinity of the urn box, could write down the voter's name on his counter-list (*Stenographische Berichte des Deutschen Reichstages* 1893: encl. 354).

Ballots could also be differentiated in other ways. In Trier's sixth electoral district, Freiherr von Stumm, the owner of a large iron mill (*Eisenhütte*), printed his ballots on very thick, "cardboard-type paper" (*Stenographische Berichte des Deutschen Reichstages* 1890: encl. 346). During the 1881 election, candidates in Trier's sixth district attempted to differentiate between the ballots by their weight (*Stenographische Berichte des Deutschen Reichstages* 1881: encl. 103). In Dittersbach, the owner of a steel mill was reported to have "printed additional ballots in his office, which were clearly distinguishable on the basis of their shapes and the quality of the paper on which they were printed" (*Stenographische Berichte des Deutschen Reichstages* 1878: encl. 1986). In Arnsberg's sixth district, owners of steel mills were reported to have changed the appearance of the ballot every hour. This strategy allowed them to monitor the electoral choices made by voters from their companies. As one witness testified, it was impossible for workers to submit a different ballot from that given to them by their supervisor.

At the same time, imperfections in the design of the ballot created slim but welcome opportunities for opposition candidates to express dissent. In Arnsberg's fifth district, the Catholic party distributed to its supporters small pieces of paper bearing the name of the Zentrum candidate. These pieces of paper had glue on the back, and voters were instructed to paste them over the name in the ballots of the candidate favored by the local employer. In the words of the local electoral committee of the Zentrum in this district, this strategy represented "the last bastion of hope in the face of the electoral terror of the large companies" (*Stenographische Berichte des Deutschen Reichstages* 1884: encl. 57).

When used together, these electoral strategies allowed employers in areas with high levels of economic concentration to observe the voting choices made by their employees and to engage in post-election reprisals. Employers used the extensive information about voters that they collected during voting to punish "rebel" voters, including those who had refused to take the ballot that had been handed to them by representatives at the "agitation table" and those who were observed to have slipped the "wrong" ballot in the urn. During the 1881 election, the management of the Badische Anilin und Sodafabrik supported the candidacy of the National Liberal candidate, Dr. Gross. On the day of voting, workers were assembled and instructed that "[w]hoever does not vote for Dr. Gross will be unemployed tomorrow" (*Stenographische Berichte des Deutschen Reichstages* 1881: encl. 116). The firm followed up on this threat and laid off the voters who had refused to follow orders, irrespective of their skill or experience. Such was the case for Georg Martin, who had been employed by the firm for more than seven years. During the election, Martin had refused to accept a ballot for Dr. Gross, saying that he already had a ballot for the Social Democratic candidate (*Stenographische Berichte des Deutschen Reichstages* 1881: encl. 116). Another worker met the same fate after refusing to "exchange" his Social Democratic ballot for that of Dr. Gross.

Employers used the local publications they controlled to express their disappointment about particular voting results and to issue threats of layoffs. Consider the following article, "Who Wants to Hear – He Can Hear!," which was published by Egmon Tielsch, a porcelain manufacturer from Breslau Waldenburg in the immediate aftermath of the 1887 election:

My workers! The election to the Reichstag on February 21st has demonstrated in the results in those precincts where you live that you do not follow my admonitions and that you are supporting the Free Liberal causes, which cannot represent your true interests. You are justified to have your own opinions, and I make no accusations because of your voting decisions. However, I will also modify my behavior toward you at times when the economic conditions change and when company reorganizations are necessary. I hope we will be able to avoid these conditions, but if this is not possible, I would like to let you know that I will be reluctant to employ workers who are opposed to the noble aspirations of our Emperor. (*Stenographische Berichte des Deutschen Reichstages* 1887: encl. 105)

In addition to layoffs, employers engaged in other post-electoral punishments. These included withdrawing the discretionary social policy benefits that had been provided by the companies from those workers who had not made the correct electoral choice. One such benefit was housing. Following the 1884 election in Arnsberg's fifth district, voters who had refused to take the ballot handed to them by the company's overseer lost their company housing (*Stenographische Berichte des Deutschen Reichstages* 1884: encl. 57).

In concentrated economic areas, the threat of layoffs was more credible because of the informal agreement between employers of the region not to hire workers who had been laid off by other firms in the region. The electoral reports refer to these ongoing practices as "public electoral secrets." In Bochum, one report noted:

[I]t is a reality that workers that were laid off at one of the jobs in the region can find work only with great difficulty or not at all. It is a public secret that the layoff slips (*Entlassungsscheine*) contained certain agreed-upon signs that were noticeable only with difficulty. The latter contained information about the laid off workers as well as an indication not to rehire them, making further correspondence between these employers unnecessary. (*Stenographische Berichte des Deutschen Reichstages* 1884: encl. 320)

Voters from concentrated regions thus experienced a double punishment for their political views: a loss of employment and the need to change their occupation, because employment in their original occupation was no longer available to them.

The evidence presented by the electoral reports allows us to reconstruct the dense apparatus of political control established by employers in areas with high levels of economic concentration. In these districts, employers took advantage of their control over a large share of the total number of eligible voters to influence electoral outcomes. Employers in these districts exercised tight political control over all stages of the voting process, including the campaign, mobilization on the day of voting, and the vote itself. Nevertheless, we find that private actors chose to expend a remarkable amount of effort to control political activities at the moment of voting. By positioning representatives of the company in the voting place and by taking advantage of imperfections in electoral technology, employers succeeded in eliminating electoral secrecy. At the beginning of this chapter, I posed the question of which stage of the electoral process was most open to electoral manipulation by employers. In the case of districts characterized by high levels of economic concentration, it was unambiguously the act of voting.

4.3. PRIVATE ELECTORAL INTIMIDATION IN DECENTRALIZED REGIONS

In this section, I examine private electoral intimidation in regions characterized by high levels of economic heterogeneity. In these regions, private actors are expected to face higher costs of electoral repression as compared to regions with high economic concentration. Firms in these regions encountered higher levels of product market competition from companies with similar production profiles. As a result, the decision to lay off workers for their electoral choices carried higher economic costs. Similarly, higher levels of occupational heterogeneity in these regions increased the employment options available to workers, which further lowered the penalties that employers could impose on workers for their political choices. When combined, these two effects likely reduced employers' incentives to engage in the electoral harassment of voters.

How pervasive was private electoral intimidation in decentralized regions? I examine electoral intimidation in Saxony and Württemberg, two regions characterized by high levels of economic heterogeneity. Most economic historians of nineteenth-century Germany characterize Saxony and Württemberg as decentralized economic regions. In autarchic regions of the Ruhr, output and employment were controlled by a small number of large firms, whereas the economic landscapes of both Saxony and Württemberg were dominated by small-scale industrial production (Herrigel 1996). The measure of occupational heterogeneity confirms this characterization. For Saxony, the values of occupational heterogeneity are significantly lower than the average level of occupational heterogeneity for the entire German Empire in both the 1895 and 1905 censuses. The measures of occupational heterogeneity for Württemberg fall close to the average level for Germany.

The skill composition of the labor force differed significantly between these two regions. Using detailed information about the skill profile for more than 180 occupations and about the occupational composition in each locality, I have computed measures of the skill profile for the German labor force. Chapter 5 discusses the methodology used in computing these measures at greater length. When we aggregate these measures at the regional level, we find that Württemberg's skill profile was close to the German average. In Württemberg, the ratio of skilled workers to the total labor force was 30 percent, as compared to 33 percent for the entire Reich. By contrast, using the same metric, Saxony's skill profile was 46 percent. If the presence of skilled workers acted as an economic constraint on the ability of employers to engage in electoral intimidation, one would expect to find significant variation in the occurrence of private electoral intimidation across these two regions and lower levels of private intimidation in Saxony than in Württemberg.

Saxony and Württemberg differ with respect to their overall levels of electoral irregularities. As discussed in Chapter 2, Saxony experienced overall levels of electoral irregularities that were significantly higher than those found in other German provinces. By contrast, in Württemberg, the share of contested elections as a percentage of total elections was below average. How significant was private electoral intimidation in these regions? To assess the incidence of such intimidation, I rely on the same subsample of electoral fraud reports coded in Section 4.1. The level of electoral intimidation perpetrated by private actors is remarkably low across both regions. In the subsample of electoral reports I coded, I found eleven cases of allegations of electoral intimidation by private actors in Saxony and Württemberg during the entire period. The instances of private electoral intimidation detected in this subsample of cases are disproportionally concentrated during the earliest elections of the period. I also found a higher incidence of private electoral intimidation in Saxony than in Württemberg.

The repertoire of electoral intimidation strategies used by private actors in decentralized regions was much more limited than that used by employers in the Ruhr and Saarland. We do not find any reference to the complicated political machinery set up by employers in "autarkic" regions to give them the ability to monitor the choices of each and every one of their employees. Electoral reports from Saxony and Württemberg describe two main strategies of electoral intimidation used by employers. The first were pre-electoral pressures to secure political support for particular candidates. Consider the case of the 1884 election in Saxony's ninth electoral district. The election was won by Merbach, the owner of a local company. A protest brought to the attention of the electoral commission of the Reichstag alleged that Merbach had engaged in "systematic electoral terrorism directed against the workers in the iron and steel works as well as in mining." As part of his campaign, Merbach had directed workers from the local companies to sign official announcements in the local newspaper expressing their support for his candidacy. Some of these announcements were signed by hundreds of voters. One such announcement, which was signed by the "personnel of the machine tool factory Konstantinhütte from Klettaschrawa" and published on October 28 in the *Freiberger Amtsblatt*, read as follows: "Workers, today, Tuesday October 28, the day of election, vote together (*Mann für Mann*) for *Oberbergrat* Merbach" (*Stenographische Berichte des Deutschen Reichstages* 1884: encl. 328).

We find reports of threats of layoffs in both Württemberg and Saxony, but their incidence is low because of the low number of cases of private electoral irregularities in general. During the 1881 election, in Württemberg's fourth electoral district, the owner of the Königliche Hüttenwerke is reported to have pressured workers to vote for the candidate Riekert or else "look for employment in other companies" (*Stenographische Berichte des Deutschen Reichstages* 1881: encl. 113). Threats of "electoral layoffs" were also reported in Saxony during the 1877 election in Zittau and Haynewalde. There, employers at the local spinning factory threatened workers with layoffs. These employers were also reported to have gathered all of the employees of their firms into three columns and to have led these columns to the polls (*Stenographische Berichte des Deutschen Reichstages* 1877: encl. 121).

Evidence of the presence of employers at the moment of voting and of their intense pressuring of voters is also limited in both Saxony and Württemberg. The exception was Saxony's eighth district during the 1884 election. At that time, employers of a local iron company were reported to have kept counter-lists during voting to control the votes of workers from their company. Testimony from voters at the time indicates that employers were able to identify the votes of all but seven of their workers (*Stenographische Berichte des Deutschen Reichstages* 1884: encl. 328).

We find significant differences in the incidence of private electoral intimidation between regions with high economic heterogeneity and those with low economic heterogeneity. Employers played a pervasive role as agents of electoral intimidation in the areas with high economic concentration. By contrast, intimidation was a less important electoral phenomenon in regions with low occupational heterogeneity. In Saxony, a region that experienced higher than average levels of electoral intimidation, most of this intimidation came from state employees and not from private actors. These differences provide initial support for the conjecture that higher occupational heterogeneity in a district raises employers' costs of electoral intimidation. Second, we find a difference in the intensity of the electoral intimidation between concentrated and heterogeneous areas. In concentrated areas, employers developed an intensive apparatus of control during all stages of the electoral process. As shown earlier in this section, employers in the Ruhr and Saarland regions exercised particularly strong control over their workers at the moment of voting. This monitoring of the choices of voters was virtually nonexistent in areas with high levels of economic heterogeneity. In those regions, private electoral influence took place instead during the stage of electoral mobilization, but employers lacked the institutional capacity to control voting decisions.

4.4. PRIVATE ELECTORAL INTIMIDATION IN RURAL AREAS

Chapter 3 documents the pervasive electoral irregularities perpetrated by public election officials in rural areas. In those districts, policemen, tax collectors, and public officials played a ubiquitous role during elections. One of their most important electoral objectives was to prevent opposition parties from canvassing, distributing ballots, and thus reaching voters. In that chapter, I also show that the strategies of state employees to engage in electoral intimidation were constrained by political competition. Most notably, higher levels of fragmentation among right-wing parties constrained the ability of candidates to deploy public officials during elections and led to the use of "noiseless" and less intrusive forms of electoral intervention.

In the Prussian countryside, acts of intimidation by employees of the state – such as policemen and tax collectors – made up the overwhelming share of electoral irregularities. Other historical studies of the period by Robert Arsenschek, Thomas Kühne, and Dan Ziblatt provide similar characterizations of patterns of electoral intimidation in the Prussian countryside. "Private" electoral intimidation by landowners was also pervasive. Just like "bread lords" in urban areas, rural landlords attempted to capitalize on their economic control over rural voters and attempted to transform their economic power into a source of political advantage.

The presence of rural landlords during elections and the intensity of their strategies of electoral intimidation vary dramatically across German districts. To illustrate this point, let me consider again the distribution of the incidence of private intimidation identified in the subsample of electoral reports submitted to the Reichstag. If we restrict the analysis to the rural districts (in other words, those districts where the percentage of workers employed in agriculture exceeded 70 percent), we find the highest incidence of private electoral intimidation in Silesia: all twelve districts of Oppeln experienced electoral contestations during at least one of the elections of the period. In addition, we find numerous cases of private electoral intimidation in Silesia.

Both economic and political conditions in Silesia created a favorable terrain for private electoral intimidation. Klein characterizes these political preconditions by describing the region as having been dominated by a "coterie of large landowners" that controlled local political conditions (Klein 2003: 137).

The statistical information about patterns of employment distribution across farms of different sizes collected by the Prussian statistical office as part of Prussia's 1905 occupational census reinforces this characterization (*Königliches Preussisches Statitisches Landesamt* 1907). Levels of agricultural employment in farms of more than 200 hectares was high in many of Silesia's communes (such as Rosenberg and Neustadt in Oppeln or Nimptsch in Breslau). In addition, Silesian localities displayed unusually low levels of educational achievement, as compared to those in other German provinces. More than one-quarter of the population above the age of ten was illiterate (Klein 2003: 117).

Silesia's political clan – the Hohenlohe family – was widely known for its practices of electoral intimidation. Several of the Hohenlohe politicians who would have lost their electoral seats as the result of contestation resigned pre-emptively, anticipating this outcome. This was the case, among others, of Fürst von Hohenlohe-Oehringen, who lost his seat in Gross Strehlitz-Kosel during the 1875 election, Prince Karl von Koschintin (also from the Hohenlohe family), who resigned from his seat in Lublinitz-Tost Gleiwitz in 1876, and Christian Krafft zu Hohenlohen-Oehringen, who also lost his seat after an invalidation by the electoral commission (Anderson 2000: 165). Lavinia Anderson characterized the electoral politics in Silesia as follows:

> Against voters who ignored their wishes, the agents of the Hohenlohes employed all the usual means by which a landlord could make life hard for his dependents. They withdrew the small offices (such as the supervision of the town clock) that enabled a man to earn a tiny income. They terminated gleaning and grazing privileges. They called in outstanding debts, raised taxes, and canceled tenancies. They evicted. In the case of the Prince of Pless – who was exacting revenge for the defeat of the Duke of Ratibor – whole villages were cut off from poor relief. (Anderson 2000: 165)

The two most common strategies of electoral intimidation used by rural employers consisted of the pre-electoral intimidation of voters and the close monitoring of the choices made by voters at the polling place. Consider first the strategy of pre-electoral intimidation. During the 1874 election in Niewische, Silesia, one of the localities of the district, Schulze Czapla, was reported to have warned voters: "[You must] give your vote to the prince; otherwise you will lose your job and the lease that you have received from Herzog von Ujest" (*Stenographische Berichte des Deutschen Reichstages* 1874: encl. 159). In neighboring villages, another landlord was reported to have threatened voters with immediate dismissal if they were not willing to support Prince von Hohenlohe (*Stenographische Berichte des Deutschen Reichstages* 1874: encl. 159). In Drengfort, a locality in the Königsberg's tenth district, local inspectors reportedly threatened to lay off people working on the Gut Serwillen if they refused to vote for Udo zu Stolberg-Wernigerode, the conservative candidate (*Stenographische Berichte des Deutschen Reichstages* 1892: encl. 126, 737).

Employers also carried out these threats. In Merseburg's eighth district, the landowner Schmidt from Aupitz is reported to have laid off workers who engaged in Social Democratic agitation. When letting these rural workers go, this landlord reportedly stated: "[L]et Hoffmann [the Social Democratic candidate] pay you your wages" (*Stenographische Berichte des Deutschen Reichstages* 1890: encl. 297).

Some of these threats were powerful and lingered over time. In Reichenbach-Neurode in Breslau, Freiherr von Richthofen-Brechelshof, a local landlord, published a threat in the official publication of the locality to lay off workers who voted for opposition candidates. The fear of dismissals persisted over time. During the following election, witnesses recalled this threat as a factor that constrained their political freedom (*Stenographische Berichte des Deutschen Reichstages* 1881: encl. 104).

On some occasions, electoral reports present evidence of sectoral agreements between rural employers in some localities to prevent workers that had been laid off for political reasons from finding alternative employment in a particular industry. Such practices were reported, for instance, during the 1881 election in Reichenbach-Neurode. At the time, forest wardens attempted to coerce rural workers to vote for the conservative candidate, Dierig. As the parliamentary report noted, the "phantom of unemployment was particularly powerful for these workers because they were unable to find similar jobs either in this locality or in its vicinity" (*Stenographische Berichte des Deutschen Reichstages* 1881: encl. 104).

As with urban employers, rural landlords attempted to take advantage of several imperfections in the voting process to exercise influence over voters. In Stolberg Wernigerode, Königsberg, the local landowner inspected each and every ballot and decided to lay off seven workers who had not voted for the conservative candidate (*Stenographische Berichte des Deutschen Reichstages* 1890: encl. 126). During the same election, in Langendorf, a village in Merseburg's eighth district, the local estate owner Bartels also acted as the president of the polling station. When one of the employees from his manor, a milkman, approached to vote, Bartels decided to open the milkman's ballot. Upon seeing that the milkman had voted for Hoffmann, a Social Democratic candidate, Bartels exclaimed: "You are working for me and you want to vote for one of these (*und willst do so einen wählen*), you dirty dog (*Misthund*)." The landowner offered the milkman a ballot for Günther, a National Liberal candidate, and asked him to place this alternative ballot in the urn (*Stenographische Berichte des Deutschen Reichstages* 1890: encl. 297).

Intimate knowledge of one's neighbors in small communities in the countryside increased electoral pressure. During the 1881 election in Reichenbach-Neurode, the chairman of the polling station was known for his political support of the conservatives; he had lived on the same farm for more than twenty years and reportedly knew all of the workers who lived there. As the electoral commission examining irregularities concluded, this intimate knowledge increased the sense of constant supervision experienced by voters and increased the costs for voters of supporting opposition candidates:

The president of the polling station in the district where these workers voted, Justizrat Rosemann, had been living for more than twenty years on this farm. He knew all the workers who were employed on this farm and was also known as a strict conservative supporter. One also has to clarify that Inspector Jäckel was the other committee member of this polling station. One could argue that these workers had the freedom to bring a ballot for another candidate and to shape that ballot in the same way as the ballot received from Inspector Jäckel. This assumption, however, is very improbable because of the well-known fear of the voters of employment loss and because of the fact that the president of the polling station, Rosemann, collected the ballots before they were introduced in the urn. (*Stenographische Berichte des Deutschen Reichstages* 1881: encl. 104)

4.5. TEMPORAL VARIATION IN ECONOMIC INTIMIDATION BY PRIVATE ACTORS

The previous sections documented the existence of significant cross-sectional variation in the incidence of private electoral intimidation and in the intensity of terror exercised by private employers during elections. We now turn to an analysis of the temporal variation in the electoral strategies used by German bread lords. Did the use of electoral intimidation by private actors vary over time? Do we find variation in the intensity of repression tactics deployed by private actors during elections? If so, what factors explain the level of intensity in the strategies deployed by German employers?

Table 4.1 presents descriptive evidence of the temporal variation in private electoral intimidation. The source for this information is the subset of fraud reports (consisting of 15 percent of the cases for twelve out of the thirteen elections that occurred during the period) for which I have coded instances of private electoral intimidation. The descriptive statistics presented in the table show that the incidence of private electoral intimidation declined over time. I find the highest level of electoral involvement by employers during the earliest elections of the period and then a decline in private electoral intimidation over time, especially after the 1898 election.

Two factors may account for this decline over time. The first is a change in economic concentration. The information collected in the two economic censuses of the period (the 1895 and 1905 censuses) show that Germany's occupational heterogeneity increased during this time. This increase, however, was not evenly distributed across regions. Many districts in the Ruhr region experienced low changes in economic concentration over time and maintained the high levels of economic concentration that were assessed as part of the 1895 census. The increase in economic diversification was, however, more pronounced in

TABLE 4.1. *Temporal Variation in the Incidence of Private Employer Intimidation*

Election	Cases of Employer Fraud	Number of Petitions (15% of Sample)	Percentage of Employer Fraud in Sample
1874	4	7	0.57
1877	3	8	0.37
1878	7	10	0.67
1881	5	9	0.56
1884	6	12	0.49
1887	3	9	0.31
1890	5	12	0.42
1893	8	15	0.50
1898	2	13	0.15
1903	3	12	0.24
1907	4	13	0.31
1912	4	11	0.37

central and southern Germany than it was elsewhere. As hypothesized, the costs of electoral intimidation for private actors were lower in districts with low economic concentration. These broad economic trends can account for some of the decline in private electoral intimidation across German elections over time. By contrast, in districts where high levels of economic concentration persisted throughout the period, electoral intimidation perpetrated by private actors did not decline. As an example, at the end of this section, I discuss the persistence of electoral intimidation in Trier's fifth electoral district.

Throughout this period, dramatic economic changes in the German countryside also contributed to an increase in the costs of electoral intimidation for private economic actors. German agriculture experienced high levels of migration during this period. The central economic problem experienced by German agriculture during the period was *Landflucht*, or migration from land (Quante 1933; Quante 1959; Bade 1980). As early as 1890, a statistical study commissioned by the Prussian Ministry of the Interior concluded that the "labor shortage that affected the Eastern regions of the Prussian monarchy can lead to the death (*Lebensunfähigkeit*) of German agriculture" (Remarks of Lodemann, director of the Prussian Ministry of the Interior, cited in Bade 1980: 280). Migration intensified in the following decades. Between 1895 and 1905, several districts of East Prussia – such as Gumbinnen, Allenstein, and Posen – experienced migration rates that exceeded 10 percent of the population (Brösicke 1907). Migration transformed the employment relations in the countryside. Regions that only a few decades earlier had enjoyed relative surpluses in the supply of available rural workers experienced labor shortages ("*Leutenot*") (Rieger 1914). Contemporary accounts decried the shortages as the "main calamity" (*"Hauptkalamität"*) of their localities, because the shortages pushed up the level of wages in agriculture and contributed to the economic collapse of many farms (Kehri 1908).

The emergence of labor scarcity in regions that had previously enjoyed labor abundance had political implications for electoral competition in rural districts because it affected the costs of electoral intimidation. In electoral districts with a relative abundance of agricultural workers, electoral intimidation carried relatively low political costs for rural employers. In conditions of labor surplus, the economic bargaining power is tilted toward employers. In such districts, one expects the threat of electoral layoffs to be relatively powerful and the willingness of voters to support opposition political candidates to be relatively low. By contrast, one expects that a shortage of agricultural workers constrains the economic power of local landlords, raising the costs of electoral intimidation. One contemporary account discussed the implications of labor scarcity for electoral politics in rural districts:

In earlier times, the electoral pressures of landowners on rural workers were certainly not low. In later periods, landowners had to use this means of power (*Machtmittel*) very carefully because of the labor shortage that existed in the countryside. One was happy if one could keep one's employees, and one was careful to not antagonize the employees through electoral harassments and to not drive them to the cities. (Wulff 1922: 13)

In Chapter 7, I explore at greater length the consequences of labor scarcity for electoral politics in Prussia's rural districts. At this point in my analysis, I note only that this variable may be a possible factor that increased the costs of private electoral intimidation.

The third factor that may explain the decline in electoral intimidation perpetrated by private actors over time is the change in the electoral law. In 1903, German lawmakers introduced electoral legislation that mandated ballot envelopes and "isolating spaces" (*Isolierräume*) in the voting area. The explicit goal of this legislation was to protect voters against possible economic retaliation for their political choices. This legislation made it more difficult for employers to exercise unmediated control over the voting choices of their employees and to engage in practices such as using counter-lists. As Chapter 7 demonstrates, this change in the electoral rules had a significant effect on the willingness of voters to support opposition candidates.

Together, these economic and political changes increased the costs of electoral intimidation for private actors. Whereas the 1903 electoral law reduced the possibility of closely monitoring the decisions of voters in the ballot booth, it did not increase the costs of other strategies of electoral intimidation used by German employers, such as monitoring turnout. Such forms of electoral intimidation persisted in areas with high levels of economic concentration, such as the Ruhr and Saar regions.

To illustrate the persistence of electoral threats issued by employers in districts with high levels of economic concentration even after the adoption of legislation protecting electoral secrecy, I conclude this chapter with a summary of electoral practices in Saarbrücken, Trier's fifth electoral district, during the 1912 election (*Stenographische Berichte des Deutschen Reichstages* 1912: encl. 1639). During this election, the district was contested between Ernst Bassermann, who competed for the National Liberal Party, and Sauermann, a local employer in mining who represented the Zentrum. Basserman won by a very narrow margin during a runoff.

The results of the election were contested on a number of grounds. Among them were violations of the electoral freedom of the voters. Protesters invoked the harsh atmosphere of electoral terror perpetrated by the owner of the Burbacher Hütte, a company that employed more than 5,000 workers. The electoral announcement posted on the company entrance illustrates the tenor of that electoral pressure. In it, employers fearlessly threatened layoffs and invoked punishments that had been used in previous elections. Consider a few statements from this electoral call (*Wahlaufruf*):

A question of honor for each worker is to vote for Bassermann. Workers, trust your employer! We are loyal to you; you need to repay the trust that we have placed in you and vote for candidate Bassermann. [By voting for Bassermann], voters need not fear meeting the same fate as those workers in previous years that did not vote for the candidate of the iron works. In previous years, those workers found themselves without bread and country (*brotlos und heimatlos*) and without any prospect of finding a job anywhere in the mining industry of the Saar, because the companies here have an agreement not to accept a mutual exchange of workers.

The electoral committee of the Zentrum, which submitted the complaint against the violation of electoral freedom, noted that "this explicit reference to the dense network of firms in the region that 'cooperated' by denying employment to the workers that chose to withstand the pressures of their employers justifies the reference to the region as 'Saarabia' (*Saarabien*)" (*Stenographische Berichte des Deutschen Reichstages* 1912: encl. 1639).

The pressure on voters did not end with this *Wahlaufruf*. Local employers also turned to other strategies of electoral intimidation that had been used during previous elections. In Saarbrücken, the head of the local company (Burbacher Hütte) summoned groups of workers to his office on election day. There, he informed them that in the upcoming election, only Bassermann was an acceptable candidate. After his speech, he distributed Bassermann ballots and instructed the workers not to accept any other ballots. After that, the workers were led in groups to the polls by a foreman and were watched by a guard (*Stenographische Berichte des Deutschen Reichstages* 1912: encl. 1639).

However, the lengthy report of electoral irregularities in this district contains no reference to practices of intimidation in the polling place or to the supervision of workers' choices by representatives of the firms. The provisions of the 1903 electoral law, which attempted to protect voters against intimidation by introducing ballot envelopes and isolating spaces appear to have succeeded in creating a modest space of political freedom. In Chapter 7, I discuss the effect of the 1903 reform on the willingness of voters to support Social Democratic candidates and provide additional evidence of the political freedom gained by German voters following these changes in voting technology.

4.6. CONCLUSION

Private electoral intimidation was pervasive in German national elections. The electoral involvement of employers has been widely noted by contemporary observers of German electoral practices, such as Max Weber, and has been documented by historians of Imperial Germany, such as Lavinia Anderson (Weber 1958; Anderson 2000). In this chapter, I formulated a number of hypotheses that seek to account for the cross-sectional and temporal variation in private electoral intimidation. Using a subset of the total number of electoral petitions submitted to the Reichstag, I identified the occurrence of private electoral intimidation. I also used the rich qualitative information available in the reports submitted to the electoral commission of the Reichstag to examine whether the types of electoral strategies used by private actors during elections and the intensity of the pressure put on workers by employers varied systematically across German localities.

The analysis of the variation in the incidence of economic intimidation by private actors provides support for my hypotheses. Economic concentration emerges as a powerful predictor of private electoral intimidation. The highest number of electoral irregularities that included electoral intimidation by private actors was reported in the Saarland and the Ruhr, two regions characterized by high levels of economic concentration. Instances of electoral intimidation by landowners were also reported in rural Prussian districts. In East Prussia, Silesia reported the most electoral irregularities. By contrast, private electoral intimidation was virtually absent in regions characterized by high levels of economic heterogeneity, such as Saxony and Württemberg. These findings are consistent with the hypothesis that occupational heterogeneity increased the costs of electoral intimidation for economic actors.

The analysis of the qualitative information presented in the electoral reports allows me to document strong variation between economically concentrated and economically diversified regions in the intensity of the strategies that private actors used in their attempts to control electoral choices. What is striking about the strategies of electoral intimidation used by private actors in areas of high economic concentration is their effort to control nearly all aspects of the electoral process, from the announcement of candidacy, to the unfolding of the campaign to the mobilization during the election, and to the moment of the vote. Employers in these regions exploited their control over a large pool of potential voters. They ensured that workers reached the voting place equipped with the proper ballots. They exploited imperfections in voting technology to keep tabs on the electoral choices made by their workers, and they engaged in post-electoral reprisals against workers making the wrong electoral choices. By contrast, employers in districts characterized by high levels of economic heterogeneity lacked the means to establish similar levels of control over the political choices of their voters. Because of the economic makeup of the districts, political layoffs for choices made at the ballot box were much costlier for firms in Germany's diversified economic regions than they were for companies in economically concentrated regions.

5

The Production of Irregularities during Elections

A Quantitative Analysis

In Chapters 1–4, I presented an account of the main forms of electoral irregularities that were present in German elections. The most important actors engaged in the perpetration of electoral intimidation were state employees and private actors. I presented a range of hypotheses about the political factors affecting the candidates' demand for electoral support from employees of the state and private actors. The decisions of state employees and private actors to supply electoral services to candidates were not entirely costless and were constrained by the range of political and economic conditions in a district. In Chapter 2, I developed a number of hypotheses about the most significant constraints on the electoral involvement of state employees and private actors. The actions used by those agents during elections violated a number of provisions of the German electoral law, which provided opportunities for candidates who lost their races to contest the outcome. Many contemporary observers of German electoral practices noted the intense legalism in the contestation of elections.

In this chapter, I subject the hypotheses about the economic and political determinants of electoral irregularities to a quantitative test. The dependent variable for the analysis includes all of the reports of electoral irregularities submitted by the parliamentary commission of the Reichstag (*Wahlprüfungs-kommission*), whose goal it was to establish the validity of the electoral outcomes. This complete dataset of electoral irregularities in German national elections during the period between 1870 and 1912 can be found in two separate historical sources. A study by Klein includes a collection of this data based on historical records assembled by the electoral commission of the German parliament (Klein 2003: 501–511). More recently, Robert Arsenschek and Dan Ziblatt created a new dataset of electoral irregularities in Imperial

Germany that differs only in minor ways from the original data published by Klein (Arsenschek and Ziblatt 2008). To ensure comparability to existing results in political science, I use the more recent dataset in my empirical analysis.

The empirical analysis in this chapter builds on the existing research of the determinants of electoral irregularities in several ways. The first contribution comes in the generation of new data that allows me to provide a systematic test of a range of economic hypotheses about the determinants of electoral irregularities. More specifically, the empirical analysis presented in this chapter uses for the first time the economic data collected by the German Statistical Office as part of the German occupational census (*Gewerbezählung*). This comprehensive empirical source includes detailed information about the employment structure for more than 200 occupations across 1,000 German localities (*Gemeinde*). For this study, I digitized two waves of the German occupational census – conducted in 1895 and 1905 respectively – to develop a range of variables that capture both cross-sectional and temporal variation in the occupational heterogeneity across Imperial Germany. I make use of additional information about the ratio between skilled and unskilled workers for 200 occupations to compute district-level measures of the skill profile of the labor force.

I also seek to refine existing explanations of the political determinants of electoral irregularities. Building on the hypotheses formulated in Chapter 2, I examine how different district-level measures of political competition – such as the tightness of a race, the political fragmentation among right-wing candidates, and the electoral strength of the main opposition candidate – affect candidates' demand for political support (which may result in the production of electoral irregularities) and the willingness of electoral agents to supply political services during elections in different ways. Although much of the previous literature hypothesizes that electoral competition contributes to a higher number of electoral irregularities, I seek to disaggregate this variable and analyze how different measures of electoral competition affect in different ways the demand made by candidates for political support and the decisions made by agents acting on behalf of those candidates who have the capacity to supply electoral irregularities.

The chapter is organized as follows. I begin in Section 5.1 with a brief analysis of the descriptive variation in the incidence of electoral irregularities in national elections to the Reichstag in Imperial Germany. Section 5.2 then restates the main hypotheses developed in Chapter 2 about the economic and political factors affecting the incidence of electoral fraud. Section 5.3 discusses the construction of some of the variables used in the analysis on the basis of the newly digitized historical data. Section 5.4 presents an empirical test of my model and is followed in Section 5.5 by robustness checks of the main empirical results to different specifications.

5.1. THE INCIDENCE OF ELECTORAL FRAUD IN GERMAN ELECTIONS AS ASSESSED BY THE REPORTS OF ELECTORAL IRREGULARITIES TO THE REICHSTAG

The main sources for the empirical analysis presented in this chapter are petitions alleging various electoral irregularities submitted by the electoral commission (*Wahlprüfungskommission*) of the Reichstag to the entire chamber. Before discussing the variation in electoral irregularities across German regions, it is important to understand the data generation process for these reports. The German electoral law that governed the administration of national elections during the period between 1870 and 1912 was characterized by its remarkable effort to give individual voters the unrestricted ability to contest the outcomes of elections. In practice, any eligible voter could submit a complaint for electoral misconduct to the parliament (Hatschek 1920). This contrasts the electoral laws of other countries that attempted to limit the contestation of electoral outcomes either through property qualifications or through high administrative burdens (Arsenschek 2003: 31). The electoral commission of the Reichstag investigated complaints about possible electoral irregularities, submitting to the Reichstag cases that demonstrated violations of the provisions of electoral rules. The dependent variable of this chapter comprises all cases submitted by the electoral commission to the Reichstag. Out of the 5,152 seat contestations in Germany during the thirteen elections held between 1871 and 1914, the commission submitted 974 complaints to the parliament. The contestation rate of German elections was close to 19 percent.

To explore some of the regional variation in the incidence of electoral fraud, Figure 5.1 presents information about the cumulative number of contested elections across Imperial Germany's 397 districts. For each district, I computed the number of electoral complaints considered by the parliamentary commission of the Reichstag as a share of the total number of elections. The darker-shaded districts in Figure 5.1 are districts where a high number of electoral irregularities took place during the thirteen elections of the period. Some of the descriptive patterns displayed in Figure 5.1 are already familiar from the empirical analysis presented in Chapters 3 and 4, which discussed the incidence of electoral irregularities in four provinces in Imperial Germany: Prussia, Saxony, Baden, and Württemberg. Figure 5.1 places these four regions within the broader political context of Imperial Germany. As discussed in Chapter 3, the incidence of electoral fraud was particularly high in Prussia and Saxony but much lower in Baden and Württemberg. Electoral fraud was also relatively high in the small German principalities (such as Schwarzburg, Reuss, Waldeck, and Schaumburg Lippe) and in the Hanseatic cities (Lübeck, Bremen, and Hamburg). Elsaß Lothringen, the region annexed by Germany in 1870, was electorally contested between independent parties, Social Democrats, the Zentrum, and representatives of various splinter liberal movements, and it also experienced

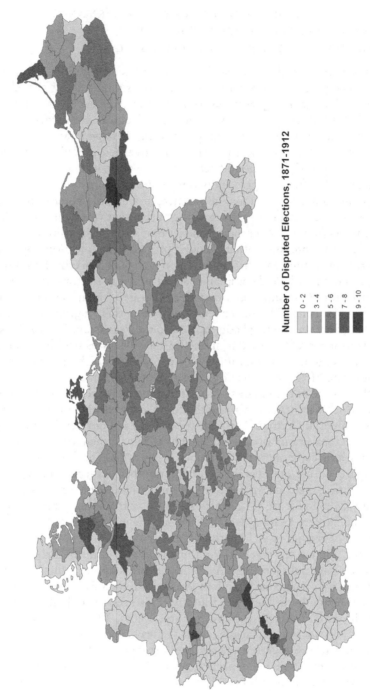

Number of Disputed Elections, 1871-1912

0 - 2
3 - 4
5 - 6
7 - 8
9 - 10

FIGURE 5.1. The incidence of disputed elections in Germany.

very high levels of electoral fraud. By contrast, Bavaria experienced remarkably low levels of electoral contestation throughout this period.

This preliminary analysis of the cross-sectional variation in the incidence of electoral irregularities reveals the existence of a strong north-south division. The incidence of electoral fraud was significantly higher in northern German states, such as Prussia and other small principalities, and much lower in the southern German provinces, such as Bavaria, Baden, and Württemberg. Whereas levels of landholding inequality differ significantly between northern and southern German regions, other variables that may affect the incidence of electoral irregularities also vary significantly across northern and southern Germany. These include occupational heterogeneity and right-wing political fragmentation.

A second observation about the variation in the levels of electoral irregularities across German provinces is that one finds high levels of irregularities both in the rural areas of East Prussia and also in some of the most advanced and developed regions of Germany. These include the Ruhr, Saxony, and the Hanseatic states. This variation challenges explanations that are based on a simple dichotomy between a backward, repressive Prussia and a modern Germany in which employers and employees have made investments in "specific skills" that guarantee harmonious and cooperative industrial relations. Exploring the variation in electoral irregularities is interesting precisely because it challenges this dichotomy.

A closer investigation of the regional variation in levels of electoral fraud suggests, however, that the distinction between highly unequal but highly corrupt regions and equal but less corrupt regions does not capture the range of empirical variation in the incidence of electoral irregularities in German elections. As discussed at the beginning of this chapter, the difference in the incidence of electoral fraud between East Prussia and other German regions is not statistically significant in many elections during this period. What is more problematic for an explanation that stresses the importance of rural inequality is that high levels of electoral fraud also occurred in some of the more modern and economically developed regions of Imperial Germany, such as Saxony and the Ruhr region. Similarly, the Hanseatic states also experienced higher than average levels of electoral irregularity. This suggests that additional economic and political characteristics in these districts explain both the motivation and also the capabilities of political actors to engage in electoral irregularities. I now turn to a test of the propositions developed in Chapter 2 that seek to account for the variation in electoral intimidation in German elections.

Table 5.1 maps some of the temporal variation in electoral irregularities across Germany's largest regions. The entries in each cell are the percentages of districts in each election and region that experienced electoral irregularities. The table illustrates the existence of significant cross-regional variation in the incidence of electoral irregularities across Germany. Electoral irregularities are significantly higher in Prussia and Saxony as compared to the other regions

TABLE 5.1. *Probability of Electoral Fraud by Region and Year*

Region	1871	1874	1877	1878	1881	1884	1887	1890	1893	1898	1903	1907	1912
East Prussia	0.18	0.13	0.13	0.28	0.22	0.21	0.17	0.23	0.31	0.32	0.25	0.24	0.31
West Prussia	0.13	0.09	0.18	0.13	0.16	0.22	0.21	0.24	0.34	0.23	0.22	0.28	0.22
Bavaria	0.10	0.19	0.02	0.02	0.08	0.06	0.06	0.06	0.17	0.13	0.13	0.15	0.02
Saxony	0.09	0.13	0.22	0.09	0.30	0.39	0.22	0.30	0.22	0.17	0.09	0.09	0.09
Württemberg	0.00	0.06	0.06	0.06	0.06	0.18	0.06	0.12	0.12	0.12	0.00	0.00	0.06
Baden	0.07	0.21	0.29	0.07	0.00	0.14	0.21	0.07	0.14	0.07	0.00	0.00	0.07
Hessen	0.11	0.00	0.00	0.22	0.00	0.33	0.22	0.22	0.00	0.00	0.22	0.22	0.22
Small Principalities and Hanseatic States	0.23	0.14	0.11	0.31	0.06	0.23	0.20	0.26	0.20	0.14	0.34	0.29	0.11
Alsace and Lorraine	0.00	0.00	0.13	0.27	0.00	0.13	0.00	0.00	0.20	0.27	0.27	0.33	0.00

in the Empire. The table also illustrates the existence of significant temporal variation in the incidence of electoral irregularities. Across all regions, the incidence of electoral irregularities increased over time and was highest during the mid-1890s, but it then declined (East Prussia represents an important exception to this trend). The broad patterns of political competition discussed in Chapter 3 predict these temporal trends: an increase in political fragmentation of parties on the right, coupled with an increase in the number of elections whose outcomes were determined in runoffs, is expected to limit candidates' incentives to use employees of the state during elections.

5.2. THE PRODUCTION OF ELECTORAL IRREGULARITIES: UNPACKING THE CALCULATIONS OF CANDIDATES AND THEIR POLITICAL AGENTS

In Chapter 2, I formulated a number of hypotheses about the main factors that influence the production of electoral irregularities during elections. I distinguished between factors that affect the demand made by candidates for electoral activities that trespass and violate some of the provisions of electoral laws and factors that affect the incentives of a variety of agents who are deployed by candidates during elections to engage in irregularities. The two types of actors that were deployed most significantly in German elections were state employees and private actors. The calculations of these actors about the costs of electoral repression were affected by a combination of different factors. Although the considerations of state employees were affected by political factors, the calculations of employers to supply irregularities during elections were affected primarily by economic variables. I refer the reader to Chapter 2 for a fuller presentation of the hypotheses. This section only briefly summarizes the longer discussion presented in Chapter 2.

5.2.1. Candidates' Demand

Candidates' demand for additional political support during elections, which could, at times, trespass the boundaries of the electoral law and result in the production of electoral irregularities, was affected by a range of political factors in a district. I consider three such factors: the tightness of a race, the strength of Social Democratic opponents, and the fragmentation of right-wing opposition in conditions where runoffs occurred.

I hypothesize that candidates' incentive to reach out to loyal agents who could be mobilized for electoral purposes was higher in tighter races. This conjecture builds on a large existing literature in political science that has found a positive relationship between the tightness of a race and the incidence of electoral irregularities. In tighter races, I conjecture, candidates were more likely to engage in risk-seeking behavior that could result in a violation of the electoral law.

Not all candidates posed a similar threat to candidates on the right able to deploy the resources of the state apparatus. Social Democratic candidates posed a particular threat because of the radical ideology espoused by the party encouraging the overthrowing of the existing economic and political order. Social Democrats were the *Reichsfeinde*, or the enemy of the Empire. One of the most important motivations for the deployment of the bureaucratic apparatus during an election was the desire to prevent a Social Democratic candidate from winning office and to eradicate Social Democratic organizations from a district. In Chapter 2, I hypothesized that the relationship between Social Democratic strength in a district and candidates' demand for additional support from agents was likely to be nonlinear. Although this demand increased as the strength of the Social Democratic opponents increased, it was likely to taper off with very high levels of support for Social Democrats. In these cases, the marginal political returns from electoral intimidation were likely to be low, seeing as intimidation was unlikely to affect the outcome of the race. All other things being equal, candidates had the strongest incentives to deploy their agents in elections in districts with intermediate levels of electoral support for Social Democratic candidates.

A final dimension of electoral competition likely to affect candidates' demand for the production of electoral irregularities was the fragmentation on the political right in races that were determined in runoffs. Although the level of electoral competition and the strength of the Social Democratic Party were likely to increase candidates' incentives to deploy all necessary means to win a race, right-wing political fragmentation was likely to lower these incentives. This moderating effect of right-wing political fragmentation on the demand for electoral irregularities was particularly pronounced in elections determined in runoffs. In these cases, candidates on the right needed to coordinate around the winners of the first round. This need for electoral coordination was likely to constrain candidates from using policemen, tax collectors, or employers as their agents against other candidates on the right. I expect that the incidence of electoral irregularities was lower in districts with high levels of fragmentation on the right whose electoral outcomes were determined in runoffs.

5.2.2. The Supply of Electoral Intervention by State Employees

As Chapter 3 documented, the state employees that were the most involved during elections were policemen and tax collectors. Let us turn to these actors and explore what factors affected their consideration to exert "political effort" on behalf of candidates. As Susan Stokes and others demonstrated in a recent study on electoral clientelism, the incentives of brokers are not necessarily aligned with those of their partisan agents (Stokes et al. 2013). Electoral politics in Imperial Germany may illustrate these divergent interests between politicians and their agents.

As I conjectured in Chapter 2, tighter races created incentives for state employees to intervene in elections that were different from those of their political principals. The uncertainty of a future political incumbent in a district was higher in more competitive districts. This uncertainty increased the fear of state employees about possible post-electoral sanctions for electoral interventions. Thus, I hypothesize that in tighter races, state employees had lower incentives to intervene.

Higher fragmentation on the political right was also likely to increase the uncertainty about the future political principal and was likely to deter state employees from exerting excessive pressure during elections. One expects that in districts where one party benefited from strong political support, state employees were more likely to exert greater effort in elections because they did not fear punishment in the aftermath of the race. Political fragmentation on the right increased the number of possible political principals and was likely to deter state employees from intervening during elections. As a result, I expect that in districts with higher levels of political fragmentation on the right, state employees exerted lower levels of effort in elections on behalf of politicians.

Finally, the Social Democratic strength in a district affected in similar ways candidates' demand for political support and the considerations of state employees to supply irregularities during elections. As Chapter 3 demonstrated, policemen and tax collectors intervened with especial brutality and harshness against the Social Democratic candidates in a district. I conjectured in Chapter 2 that the intensity of their effort was likely to be strongest when Social Democratic candidates exhibited intermediate levels of strength. At very high levels of political support for Social Democratic candidates, such intervention may have been counterproductive.

5.2.3. The Considerations of Employers about the Supply of Political Effort

Employers were important actors whose electoral intervention often resulted in electoral irregularities. Chapter 3 documented the large number of strategies of intimidation used by employers in elections. These included pre-electoral activities, such as turnout boosting or turnout repression, the systematic monitoring of the decisions of voters, and the post-electoral punishment of voters who had disobeyed the orders given by their employers. The political involvement of employers differed significantly across the different regions of the German Empire.

Electoral intervention was not entirely costless to employers. The systematic harassment of workers for their political views and the imposition of economic sanctions on voters who had "undesirable" political views could have repercussions on the economic bottom line of a firm. Political harassment could lead to the resignations of valuable employees. Practices such as electoral layoffs could also be potentially costly, especially if those workers could find reemployment in competing firms without incurring any relocation costs. Firms' decisions to provide political support to candidates during elections took into account these costs of electoral repression. Firms only intervened if the benefits of their repressive activities outweighed the costs of their political activities. The most likely benefits were associated with the election of business-friendly candidates, and they came in the form of favorable industrial and trade policies and low taxation.

In Chapter 2, I conjectured that the most salient variable affecting the costs of electoral intimidation by employers was the economic concentration of a district. The economic costs of political involvement were low in economically concentrated districts, but they increased with an increase in economic hetero-geneity. When one single firm controlled the employment and output of a district, the firm encountered low costs for monitoring the political choices made by its employees at the ballot box and incurred low costs to harass voters, because voters had no immediate opportunities for reemployment. As such, I expect that the willingness of employers to engage in the harassment of voters was higher in economically concentrated districts.

In addition to economic concentration, I also conjectured that the skill level of the workforce was likely to increase the costs of electoral repression for employers. Employers that had made significant investments in the skills of their employees were likely to exercise more restraint in harassing those employees for their political choices out of fear that such undue pressure might result in the loss of valuable employees. The implication of this conjecture is that the level of electoral intimidation should be lower in districts with a higher share of skilled workers.

A final economic variable that may affect the costs of electoral intimi-dation for employers was the inequality in the distribution of farms. High inequality in landownership may confer on landlords either more economic resources or the ability to control a larger pool of workers, which may lower the costs of repression for rural landlords. In recent years, Dan Ziblatt has empirically investigated the relationship between landholding inequality and the incidence of fraud. Let me note, however, that this theoretical expec-tation about the relationship between landholding inequality and the inci-dence of electoral fraud differs in an important way from the explanation proposed by Ziblatt. Ziblatt argued that in highly unequal districts, conserva-tive landowners "captured the state," which in turn explains the production of electoral irregularities. Such an analysis is theoretically underspecified and does not consider the range of additional factors that influenced the politi-cal calculations made by state employees when deciding to supply political support to candidates. As Chapter 3 demonstrated, the incentives for state employees to intervene electorally varied significantly across elections, even in districts with high levels of landholding inequality, and they were primarily affected by the level of political competition in these districts. An explanation premised on the notion of "state capture" cannot account for this within-district variation.

To sum up, predicting the incidence of electoral fraud in elections is not straightforward because of the fact that political principals (politicians) and electoral agents (state employees and employers) respond to different sets of incentives. What complicates this analysis is that the most salient political variables – such as the tightness of a race – have offsetting effects on the demand by candidates for higher levels of electoral irregularities and on the incentives of some of the agents to supply these irregularities. It is theoretically uncertain which of these effects prevails; I therefore use empirical analysis to examine which effects prevail. In the following section, I disentangle the relative importance of a range of political and economic variables in understanding variation in the production of electoral irregularities.

5.3. A QUANTITATIVE TEST: EXPLAINING THE INCIDENCE OF ELECTORAL FRAUD IN GERMAN NATIONAL ELECTIONS

To test these theoretical hypotheses, I examine the effects of the political and economic conditions in a district on the incidence of electoral fraud. The dependent variable uses records of disputed elections that were considered by the German electoral commission (*Wahlprüfungskommission*) of the Reichstag during the period between 1870 and 1912.

Is the existence of a petition that alleged electoral irregularities a good measure of the incidence of electoral fraud? As discussed in Section 5.1, the procedures set up by the German electoral law allowing voters to dispute the outcomes of elections were remarkably open. Any citizen of the Reich could submit an electoral complaint after an election. This openness to contestations weakens concerns about possible sources of bias in this measure. The electoral commission acted as an initial gatekeeper that was supposed to eliminate the "frivolous" cases and submit to the Reichstag those in which evidence of violations of some provisions of the electoral code existed. The dependent variable in this chapter uses the petitions submitted by the commission for full consideration in the Reichstag, and these include more than 90 percent of the total number of petitions submitted to the commission. The political composition and ideological polarization of the commission of the Reichstag could affect the selection of cases. To control for this potential bias in the statistical analysis, I follow the empirical strategy used by Ziblatt (2009) and include several variables that capture variation in the political composition of the electoral commission.

5.3.1. Political Conditions in a District

As discussed in Section 5.2, a range of electoral variables may affect the demand for and supply of electoral intimidation. To test the political hypotheses outlined in that section, I construct a number of measures using the ICPSR dataset on German elections (ICPSR 1984), including the following variables:

MARGIN: Margin is a measure of the tightness of a race and is computed as the difference in electoral victory between the winner and the runner-up in the decisive electoral round (ICPSR 1984). As elaborated in the previous section, the theoretical predictions about the relationship between margin and the incidence of electoral fraud are ambiguous. In tighter races, the demand by candidates for electoral irregularities is likely to increase. By contrast, the incentives for state employees to supply electoral support is likely to be lower in tighter races. I also include a control for the decisive round of the election by including a variable that takes the value of 1 if the election was determined in the second round and zero otherwise (SECOND ROUND).

STRENGTH OF SOCIAL DEMOCRATIC CANDIDATES: To estimate the relationship between the political strength of the main opposition parties and the incidence of electoral fraud, I use a measure of the vote share of Social Democratic candidates during the first electoral round. As discussed in Section 5.2, I hypothesize that the relationship between this variable and the incidence of electoral fraud is nonlinear and highest at intermediate levels of Social Democratic strength. As such, I include both the measure of Social Democratic vote share and its quadratic in the specification (SOCIAL DEM VOTE SHARE, SOCIAL DEM SQ).

EFFECTIVE NUMBER OF RIGHT-WING PARTIES (ENRP): To examine the relationship between the political fragmentation among right-wing parties and the incidence of electoral fraud, I construct a measure of the effective number of right-wing parties in a district. If right-wing political fragmentation constrained the incentives of candidates on the right to use the apparatus of the state during elections, then the relationship between this variable and the incidence of fraud has a negative sign. To test the related hypothesis that the reliance of candidates on electoral intimidation was lower in districts where the race was decided during runoffs, I combine the measure of electoral fragmentation among right-wing parties with a variable taking the value of 1 if the race was decided during runoffs (ENRP*RUNOFFS). I expect a negative relationship between this variable and the incidence of electoral fraud.

5.3.2. Economic Conditions

As hypothesized in Section 5.2, a variety of economic conditions in a district may affect the costs of electoral intimidation incurred by private actors. To develop precise measures that allow us to test these hypotheses, I digitized the statistical information collected by the German Statistical Office's occupational census. The occupational census was one of the most remarkable accomplishments of European data collection at the turn of the twentieth century.

I use both the 1895 and the 1905 waves of the occupational census to construct very precise measures of occupational heterogeneity and skill composition in German localities. The sources for the construction of these variables include the following. For the 1895 census, I use the publications titled *Gewerbestatistik der kleineren Verwaltungsbezirke*, which was published by the German Statistical Office in two volumes in 1897 (Statistisches Reichsamt 1898a, 1898b). For the 1905 census, I use the two volumes of the *Gewerbliche Betriebstatistik* published in 1909 (Statistisches Reichsamt 1909a, 1909b). Each of the two censuses contains more than 400,000 lines of information that provide extremely fine-grained information about employment levels for 180 occupations across 1,000 municipalities throughout the German Empire. I aggregate these variables to the 397 electoral districts, using the mapping of localities into districts reported in Reibel (2007). Germany experienced no redistricting for the elections to the Reichstag, which makes the mapping of localities to districts relatively straightforward.

5.3.3. Occupational Heterogeneity

I hypothesize at repeated points in this book that the costs for private actors to participate in the electoral intimidation of voters were lowest in districts with high levels of employment concentration. In the extreme case of one single firm controlling the labor supply of a district, the firm faced no economic costs for electoral repression and could arbitrarily lay off workers for their political choices at the ballot box. The costs of electoral intimidation for private actors increased, however, as the occupational heterogeneity of a district increased.

The first measure of economic concentration at the district level is the Herfindahl-Hirschman Index (HHI) of employment concentration. As it is conventionally used in the literature on industrial organization, the Herfindahl-Hirschman Index refers to the sum of the squares of employment shares of all occupations in a particular district. I construct

$$HHI = \sum_{i=1}^{n} (S_i)^2,$$

where S stands for the employment share of occupational employment in each occupation i. Higher values of the HHI indicate concentrated economic structures, and lower values represent more decentralized economic conditions. This variable is logged to deal with the skewness in the raw data. One possible concern with this index is that it measures employment concentration at the occupational level and does not fully capture employment structure at the firm level. However, the highly disaggregated nature of this data (for each locality, we have information about employment shares in 183 occupations) allows us to assume that for each locality, one occupational category approximates one firm. I also present a number of alternative models that use a weighted HHI measure that weighs the employment share by the number of firms in each occupation.

The disaggregated occupational data is available only for the 1895 and 1905 censuses. I use a conservative approach to interpolate data for the years before and after those measurements. I use the 1895 values for proposals submitted before 1895 and the 1905 measures for those introduced after 1905. For proposals in between the two censuses, I use a weighted average (based on time from/to the last/next census). The emerging patterns are flat-steep-flat, such that the measures are constant between 1875 and 1895, they grow or fall during the time between the two measures, and they remain stable after 1905.

Economic heterogeneity plays an important role in existing economic and historical scholarship of German economic development (Fremdling and Tilly 1979; Sabel and Zeitlin 1996). Gary Herrigel's seminal study *Industrial Constructions: The Sources of German Industrial Power* is a prominent account of the importance of economic heterogeneity for the long-term variation in economic development across German regions. Critiquing the Gerschenkronian view of unitary industrial development, Herrigel convincingly argues that Germany's economic structure during this period was bifurcated between an undiversified ("autarkic") region dominated by a small number of large employers and a "decentralized economic structure" characterized by high levels of occupational heterogeneity (Herrigel 1996). In the latter,

industrialization occurred in a distinctly decentralized way.... Growth in these decentralized systems of production over the course of the nineteenth century generally produced three developments: 1) the slow decline of industrial employment in homework, 2) the proliferation of small and medium-sized establishments and 3) the diversification of the industrial base of the region.... Production was located, organized and technologically outfitted in different ways in different phases in the production of a single product and, in the case of the *geteilte Betriebe*, it even occurred in different ways and locales within the same phase of production. (Herrigel 1996: 39–40)

For Herrigel, the Ruhr area is an example of an autarkic, or undiversified, economic region, and Württemberg and Saxony are examples of decentralized regions (Herrigel 1996: 34–40). My book uses for the first time the rich economic and occupational data collected by the German statistical authority to provide a more productive empirical evaluation of the differences in economic heterogeneity across Germany's regions. Whereas Herrigel's study was concerned with the consequences of economic heterogeneity on long-term *economic* growth, this study examines the *political* consequences of the differences in economic heterogeneity.

Figure 5.2 displays the variation in economic heterogeneity across German electoral districts as measured by data collected in 1905. Darker-shaded

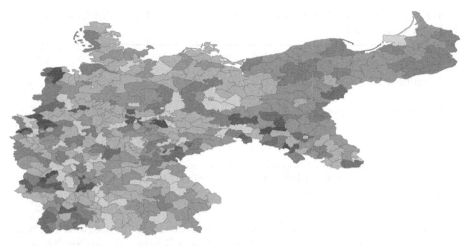

FIGURE 5.2. Variation in employment concentration across German districts.

districts represent higher levels of economic concentration, and lighter-shaded areas represent regions characterized by high economic heterogeneity. The visual presentation of the data is highly consistent with Herrigel's characterization of the differences in economic diversification across German regions. The autarkic areas are found in the Ruhr, Saarland, and Silesia. The level of economic heterogeneity of the Arnsberg province in the Ruhr is two standard deviations higher than the average for Germany. By contrast, the economic heterogeneity in Württemberg and Saxony-Weimar is below the average. Saxony exhibits values of economic heterogeneity that are close to the national level.

5.3.4. Vocational Skills

A number of recent studies have argued that human capital was an important predictor of political democratization during the nineteenth century (Cusack et al. 2009, 2011). Despite their emphasis on "co-specific assets" and skills as explanatory variables, these studies do not provide direct measures of the variation in the skill profile of workers across German regions. Cusack et al. evaluates these hypotheses about the importance of human capital by creating composite institutional measures of the strength of guilds, rural cooperatives, and associations of employers at the national level (Thelen 2004; Cusack et al. 2011, based on Katzenstein 1984 and Crouch 1993; see Kreuzer 2011 for a critique of these measures). Thus, hypotheses about the political consequences of skills remain untested, even in publications that seek to predict subnational political outcomes across Germany. This is the case, for example, of the Cusack et al. (2011) article, which seeks to explain the adoption of proportional representation at the subnational level in Germany.

TABLE 5.2. *Structure of Occupational Categories According to the German Occupational Census*

Sector	Vocation	Type
1. Agriculture	I. Nursery	
	II. Livestock	
2. Mining and Industry	III. Metalworking	a. Working with Gold and Silver
		b. Working with Copper
		c. Working with Steel
3. Trade and Commerce		

Note: Structure of the fine-grained classification of vocational categories in the German occupational census. Example: goldsmith.

In this book, I seek to remedy this empirical deficit in the existing literature by developing precise measures of skill profiles in German localities. The data of the skill composition of the labor force has two different inputs. The first measures the ratio of skilled workers to unskilled ones. As part of its 1895 census, the German Statistical Office collected information about the ratio between skilled workers and unskilled workers in 183 occupations, including 161 industrial occupations and 22 occupations in services. The German Statistical Office's definition of skilled workers (*gelernte Arbeiter*) is straightforward, if somewhat laconic: "Skilled workers are those workers who had experienced some training. By contrast, unskilled workers (*ungelernte Arbeiter*) – in other words manual workers, handymen, and other workers in services – do not have training" (Kaiserliches Statistisches Amt 1899: 73). Officials of the German Statistical Office noted that the number of skilled workers was very high in Germany (nearly 50 percent of workers), and argued that "The economic relations in industry – which require particular abilities and skills that can be learned or acquired through persistent exercise – are the decisive factor that explains this high ratio of skills" (Kaiserliches Statistisches Amt 1899: 73).

The data on skill distributions has the following structure. Every occupation is broadly classified as belonging to the agriculture, mining and production, or trade and commerce industries. Within these categories, there are two additional levels. To illustrate this, consider the occupational classification of goldsmiths (Table 5.2). These people make jewelry and are therefore employed in the second sector (mining and production industry), but within that sector, they belong to the vocational group "V" (metalworking class). If a goldsmith does not use copper but instead uses gold, he or she belongs to the vocational group "V" and type "a" (metalworking with gold or silver). Germany's 1895 occupational census collected information about the ratio of skilled workers to unskilled workers at this very detailed level of occupational aggregation. We know exactly how many people employed in "Va" were skilled and how many were unskilled.

The second input for the construction of the skill variable also comes from Germany's occupational census. In addition to data on skill profiles, I use the extreme disaggregated information about the employment share across all occupations (which I also used to compute the measure of occupational heterogeneity). These two inputs allow me to calculate the ratio of skilled to unskilled workers for each locality. In the final stage, I aggregate localities to electoral districts to obtain measures of the density of human capital across the 397 electoral districts of Germany. Using the number of skilled workers in each district as an input, I compute two measures of skill profiles that differ in their respective denominators. The first is a measure of skills as a percentage of workers employed in the industry (SKILL INDUSTRY). The second is a ratio between the skilled workers and all the workers in the district (SKILL ALL).

Unfortunately, the German Statistical Office did not collect similar data measuring the ratio of skilled to unskilled workers for each occupation as part of its 1905 census. The only comparable information from the 1905 census was a comparative table showing the number of apprentices (*Lehrlinge*) for each occupation. The table compares the 1895 and 1905 censuses and reveals that the changes in skill formation over time were very small. As a result, one can assume that the skill ratio remained constant over time for each occupation. What changed, however, was the occupational makeup of the districts. This requires us to recalculate the skill ratio using the information that was collected as part of the 1905 census. I employ the same procedure as in the calculation of the skill ratios for 1895, using the information about the distribution of workers across occupations presented in the 1905 census (Statistik des Deutschen Reiches 1909a, 1909b). But because the 1905 census does not have data on all agricultural workers in each occupation at the most disaggregated level (the locality), I can only compute a measure of skilled workers that uses the number of industrial workers in its denominator. SKILL INDUSTRY is, thus, the only time-varying measure of human capital.

5.3.5. Landholding Inequality

To test whether rural inequality affected the capability of private actors to engage in electoral intimidation, I rely on the measure of rural inequality computed by Ziblatt (2009). The Gini measure of LANDHOLDING INEQUALITY calculates the magnitude of the deviation from a perfectly equal distribution of agricultural land among landholders. Higher values of the Gini Index indicate that larger farms accounted for a greater proportion of total agricultural land, whereas smaller values suggest that total farm acreage was relatively equally distributed among farms of different sizes. The variable was computed by Ziblatt using data from the 1895 agricultural census (Statistik des Deutschen Reiches 1898a, 1898b). Ziblatt's study reveals considerable variation in patterns of landholding inequality but high average values for the measure of landholding inequality in Imperial Germany in 1895. Ginis of landholding inequality ranged from 0.46 to 0.95, with an average of 0.73. To put these figures in a comparative context, in 1860, the Gini of land inequality across the states of the United States ranged between 0.34 (Connecticut) and 0.83 (Louisiana), with an average Gini of 0.54.

5.3.6. Additional Controls

The electoral commission of the Reichstag used its prerogative to reject some of the petitions as "frivolous." Commissions with different political compositions could thus introduce specific biases when selecting cases of electoral irregularities. To control for these commission-specific effects, the various specifications include a battery of controls that code differences in the composition of the electoral commission, which were constructed by Ziblatt (2009). They include a control for the number of members of the commission belonging to political parties that represented the interests of landowners (including the Conservative and Imperial parties) and a measure of the "professionalism," or "neutrality," of the commission chair (Ziblatt 2009). The final measure is a measure of the ideological polarization of the election commission, which is constructed by multiplying the number of seats in a commission held by different members with a measure of the ideological score of their respective parties.

All specifications include a battery of additional variables to control for other sources of variation across German districts. To control for differences in economic development, the models include a measure of the percentage of the population employed in the non-agricultural sector (ECONOMIC DEVELOPMENT). The source for this measure is Reibel (2007). Because the values were only measured in 1895 and 1905, I use the flat-steep-flat method of interpolating missing values that I outlined in Section 5.3.3. I also control for the religious differences across districts by including a measure of the percentage of Catholics in the population (CATHOLICS). The source for this variable is the ICPSR dataset on German elections (ICPSR 1984).

5.4. EMPIRICAL ANALYSIS: EXAMINING THE INCIDENCE OF FRAUD IN GERMANY

5.4.1. Explaining the Incidence of Electoral Irregularities

This section examines the political and economic determinants of electoral fraud in national elections to the German Reichstag during the period between 1870 and 1912. I begin by presenting a set of models that test my hypotheses about the determinants of the demand for electoral fraud. These simplified models leave out a number of economic factors that may account for the decisions of employers to supply electoral irregularities, and they examine only the relationship between the political variables in a district and the incidence of electoral irregularities. Because the dependent variable is binary, I estimate a logistic model with fixed effects for the different provinces of Imperial Germany to control for unobserved region-specific characteristics.

The inclusion of these regional fixed effects can be justified both statistically and substantively. A Hausman test rejects the null hypothesis that there is no systematic difference between the coefficients in the random and fixed effects models at the 1 percent level, which suggests that the model with fixed effects for regions is preferable. In substantive terms, the inclusion of fixed effects is justified because of the large differences in electoral laws that governed subnational elections across German regions. As argued by prominent historical scholars of the period, subnational electoral practices exerted persistent effects on electoral practices in national elections (Klein 2003; Arsenschek 2003). Regional fixed effects are one way to reduce this unobserved heterogeneity and minimize omitted variable bias.

Table 5.3 displays the results of these demand-side models, which test the hypotheses presented in Chapter 2. It examines the relationships between three factors – the electoral strength of Social Democratic candidates, the tightness of a race, and the amount of political fragmentation among right-wing parties (both in the presence and absence of runoffs) – and the incidence of electoral fraud. These models reported in Table 5.3 also control for the religious fragmentation (CATHOLICS), POPULATION, and level of ECONOMIC DEVELOPMENT (percentage of non-agricultural employment) in a district, as well as for the composition of the electoral commission. The models also include a lagged dependent variable for the presence of electoral irregularities during the previous election.

Model 1 reports a baseline specification that includes the political variables that are hypothesized to affect the incidence of fraud and some of the demographic controls. To examine the relationship between the electoral strength of opposition candidates and the incidence of electoral fraud, Model 1 includes both a linear measure of the vote share of the Social Democratic candidates in a district and its quadratic (SPD VOTE SHARE, SPD VOTE SQ). The coefficient of the vote share of Social Democrats is negative, and that of its quadratic term is positive. Both coefficients are statistically significant at conventional levels of statistical significance. These results lend support to the hypothesis that candidates' incentives to trespass the boundaries of the electoral law and engage in electoral intimidation were highest when Social Democratic candidates were at intermediate levels of strength. As conjectured, the incentives for candidates to rely on electoral intimidation increased as the electoral strength of opposition candidates increased, but the marginal political returns of intimidation diminished at very high levels of Social Democratic electoral strength.

TABLE 5.3. *Political Determinants of Electoral Irregularities*

Equation	Variables	Model 1	Model 2	Model 3	Model 4	Model 5
Political Variables	SPD Vote Share	5.34***	5.42***	5.36***	5.35***	5.39***
		(0.91)	(0.91)	(0.91)	(0.91)	(0.91)
	SPD Vote Squared	-11.75***	-11.85***	-11.83***	-11.76***	-11.77***
		(1.64)	(1.64)	(1.64)	(1.64)	(1.64)
	ENRP	0.37***	0.34***	0.36***	0.36***	0.36***
		(0.09)	(0.09)	(0.09)	(0.09)	(0.09)
	Second Round	1.11***	1.09***	1.11***	1.11***	1.08***
		(0.25)	(0.25)	(0.25)	(0.25)	(0.25)
	ENRP*Second	-0.44***	-0.43***	-0.44***	-0.43***	-0.43***
		(0.11)	(0.11)	(0.11)	(0.11)	(0.11)
	Margin	-0.01**	-0.01***	-0.01**	-0.01**	-0.01***
		(0.00)	(0.00)	(0.00)	(0.00)	(0.00)
	Catholics	-0.01***	-0.01***	-0.01***	-0.01***	-0.01***
		(0.00)	(0.00)	(0.00)	(0.00)	(0.00)
	Population	1.89**	1.89**	1.93**	1.89**	1.87**
		(0.75)	(0.75)	(0.76)	(0.75)	(0.75)
Economic Variables	Economic Development	-0.01***	-0.01***	-0.01***	-0.01***	-0.01***
		(0.00)	(0.00)	(0.00)	(0.00)	(0.00)
	Fraud Lagged	0.40***	0.40***	0.40***	0.40***	0.40***
		(0.09)	(0.09)	(0.09)	(0.09)	(0.09)
	Time	0.05***	0.05***	0.04**	0.05***	0.04**
		(0.01)	(0.02)	(0.02)	(0.02)	(0.02)
	Time Squared	-0.00***	-0.00***	-0.00**	-0.00**	-0.00**
		(0.00)	(0.00)	(0.00)	(0.00)	(0.00)

Commission-Level Variables					
Partisan Center of Gravity Election Commission		0.36*			1.08***
		(0.19)			(0.41)
Neutrality of Election Chair			0.09		−0.17
			(0.09)		(0.14)
Conservative Seat Share of Election Commission				−0.31	3.77**
				(1.10)	(1.83)
Constant	−1.91***	−2.99***	−1.86***	−1.82***	−6.28***
	(0.32)	(0.65)	(0.32)	(0.45)	(1.73)
Observations	4,702	4,702	4,702	4,702	4,702
Log Pseudo Likelihood	−2,079	−2,077	−2,078	−2,079	−2,075
Pseudo R²	0.0889	0.0897	0.0891	0.0889	0.0906
χ^2	370.6	371.9	371.2	370.6	371.9

Notes: Robust standard errors are in parentheses; *** $p < 0.01$; ** $p < 0.05$; * $p < 0.10$.

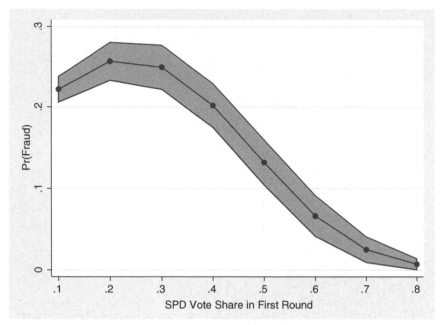

FIGURE 5.3. Predicted relationship between Social Democratic vote share and incidence of electoral fraud.

Figure 5.3 plots the predicted relationship between the political strength of Social Democracy and the incidence of electoral fraud. As can be seen in the figure, the predicted incidence of electoral fraud peaks when levels of Social Democratic strength were around 30 percent, but it declined as the level of Social Democratic strength in the district increased above these values. Holding all other variables in the regression at the mean, the predicted probability of fraud at very low levels of Social Democratic vote share (lowest decile) is 0.16. The predicted levels of electoral fraud in districts where Social Democratic strength is average for the sample is at 0.22. By contrast, in districts with very high levels of Social Democratic vote share (highest decile), the probability of electoral fraud is only 0.007 percent.

Model 1 also examines the relationship between the fragmentation among right-wing parties, runoffs, and the incidence of electoral fraud. I hypothesize that in races that were decided during runoffs, candidates on the right need to coordinate. This dampened the incentives for candidates on the political right to rely on electoral intimidation. I also examine whether right-wing political fragmentation would be associated with lower levels of fraud even in the absence of runoffs. This could be the case if the incentives for state officials to engage in electoral irregularities were lower in districts with a fragmented right than they were in districts with a coordinated right. To test these hypotheses, I include both measures of right-wing political fragmentation (ENRP), runoffs

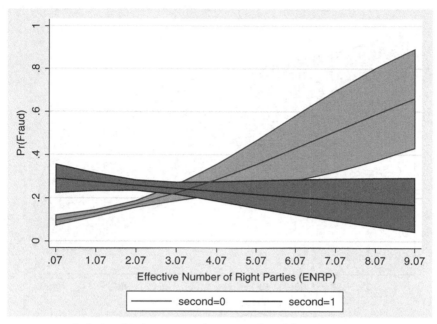

FIGURE 5.4. Relationship between right-wing political fragmentation and the incidence of electoral fraud in races decided in the first round and runoffs.

(SECOND), and their interaction (ENRP*SECOND). Figure 5.4 displays the findings graphically. The results confirm only one of the hypotheses: I find support for the political hypothesis that electoral fragmentation on the right constrained actors from using electoral intimidation in races that were decided during runoffs. My second hypothesis is, however, disconfirmed. In the absence of runoffs, I find that right-wing political fragmentation did not constrain the incidence of electoral fraud. The relationship between the measure of political fragmentation of the right and the incidence of fraud is positive if a race was decided during the first round.

Finally, I find that the incidence of electoral intimidation was higher in tighter races. As discussed in Section 5.2, the theoretical expectations about the relationship between the tightness of a race and the incidence of electoral irregularities were ambiguous. Although the demand made by candidates for electoral irregularities was likely to increase as the race became more competitive, the uncertainty of political outcomes could deter state employees from intervening in elections. The empirical results suggest that the demand-side considerations of the candidates outweighed the supply-side considerations of actors and affected the latter's willingness to intervene during elections. This empirical result linking more competitive races with a higher incidence of fraud is consistent with a large number of other studies that examine the production of electoral irregularities in other political contexts. Figure 5.5 plots the

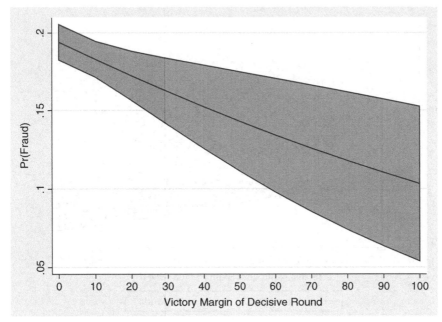

FIGURE 5.5. Relationship between margin of victory in decisive round and the probability of electoral fraud.

relationship between the tightness of a race and the incidence of electoral fraud. Holding all other variables at their mean values, a change in the margin of victory from the mean value to the maximum value decreases the probability of electoral fraud from 0.18 to 0.10, with a 95 percent confidence interval of (0.05, 0.15).

Models 2–5 examine the robustness of these results by adding various measures for the political composition of the electoral commission that investigated the electoral irregularities. As discussed in Section 5.3, the composition of the electoral commission could affect the selection of fraud cases that were submitted to the Reichstag. I use the three measures developed by Dan Ziblatt (2009) to capture various characteristics of the commission of the Reichstag. In Model 2, I add a variable that measures the political parties of the commission members. I find a positive relationship between this measure and the incidence of electoral fraud. Model 3 adds a measure for the neutrality of the commission chair. Differences in the neutrality of the commission had no impact on the types of cases of fraud that were selected. In Model 4, I add a variable that measures the share of conservative politicians on the commission to the model, but I find no relationship between this variable and the incidence of electoral fraud. Model 5 includes controls for all of these different commission-level measures. In this specification, none of these variables achieves statistical significance at conventional levels. The addition of these commission-level variables does not affect in substantive ways the magnitude and significance levels of the political variables.

In Table 5.4, I present a range of models that test both my economic and political hypotheses about the production of electoral irregularities in German elections. The most significant difference compared to the models presented in Table 5.3 is the inclusion of a range of variables that measure variation in economic conditions across districts. As I hypothesize, economic conditions in a district affect the likely costs of electoral repression incurred by private actors and their incentive to engage in electoral intimidation. The first three models reported in Table 5.4 present each of the economic variables that may affect private actors' incentives to intervene at elections. In Model 1, I add the time-varying measure of the economic heterogeneity of the district. I find a strong and positive relationship between the employment concentration of a district and the incidence of electoral fraud, and it is significant at conventional levels. The effect is also substantive in magnitude. Holding all other variables at their mean values, a change in the level of employment concentration from its mean value to its maximum value increases the probability of electoral intimidation from 0.36 to 0.56. In Model 2, I add a measure of the skill profile of the labor force in a district to the baseline specification that includes only political variables. Although the sign of the variable is negative, the relationship between this variable and the incidence of electoral irregularities does not achieve statistical significance at conventional levels. This suggests that the presence of a more skilled labor force did not constrain the decisions of private actors to engage in political intimidation. In Model 3, I add a control for the level of rural inequality in a district. In this specification, I find a positive relationship between the level of landholding inequality and the incidence of fraud, which is consistent with the results reported by Ziblatt (2009).

The sign and statistical significance of the political variables remains unaffected by the inclusion of these economic controls. Consistent with the theoretical prediction, we find a U-shaped relationship between the electoral strength of Social Democratic candidates and the incidence of fraud. The incidence of electoral fraud was higher in narrower races. Finally, when examining the relationship between the right-wing political fragmentation and the incidence of electoral fraud, I find that increased fragmentation on the right constrained candidates' incentives to use electoral fraud in districts that were decided during runoffs. By contrast, in races that were decided during the first electoral round, we find a positive relationship between right-wing fragmentation and the incidence of fraud.

Some results from the other control variables are also noteworthy. First, the incidence of electoral fraud is lower in districts with larger Catholic populations. We also find a lower incidence of fraud in more developed districts where a higher percentage of the labor force was employed in manufacturing

TABLE 5.4. *The Economic and Political Determinants of Electoral Irregularities*

		Model 1	Model 2	Model 3	Model 4
Economic Variables	Economic Concentration	2.84*** (0.78)			2.89*** (0.79)
	Skill Industry		−0.05 (0.44)		−0.28 (0.45)
	Landholding Inequality			0.96* (0.54)	0.99* (0.55)
Political Variables	SPD Vote Share	5.35*** (0.91)	5.48*** (0.96)	5.34*** (0.91)	5.42*** (0.95)
	SPD Vote Squared	−11.48*** (1.63)	−11.89*** (1.68)	−11.76*** (1.63)	−11.63*** (1.67)
	ENRP	0.38*** (0.09)	0.36*** (0.09)	0.36*** (0.09)	0.38*** (0.09)
	Second Round	0.93*** (0.24)	0.91*** (0.23)	0.91*** (0.23)	0.93*** (0.23)
	ENRP*Second	−0.37*** (0.11)	−0.36*** (0.11)	−0.36*** (0.10)	−0.36*** (0.11)
	Margin	−0.01*** (0.00)	−0.01*** (0.00)	−0.01*** (0.00)	−0.01*** (0.00)
	Catholics	−0.01*** (0.00)	−0.01*** (0.00)	−0.01*** (0.00)	−0.01*** (0.00)
	Population	1.64** (0.72)	1.87** (0.75)	1.68** (0.74)	1.44** (0.72)
	Economic Development	−0.01*** (0.00)	−0.01*** (0.00)	−0.01*** (0.00)	−0.01*** (0.00)
	Fraud Lagged	0.39*** (0.09)	0.40*** (0.09)	0.40*** (0.09)	0.38*** (0.09)
	Time	0.04** (0.02)	0.04* (0.02)	0.04** (0.02)	0.04* (0.02)
	Time Squared	−0.00** (0.00)	−0.00** (0.00)	−0.00** (0.00)	−0.00** (0.00)
Commission-Level Variables	Partisan Center of Gravity Election Commission	1.11*** (0.41)	1.10*** (0.41)	1.08*** (0.41)	1.14*** (0.41)
	Neutrality of Election Chair	−0.19 (0.14)	−0.19 (0.14)	−0.18 (0.14)	−0.20 (0.14)
	Conservative Seat Share of Election Commission	3.88** (1.83)	3.87** (1.83)	3.85** (1.83)	3.95** (1.84)
	Constant	−6.44*** (1.74)	−6.37*** (1.74)	−7.10*** (1.79)	−7.31*** (1.80)
	Observations	4,704	4,704	4,704	4,704
	Log Pseudo Likelihood	−2,072	−2,076	−2,075	−2,070
	Pseudo R^2	0.0925	0.0906	0.0914	0.0933
	χ^2	372.1	371.4	371.6	373.3

Notes: Robust standard errors are in parentheses; *** p<0.01; ** p<0.05; * p<0.10.

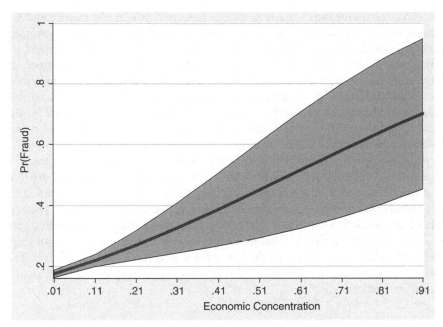

FIGURE 5.6. Predicted relationship between economic concentration and the incidence of electoral fraud.

or services. Also, we find a positive and statistically significant relationship between two of the commission-level variables – the polarization of the commission and its "conservativeness" – and the incidence of electoral fraud. Although some commission-level effects are present, I find that more conservative and more polarized commissions were more likely to allow a larger number of cases to be considered by the Reichstag.

To interpret the main results for the economic hypotheses, in Figure 5.6, I have graphed the predicted probability of the incidence of electoral fraud based on the employment concentration of a district. As discussed earlier in this section, I find a positive relationship between the employment concentration of a district and the probability of electoral intimidation. Holding all variables at their mean, the predicted probability of electoral fraud in a district that has measures of employment concentration in the lower 10 percent of the range of values for Germany is 0.17. By contrast, the predicted probability of electoral fraud for districts whose values of employment concentration that are located in the highest 10 percent of the sample is 0.6. These results are consistent with the qualitative evidence presented in Chapter 4, which suggested that the epicenter of electoral intimidation was found in areas characterized by high levels of occupational concentration, such as the Ruhr and Saarland regions.

In sum, the quantitative analysis of the determinants of electoral fraud in German elections points to the joint importance of political and economic variables in predicting the incidence of electoral irregularities. With respect to political variables, I find that the incidence of electoral fraud was higher in tighter races and in districts where Social Democratic candidates had intermediate levels of strength. Fragmentation among parties on the right reduced the incidence of electoral fraud only in districts that were decided in runoffs. By contrast, in districts that were decided during the first round, I find a positive relationship between the fragmentation of the political competition on the right and the incidence of electoral fraud. With respect to economic hypotheses, I find a positive relationship between the economic fragmentation of a district and the incidence of electoral fraud. This suggests that high levels of economic concentration lowered the costs of electoral intimidation for employers. Higher levels of economic heterogeneity were, however, more likely to constrain private actors from using electoral intimidation. By contrast, I find no relationship between the skill composition of the labor force and the incidence of electoral fraud. Vocational skills, it appears, did not constrain employers from using electoral intimidation.

5.5. ROBUSTNESS CHECK OF THE MAIN EMPIRICAL RESULTS

In this section, I present a number of additional specifications in order to examine the robustness of the findings reported in Table 5.4. These specifications either use different measures for the central economic variables or test the predictions of the models in a narrower sample that excludes the most urban areas. In the following sections, I present three different specifications.

5.5.1. Alternative Measure of Employment Concentration

One possible objection to the measure of employment concentration used in the specification reported in Table 5.4 is that the variable includes only information about employment shares in different occupations, but no information about the number of firms. To address this objection, I have created an alternative measure of employment concentration: a weighted Herfindahl-Hirschman Index of employment concentration (WEIGHTED HHI). To calculate the weighted HHI, I choose the four occupations with the largest employment shares in each district and calculated the size of a representative firm for each occupation by dividing the employment share in that occupation by the number of firms. I take the resulting number, square it, and sum it up to calculate the weighted HHI. Thus I compute

$$WHHI = \sum_{i=1}^{4} (S_i / F_i)^2,$$

where S is the employment share and F is the number of firms in each occupation.

In Table 5.5, I present the results for a number of models that examine the relationship between the weighted Herfindahl-Hirschmann Index of employment concentration and the incidence of electoral fraud. The conclusions about the relationship between industrial concentration and the incidence of electoral fraud are not affected by the type of measure. We find a positive relationship between the weighted measure of occupational concentration and the incidence of electoral fraud, and that relationship is significant at conventional levels.

One additional difference from the results presented in Table 5.4 comes from a different range of models that use this weighted HHI. The change in the concentration measure does not substantively affect the main empirical results. We find a positive and significant correlation between the weighted HHI (the new measure of occupational concentration) and the incidence of fraud. Models 3 and 4 differ from Models 1 and 2 in their use of the alternative measure of skills (whose denominator includes all types of agricultural workers). The effects of this variable are also large in magnitude. The change in this measure of occupational fragmentation does not affect the sign or the statistical significance of the relationships of any other results reported in Table 5.4.

Models 3 and 4 present another robustness check of the results reported in Table 5.4 by employing a different measure of the skill composition of the labor force. Recall that the measure of vocational skills reported in the empirical results in Table 5.4 uses a number of workers employed in industry in its denominator (SKILL INDUSTRY). As discussed earlier in this chapter, one can construct an additional measure for skill profile that uses both industrial and agricultural workers in the denominator but only for the 1895 census. Models 3 and 4 in Table 5.5 use this second time-invariant measure for skills (SKILL ALL). The main conclusion about the relationship between the skill composition of the labor force in a district and the incidence of electoral irregularities there remains unchanged. We find no statistically significant relationship between the skill level of the labor force and the incidence of electoral fraud.

5.5.2. Alternative Measure of Occupational Heterogeneity

The specifications presented in Table 5.4 use a time-varying measure of occupational heterogeneity that can be computed for both economic censuses of the period. The drawback of this measure is that it excludes information about the number of agricultural workers in a district. Complete occupational data that includes information about the number of all agricultural workers is available only for the 1895 census. To compute this measure, I add for each locality the number of agricultural employees that was reported in a special publication of the German Statistical Office, the *Berufsstatistik der kleineren Verwaltungsbezirke* in 1897 (Statistisches Reichsamt 1897).

TABLE 5.5. *Robustness Checks Using Weighted Measures of Occupational Heterogeneity*

		Model 1	Model 2	Model 3	Model 4
Economic Variables	Economic Concentration Weighted by Firm Size (WHHI)	33.88*** (6.20)	33.74*** (6.22)	33.82*** (6.22)	33.67*** (6.23)
	Skill Industry	0.05 (0.44)	−0.12 (0.45)		
	Skill All			−0.40 (0.42)	−0.42 (0.43)
	Landholding Inequality	1.17** (0.55)	1.18** (0.55)	1.27** (0.56)	1.26** (0.56)
Political Variables	SPD Vote Share	5.49*** (0.95)	5.65*** (0.95)	5.71*** (0.93)	5.78*** (0.93)
	SPD Vote Squared	−12.0*** (1.67)	−12.2*** (1.67)	−12.2*** (1.64)	−12.2*** (1.64)
	ENRP	0.37*** (0.09)	0.37*** (0.09)	0.37*** (0.09)	0.36*** (0.09)
	Second Round	0.95*** (0.23)	0.92*** (0.23)	0.94*** (0.23)	0.92*** (0.23)
	ENRP*Second	−0.37*** (0.11)	−0.36*** (0.11)	−0.37*** (0.11)	−0.36*** (0.11)
	Margin	−0.01** (0.00)	−0.01*** (0.00)	−0.01** (0.00)	−0.01*** (0.00)
	Catholics	−0.01*** (0.00)	−0.01*** (0.00)	−0.01*** (0.00)	−0.01*** (0.00)
	Population	1.79** (0.74)	1.77** (0.74)	1.90** (0.75)	1.89** (0.75)
	Economic Development	−0.01*** (0.00)	−0.01*** (0.00)	−0.01*** (0.00)	−0.01*** (0.00)
	Fraud Lagged	0.35*** (0.09)	0.35*** (0.09)	0.35*** (0.09)	0.35*** (0.09)
	Time	0.05*** (0.02)	0.04** (0.02)	0.05*** (0.01)	0.04** (0.02)
	Time Squared	−0.00*** (0.00)	−0.00** (0.00)	−0.00*** (0.00)	−0.00** (0.00)
Commission-Level Variables	Partisan Center of Gravity Election Commission		1.08*** (0.41)		1.08*** (0.41)
	Neutrality of Election Chair		−0.18 (0.14)		−0.18 (0.14)
	Conservative Seat Share of Election Commission		3.78** (1.83)		3.75** (1.83)

	Model 1	Model 2	Model 3	Model 4
Constant	−2.86***	−7.21***	−2.85***	−7.19***
	(0.56)	(1.80)	(0.56)	(1.79)
Observations	4,704	4,704	4,704	4,704
Log Pseudo Likelihood	−2,065	−2,062	−2,065	−2,061
Pseudo R²	0.0954	0.0971	0.0956	0.0973
χ²	390.7	392.8	390.5	393.1

Notes: Robust standard errors are in parentheses; *** $p<0.01$; ** $p<0.05$; * $p<0.10$.

In Table 5.6, I present estimates of the relationship between this time-invariant measure of occupational heterogeneity and the incidence of electoral fraud. The main result that links high economic concentration with a higher incidence of electoral fraud is not affected by the use of the measure of occupational heterogeneity.

5.5.3. The Incidence of Electoral Fraud in Rural Districts

The models presented in Tables 5.3 and 5.4 examine the economic and political determinants of electoral irregularities and are estimated using the full sample of German districts. An alternative interpretation of the incidence of electoral fraud in German elections presented by Dan Ziblatt downplays the importance of labor market considerations (such as occupational heterogeneity and skills) and the importance of political considerations other than the tightness of a race. For Ziblatt, the main factor that affected the incidence of electoral irregularities is the level of rural inequality.

Given the importance of landholding inequality for his explanation, Ziblatt estimated a model of the determinants of electoral irregularities that was restricted to rural districts only. To ensure direct comparability between the findings of this chapter and the empirical results in Ziblatt, I reestimate the models by restricting the analysis to rural districts. To this end, I exclude those districts with levels of agricultural employment lower than 11.7 percent, which constitutes the upper 10 percent of the sample. Table 5.7 presents these empirical results. In this narrower sample, I present models for the two different measures of skills, SKILL INDUSTRY and SKILL ALL.

The main results reported in previous tables are unchanged in this specification, which is restricted to rural districts. The main economic variable that explains the incidence of electoral fraud in a district remains occupational heterogeneity. I find no relationship between the skill profile of a district and the incidence of electoral fraud. Also, all previous results concerning the political determinants of electoral irregularities remain unchanged. The only change in these specifications concerns the relationship between landholding inequality and the incidence of electoral fraud. If one excludes urban centers from

TABLE 5.6. *Robustness Checks Using Alternative Measures of Occupational Heterogeneity*

		Model 1	Model 2
Economic Variables	Economic Concentration with Agriculture	0.67** (0.33)	0.63* (0.33)
	Skill Industry	0.53 (0.49)	0.32 (0.50)
	Landholding Inequality	1.07** (0.54)	1.07** (0.54)
Political Variables	SPD Vote Share	5.53*** (0.96)	5.67*** (0.96)
	SPD Vote Squared	−11.83*** (1.68)	−11.98*** (1.68)
	ENRP	0.36*** (0.09)	0.36*** (0.09)
	Second Round	0.95*** (0.23)	0.92*** (0.23)
	ENRP*Second	−0.36*** (0.10)	−0.35*** (0.10)
	Margin	−0.01** (0.00)	−0.01*** (0.00)
	Catholics	−0.01*** (0.00)	−0.01*** (0.00)
	Population	1.94** (0.76)	1.90** (0.75)
	Economic Development	−0.01** (0.00)	−0.01** (0.00)
	Fraud Lagged	0.39*** (0.09)	0.39*** (0.09)
	Time	0.05*** (0.02)	0.04** (0.02)
	Time Squared	−0.00*** (0.00)	−0.00** (0.00)
Commission-Level Variables	Partisan Center of Gravity Election Commission		1.07*** (0.41)
	Neutrality of Election Chair		−0.18 (0.14)
	Conservative Seat Share of Election Commission		3.77** (1.84)
	Constant	−3.28*** (0.60)	−7.55*** (1.81)
	Observations	4,704	4,704
	Log Pseudo Likelihood	−2,076	−2,073
	Pseudo R^2	0.0906	0.0922
	χ^2	375.1	375.8

Notes: Robust standard errors are in parentheses; *** $p<0.01$; ** $p<0.05$; * $p<0.10$.

TABLE 5.7. *Robustness of Analysis in Rural Districts*

		Model 1	Model 2	Model 3	Model 4
Economic Variables	Occupational Heterogeneity	0.83** (0.42)	0.85** (0.43)	0.79** (0.35)	0.73** (0.35)
	Skill Industry	0.56 (0.67)	0.56 (0.67)		
	Skill Level (with Agriculture)			0.78 (0.59)	0.52 (0.60)
	Landholding Inequality	0.76 (0.59)	0.75 (0.59)	0.80 (0.59)	0.78 (0.59)
Political Variables	SPD Vote Share	5.61*** (1.02)	5.67*** (1.02)	5.38*** (1.04)	5.52*** (1.04)
	SPD Vote Squared	−10.11** (1.82)	−10.2*** (1.82)	−9.72*** (1.85)	−9.90*** (1.85)
	ENRP	0.38*** (0.09)	0.38*** (0.09)	0.38*** (0.09)	0.37*** (0.09)
	Second Round	1.25*** (0.26)	1.23*** (0.26)	1.26*** (0.26)	1.24*** (0.26)
	ENRP*Second	−0.47*** (0.12)	−0.47*** (0.12)	−0.47*** (0.12)	−0.47*** (0.12)
	Margin	−0.01** (0.00)	−0.01*** (0.00)	−0.01** (0.00)	−0.01*** (0.00)
	Catholics	−0.01*** (0.00)	−0.01*** (0.00)	−0.01*** (0.00)	−0.01*** (0.00)
	Population	2.00 (1.43)	2.01 (1.43)	2.05 (1.43)	2.07 (1.43)
	Economic Development	−0.01*** (0.00)	−0.01*** (0.00)	−0.01*** (0.00)	−0.01*** (0.00)
	Fraud Lagged	0.33*** (0.10)	0.33*** (0.10)	0.32*** (0.10)	0.33*** (0.10)
	Time	0.04** (0.02)	0.03 (0.02)	0.05*** (0.02)	0.04 (0.02)
	Time Squared	−0.00*** (0.00)	−0.00* (0.00)	−0.00*** (0.00)	−0.00** (0.00)
Commission-Level Variables	Partisan Center of Gravity Election Commission		1.09** (0.43)		1.02** (0.44)
	Neutrality of Election Chair		−0.17 (0.15)		−0.15 (0.15)
	Conservative Seat Share of Election Commission		3.99** (1.94)		3.82** (1.95)
	Constant	−2.89*** (0.72)	−7.35*** (1.96)	−2.91*** (0.71)	−7.01*** (1.95)

(continued)

TABLE 5.7 *(continued)*

	Model 1	Model 2	Model 3	Model 4
Observations	4,245	4,245	4,245	4,245
Log Pseudo Likelihood	−1,862	−1,858	−1,861	−1,858
Pseudo R^2	0.0970	0.0988	0.0973	0.0988
χ^2	357.9	359.1	357.6	358.5

Notes: Robust standard errors are in parentheses; *** p<0.01; ** p<0.05; * p<0.10.

the analysis, one finds no relationship between landholding inequality and the incidence of fraud.

The lack of a robust relationship between landholding inequality and the incidence of electoral fraud and the absence of this relationship in the subsample of German districts where one would expect it to be particularly powerful raises a range of additional questions about the political mechanisms by which landholding inequality is expected to have affected political outcomes. How exactly did inequality in the distribution of land affect the decisions of politicians and landowners to violate the provisions of the electoral law and engage in voter intimidation? What are the advantages conferred by landholding inequality to politicians during elections? I take up the additional puzzles raised by the findings reported in Table 5.7 in Chapter 8. The goal of Chapter 8 is to examine what effects landholding inequality has in elections and to explore several of the pathways by which different dimensions of inequality affect political outcomes. To address these additional questions, the collection of more fine-grained data about the various dimensions of rural inequality is necessary.

5.6. CONCLUSION

In this chapter, I presented an additional test of the explanations for why politicians demanded – and why employees of the state and private actors supplied – activities that resulted in electoral irregularities. Building on and extending the discussion presented in Chapters 3 and 4, I specified the factors that were likely to affect candidates' demand for electoral activities trespassing the boundaries set by the electoral law and the decisions of two type of agents – state employees and private actors – to supply these political activities during elections. I then tested a range of hypotheses about the determinants of electoral irregularities in German elections considering the relative importance of the economic and political variables in a district.

I found empirical support for most of the political hypotheses presented in Chapter 2. Political conditions in a district were strong predictors of the incidence of electoral fraud. One of the main objectives of political intervention in elections was to stem the political activities of Social Democratic candidates. I found a nonlinear relationship between the strength of Social Democratic candidates and the incidence of fraud: the probability of electoral intervention was highest when Social Democracy had intermediate levels of electoral strength, but it was lower when Social Democratic candidates had either low or very high levels of political strength. In the former types of districts, the deployment of the resources of the state and of private actors was perceived as unnecessary. By contrast, in districts with high levels of Social Democratic electoral strength, the marginal returns of electoral intervention were likely to be lower than they were in districts with intermediate levels of Social Democratic strength. These considerations were likely to lower both the demand by candidates for additional electoral support from state employees and private actors and the willingness of the employees and actors to provide political support during elections.

In addition to the strength of the Social Democratic candidates, I also examined the relationship between other political factors and the incidence of electoral fraud. I found that the incidence of electoral fraud was higher in tighter races. When exploring the relationship between right-wing political fragmentation, runoffs, and the incidence of electoral fraud, I found that right-wing fragmentation lowered the incidence of electoral fraud in races whose outcome was determined during runoffs. The interpretation of this result is that in these districts, candidates on the right refrained from engaging in heavy-handed political intervention because they anticipated forming electoral coalitions with their opponents. By contrast, such strategic considerations among candidates on the right were not present in districts that were not won during runoffs. In the latter, I found a positive relationship between right-wing fragmentation and the incidence of fraud.

In addition to these political hypotheses, I examined a range of economic hypotheses about the determinants of electoral fraud. Economic conditions in a district, I conjectured, affected the incidence of electoral fraud by affecting the costs of electoral repression for private actors. Consistent with the theoretical hypothesis presented in Chapter 2, I found a strong positive relationship between the economic concentration of a district and the incidence of electoral fraud. This finding lends support to the hypothesis that the costs of electoral intimidation for private actors were lower in districts where a limited number of firms controlled output and employment, but the costs increased as the economic heterogeneity of the district increased. The results are also consistent with the qualitative empirical evidence presented in Chapter 3, which documented the epicenter of private electoral intimidation as having been located in districts that were dominated by large manufacturing employers in the Ruhr, Saarland, and Silesia.

By contrast, I found no relationship between the various measures of the skill composition of different districts and the incidence of electoral fraud. In conjunction with the findings presented in Chapter 4, which documented the pervasive electoral intimidation perpetuated by employers in the Ruhr and the Saar, this finding presents a challenge to the predictions made by a variety of capitalism scholars. The presence of high vocational skills did not constrain German employers from harassing and intimidating their employees for their electoral choices during the Imperial Period.

6

The Adoption of Electoral Reforms

Chapters 3–5 demonstrated the existence of pervasive intimidation in German national elections to the Reichstag. Although electoral law mandated universal, direct, secret, and equal suffrage, it provided insufficient protections for voters to cast their votes freely. As a result, core principles of the electoral law were systematically violated in everyday electoral practices. As Heinrich Rickert, one of the German politicians who relentlessly pushed for the adoption of additional electoral reforms, argued: "The freedom of the vote is a guarantee of one of the most important constitutional provisions in Germany. It is the foundation of our constitutional life. If we do not provide sufficient guarantees for it, then our public life will be based on hypocrisy, on pressure, and on force, and those have never led to a good outcome" (*Stenographische Berichte des Deutschen Reichstages* January 15, 1896).

This violation of the cornerstone of German constitutional life to which Rickert referred resulted from two distinct factors. The first were imperfections in voting technology. As the previous chapters demonstrated, imperfections in the design of the ballot and the design of the urn allowed representatives of political parties to "pierce" the veil of secrecy of the vote and observe the electoral choices made by voters. Second, economic inequalities that increased the dependency of voters on their employers amplified the consequences of these irregularities in voting technology. These economic conditions lowered the costs of electoral repression for employers and increased the credibility of their threat to harshly punish voters who made "incorrect" electoral choices. Economic dependence also undermined the willingness of individual voters to risk their livelihoods by casting different ballots from the ones handed to them by their employers. This combination of institutional imperfections in the electoral code and economic inequalities in the labor market explains the persistence of electoral pressure in German elections.

The goal of this chapter is to examine political efforts to reform electoral institutions and to ensure greater protection of electoral secrecy. In practical terms, these reforms attempted to protect the secrecy of the vote and "ensure that the vote cast represented the true intention of the voter" (*Stenographische Berichte des Deutschen Reichstages* January 29, 1896). First and foremost, these reforms attempted to protect the most vulnerable voters by minimizing the chances of post-electoral reprisal.

Where did the demand for the democratization of electoral practices originate? What factors explain the support for electoral reforms that would increase the political autonomy of voters? In this chapter, I examine these questions through an analysis of the cosponsorship of legislative proposals to reduce opportunities for electoral intimidation that were discussed by the German Reichstag during the period between 1870 and 1912. The main goals of the analysis are to uncover the economic and political factors that motivated politicians to support election reforms and to identify the electoral coalitions in the German Reichstag that supported or opposed the protection of voters from intimidation. I advance and test two propositions about the determinants of demand for electoral reforms that highlight the relative importance of partisan factors and district-level economic and political factors, respectively. With respect to partisan factors, I conjecture that politicians from "outsider parties" that lacked ties to agents able to engage in electoral intimidation were more likely to support the adoption of electoral reforms. With respect to district-level factors, I conjecture that politicians who encountered higher relative costs of electoral intimidation were more likely to support electoral reforms. By contrast, politicians faced with relatively low economic and political costs of electoral intimidation in their districts were likely to support the policy status quo and oppose reforms of electoral institutions.

The chapter proceeds as follows. To set the background for the political hypotheses, I begin in Section 6.1 by presenting the most significant attempts undertaken by the German Reichstag to reform electoral institutions, beginning with the adoption of the electoral law in 1869. The discussion of these deliberations seeks to identify both the normative and the practical arguments formulated by supporters and opponents of electoral reforms. In Section 6.2, I discuss the unsuccessful efforts made by politicians on the right to abolish the electoral law and replace it with legislation premised on open voting. Next, I turn to a discussion of the reforms of the existing electoral law aimed at protecting the secrecy of the vote. These sections examine three dimensions of the electoral reform considered at the time, including the adoption of ballot envelopes (Section 6.3), isolating rooms (*Isolierräume*) (Section 6.4), and changes to the design of the electoral urn (Section 6.5). The following section, Section 6.6, presents the central hypotheses about the economic and political factors accounting for the demand for electoral reforms. I hypothesize that demand for electoral reforms originated with politicians who could not take advantage of opportunities for intimidation under existing electoral rules.

Support for electoral reform, I hypothesize, can be explained by a combination of partisan calculations and district-level conditions. With respect to partisan calculations, I conjecture that support for electoral reforms originated with politicians whose parties lacked connections to the main political actors and employers able to in electoral intimidation. In their order of parliamentary importance, these parties were the Zentrum, the Free Liberals, and the Social Democrats. In addition to these partisan considerations, politicians' conceptions of the advantages of electoral reforms were also affected by district-level conditions. I conjecture that politicians facing relatively high costs of electoral repression in their district were more likely to support electoral reforms. Chapter 2 developed a number of propositions about the relationship between economic and political conditions in a district and the costs of electoral intimidation there. In Section 6.7, I test these hypotheses using a novel dataset of the cosponsorship of all electoral bills recommending better protection for the secrecy of the vote that were considered by the German parliament from 1870 to 1912. I explore systematically the effects of district-level characteristics, political partisanship, and electoral competition on politicians' calculations about whether to protect voters against intimidation.

My analysis of the determinants of support for voting autonomy includes a number of variables that test theoretical predictions from three prominent debates about the determinants of democratization. The first is the debate about endogenous democratization (Przeworski et al. 2000; Boix and Stokes 2003). In a recent extension of this line of analysis, Susan Stokes argues that the growth in the size of the industrial labor force was the crucial factor that spurred political incentives for reforms seeking to limit electoral corruption in Imperial Britain (Stokes 2011). Second, I subject to new empirical tests the proposition in recent literature on democratization that inequalities in the distribution of land slow down democratic transitions; here, I examine the relationship between inequalities in landownership and the support for democratic reforms (Acemoglu and Robinson 2000; Acemoglu and Robinson 2006; Boix 2003). Finally, I test empirical predictions formulated by "varieties of capitalism" scholarship, which argues that differences in the skill composition of a workforce affect political demand for the adoption of democratic institutions (Cusack et al. 2010). By employing very precise measures of economic conditions and of the skill composition of the labor force, this chapter provides the first ever test of the relative importance of human capital endowments on democratic reforms.

6.1. THE AGENDA OF REFORM

The passage of electoral reforms protecting voter secrecy during elections in the Reichstag was a long and arduous process. The first proposals for reform were, in fact, formulated at the same time that the national electoral law was adopted. Already at that time, a number of prominent politicians believed that the electoral law did not sufficiently protect voters against intimidation. To remedy this shortcoming, Anton Sombart, a National Liberal politician, recommended the introduction of ballot envelopes. Although the initial Sombart bill was defeated, some of its proposals established the blueprint for the electoral reform proposals that arose during the 1890s.

The investigation of electoral practices by the electoral commission of the Reichstag revealed the existence of ample electoral irregularities perpetrated by both private actors and public election officials. Reports of voters being driven like flocks of sheep to the urns, being forced to enter the voting area while holding ballots in their right hands over their heads, and being subjected to post-electoral punishments amply demonstrated that the guarantees of electoral secrecy provided by the electoral law were only nominal. Proposals for a reform of the electoral system were placed on the agenda of the Reichstag beginning in 1875. From that year onward, similar proposals were found on the agenda of the Reichstag in nearly every legislative period. During the late 1890s, members of the Reichstag voted with a large majority to adopt reforms to protect the secrecy of the vote by introducing electoral urns and isolating spaces. The proposal lingered, however, for a number of years in Germany's upper house, the Bundesrat. The decision of Bundesrat was announced by Chancellor Bülow on January 21, 1903 (*Stenographische Berichte des Reichstages* 1903: 7431). The provisions of the new legislation – also known as the Rickert law – came into effect for the first time during the elections that were held in June 1903. As Chapter 8 demonstrates, these changes in voting technology had decisive political consequences. By reducing the observability of the votes cast by individual voters and the credibility of employers' threats of post-electoral punishments, this legislation facilitated a dramatic increase in the electoral strength of the Social Democratic Party. During the 1903 election, the first election when the provisions of the Rickert law – which mandated ballot envelopes and isolating spaces for voters – were in place, the number of Social Democratic voters increased by 900,000 to slightly exceed 3 million voters.

In the next four sections, I review the most important arguments in favor and against electoral reforms that were made during the five decades during which voter protection from electoral intimidation was debated. I present these arguments in two stages. First, I begin by discussing the overarching opposition of parties on the political right to the fundamental principle of electoral secrecy. Next, I discuss the three concrete proposals for reform that were considered during these political deliberations. These included the adoption of ballot envelopes, the adoption of isolating spaces, and uniform provisions for the design of the urn.

6.2. OPPOSITION TO SECRET VOTING

Politicians who opposed the adoption of legislation seeking to introduce additional protections for voters against electoral intimidation did not shy away from expressing their disapproval of the existing electoral law. But although they shared with reformers the diagnosis that electoral practices in Imperial Germany were highly imperfect, they proposed a fundamentally different solution. For German politicians on the right, the proposed alternative solution was to eliminate the existing legislation premised on secret voting and replace it with open voting. The intention to replace secret voting with open voting was announced by prominent conservative politicians and ministers, and it was amply discussed in the conservative press during this period. Although the magnitude and credibility of the threat declined over time, this staunch opposition to the existing electoral rule contributed to the delay in the adoption of legislation protecting electoral secrecy.

In 1899, during a parliamentary discussion of electoral reform, Stumm, a member of the Free Conservative Party representing Trier's sixth district (which was also known as *Saarabien*), conceded that the existing electoral law showed serious weaknesses in implementation. Its problems, Stumm argued, would be resolved not through a piecemeal reform of the existing electoral law, but rather through its replacement by legislation premised on open voting. Open voting was preferable because the secret vote was incompatible with the "manly honor (*Manneswürde*) of the German *Volk*" (*Stenographische Berichte des Deutschen Reichstages* 1899).

Stumm's recommendation to adopt legislation premised on open voting was widely shared in conservative circles. The former Prussian ministers von Puttkammer and von Rauchhaupt interjected into this debate that they were ready to "lend a hand" to eliminate secret voting in Germany (*Stenographische Berichte des Deutschen Reichstages* March 28, 1895). Graf Mirbach, another conservative politician who represented Sensburg-Ortelsberg, a district in East Prussia, argued that "the decision to establish a new electoral law would be welcomed with euphoria in all rural districts and beyond" (*Stenographische Berichte des Deutschen Reichstages* March 28, 1895).

Although many conservative politicians agreed with the return to the open method of voting, they disagreed about how to abolish the existing electoral law. Their disagreement may partly explain why von Rauchhaupt and von Puttkammer's desire to abolish the existing electoral law never materialized. One possible strategy of reform was to use the existing parliamentary channels and wait for a favorable parliamentary majority. This strategy was announced in the Reichstag in 1899: "A law mandating the change of the electoral law for the Reichstag was already drafted last summer. There is no doubt that it will be submitted to the Reichstag as soon as we have a chamber that is willing to adopt it (*ein bewillungslustiger Reichstag*)" (*Stenographische Berichte des Reichstages* February 1, 1899: 586).

From the perspective of conservatives, a second way to change the electoral system was to sidestep parliamentary procedures and instigate a coup. Conservative politicians did not shy away from using threats of coups to signal both their dissatisfaction with the policy status quo and to preempt reformers who were pushing for changes in electoral institutions. In a meeting on March 30, 1895, Graf von Frankenberg invoked the "sword" as the method by which the constitution should be reformed. Von Frankenberg demanded the immediate dissolution of the Reichstag. Although such threats were invoked with particular frequency during the 1890s, they declined in intensity over time. With each introduction of a proposal aimed at protecting the political autonomy of voters, the political coalition supporting such reforms grew in size.

6.3. BALLOT ENVELOPES

A large number of the proposals for the protection of electoral secrecy considered by the German Reichstag recommended introducing ballot envelopes. The goals of ballot envelopes were to prevent candidates from manipulating the color or shape of ballots and from keeping a tally of how individual voters cast their ballots. As Ignaz Auer, a Social Democratic politician, argued in the Reichstag, wide differences in the designs of ballots had negated voting secrecy altogether:

It is not today that we see for the first time ballots of different sizes. Rather, this is an old experience. We know that there are ballots as large as of half of a sheet of paper and also ballots the size of stamps; we know that especially in the western industrial areas, candidates issue clear indications to distribute at certain times ballots of particular sizes and shapes that are made out of paper with different levels of thickness. We have seen ballots printed on cardboard paper and ballots printed on the thinnest transparent paper. (*Stenographische Berichte des Reichstages* February 1, 1899)

Another widely reported irregularity in ballot design was the use of ballots that had been deliberately crumpled up into balls. Because the ballots were then handed out to voters shortly before entering the voting area, voters did not have enough time to uncrumple the ballot and write in the name of a different candidate. Replacing the ballot with a different one would also single out that voter as a dissenter. Consider the following discussion of electoral irregularities in Oels Wartenberg, a district in Silesia: "In Oels Wartenberg, the ballots have been so crumpled up by the factory inspectors that the fingers of voters cannot unfold them. One cannot expect that a worker, a simple person, will have delicate and smooth enough hands to allow him the fold up the ballot in the same way after unfolding it in the first place" (*Stenographische Berichte des Deutschen Reichstages* January 29, 1896: 609).

The electoral commission of the Reichstag lacked a clear procedure for addressing irregularities that resulted from the use of ballots of different shapes or colors. Reports of these practices led to endless haggling over whether a particular case had violated the provision of the electoral law that required ballots to be printed on white paper only. One politician noted:

[C]olor blindness seemed to be acute among members of the commission when they were asked to identify the color of the ballot... Undoubtedly, the legislation prescribes that ballots have to be printed on white paper, but the opinions diverge as to what counts as white paper. The more senior colleagues in this chamber may still recall the investigation of the election of Graf von Saldern-Ahlimp, where the differences between the colors of the ballots played a decisive role. Those of us who at the time were in the minority regretted that the majority was afflicted by color blindness. The majority of this chamber decided that ballots that were printed on light green paper were, in fact, white. (*Stenographische Berichte des Deutschen Reichstages* February 1, 1899: 584)

The introduction of ballot envelopes was an attempt to resolve this problem. Once ballot envelopes were in place, questions about possible electoral irregularities that could be attributed to differently shaped or differently colored ballots became moot. This was the argument for the adoption of ballot envelopes that was used by the advocates of electoral reforms. Adolf Gröber, a politician of the Zentrum and one of the most significant advocates of electoral reforms, explained the justification for the introduction of ballot envelopes:

The question of whether a ballot is white or not entirely white, of whether it has a blue, gray, yellow, or red shade, will no longer be a valid question after the introduction of ballot envelopes. In conjunction with isolating spaces, the voters will have the opportunity to introduce the envelopes into the urn. If our proposal is accepted, the controlling of votes by controlling the color of the ballots will no longer be possible. (*Stenographische Berichte des Deutschen Reichstages* January 29, 1896: 609)

Opponents of electoral reforms made a number of procedural objections to the proposals to introduce ballot envelopes. Critics argued that the ballot envelopes themselves could be marked with signs on their exteriors or pressed together (*eingekniffen*), just like individual ballots could. Another objection raised by opponents was that ballot envelopes might slow down the voting process. One such argument, which was used by conservative politicians on many occasions, was that "placing the ballots in envelopes was not an easy thing for many voters" (*Stenographische Berichte des Deutschen Reichstages* January 15, 1890). Other criticisms of the bill invoked the difficulties with ballot envelopes that had been experienced in provinces that had adopted them for subnational elections. For example, Württemberg had introduced ballot envelopes in 1882 but decided to eliminate them after a few years (*Stenographische Berichte des Deutschen Reichstages* January 15, 1890). The decision was based on considerations that envelopes were found to slow down the voting process and increase the number of cases of contested elections (Statement by deputy Haug in the Württemberg parliament, cited in *Stenographische Berichte des Deutschen Reichstages* January 15, 1890).

6.4. ISOLATING SPACES

In addition to ballot envelopes, reformers recommended adopting "isolating spaces" (*Isolierräume*). The justification for the introduction of areas that guaranteed the privacy of voters at the time they cast their ballots, which was presented by Rickert, the architect of the electoral reforms, was that isolating spaces would ensure "that the vote expressed the true conviction of the voter and not the opinion of the minster, *Landräte*, policemen, or employers" (*Stenographische Berichte des Deutschen Reichstages* January 15, 1890). Isolating spaces were a complement to the ballot envelopes. Ballot envelopes by themselves could not entirely provide the fullest necessary guarantees of secrecy to voters. They had to be complemented by other institutions that gave voters the opportunity to "be alone and unobserved for a few seconds, so that [they] could insert in the envelope the ballots that corresponded to their true convictions" (*Stenographische Berichte des Deutschen Reichstages* January 15, 1890: 1015). Other politicians used similar justifications: "The isolating space is not a dangerous institution. Quite the contrary, it will allow voters that are pressured from all directions to reflect in silence before casting their vote" (*Stenographische Berichte des Deutschen Reichstages* February 1, 1899: 1099).

The idea of the isolating space encountered significant opposition from parties on the political right, notably Conservatives, Free Conservatives, and National Liberals. Politicians from these parties used two strategies to discredit the proposal. The first strategy was ridicule. The isolating space had a "comical feeling," conservative politicians argued (*Stenographische Berichte des Deutschen Reichstages* May 15, 1895). Prominent National Liberal publications – such as the *Kölnische Zeitung* – referred to the isolating room as a "room of fear (*Angstkammer*). Isolating spaces had to be kept dark at all times, so that no one could observe the fear of the voters" (*Kölnische Zeitung*, November 3, 1889). Other critics referred to the isolating room as a "camera obscura" (*Stenographische Berichte des Deutschen Reichstages* January 15, 1890: 1023). Conservatives coined the term "*Klosettraum*," a label that stuck when opponents referred to the bill ("Das Klosettgesetz," *Deutsche Tageszeitung*, March 9, 1903; "Nochmals das Klosettgesetz," *Deutsche Tageszeitung*, March 13, 1903).

In addition to using ridicule, opponents of the improvements in the protection of electoral secrecy raised a number of procedural objections. One such objection invoked difficulties in manufacturing such isolating spaces. On repeated occasions, conservatives argued that they lacked the means to construct isolating spaces in all voting districts in the "flat land" of the east (*Stenographische Berichte des Deutschen Reichstages* May 15, 1895). Georg Müller, a deputy of the Imperial Party representing the district of Marienwerder, argued that in Germany's eastern regions, no single space could meet the demands of the Rickert proposal (*Stenographische Berichte des Deutschen Reichstages* January 15, 1890: 1021). It was relatively easy to dismiss such arguments as exaggeration. One politician countered:

[O]ne can find carpenters everywhere, and if there are no carpenters, then one can find cabinet makers. If there are no cabinet makers, then one can find others who can build with very little effort a structure in the form of a large fire screen and place a curtain around t so that the voting table is protected and nobody can peak into it. Objections of this kind cannot be taken seriously. (*Stenographische Berichte des Reichstages* January 29, 1902)

Other politicians feared that isolating spaces could slow down the voting process and create opportunities for more electoral irregularities. One such objection was that a representative of one party could occupy the isolating space for a long period of time in an effort to prevent voters who were favorable to other candidates from having enough time to exercise their right to vote. This objection was raised, among others, by Ernst Bassermann, a prominent National Liberal politician and a supporter of other aspects of the reform, such as ballot envelopes and changes to the design of the urn (*Stenographische Berichte des Reichstages* May 15, 1895: 2287). Altogether, this line of argumentation implied that the high administrative costs associated with the introduction of isolating spaces might not be offset by the gains of fewer contested elections.

6.5. THE DESIGN OF THE URN

The 1869 electoral code did not include specific regulations for the design of the electoral urn. Choices concerning the sizes and shapes of urns were left to the discretion of local election officials. Contemporary accounts of electoral practices documented the wide variety of objects used as electoral urns (Siegfried 1903). In many East Prussian districts, soup bowls were used as electoral urns (Saul 1975: 198). Other possible vessels included "cigar boxes, drawers, suitcases, hat boxes, cooking pots, earthen bowls, beer mugs, plates and wash tubs" (Siegfried 1903). Small voting urns were particularly conducive to the violation of electoral secrecy. As the historian Brett Fairbairn noted:

[B]allots would fall in such a way that they laid flat directly on top of each other in the exact order in which they were dropped in[to the urn]. This would allow a vengeful official to compare the stack with a list of the order in which people had voted and arranged for a punishment for those that had voted the wrong way. (Fairbairn 1990: 818)

The Rickert bill adopted in 1903 introduced both isolating spaces and ballot envelopes, but it mandated no changes in the design of the urn. Following the adoption of the other two changes, reformist legislators pressed for additional changes in electoral institutions to "say good-bye to the use of soup bowls and cigarette boxes as electoral urns" (*Stenographische Berichte des Deutschen Reichstages* April 16, 1913). As with the changes proposed in the Rickert bill, disagreement persisted about the magnitude of the violations of electoral secrecy and about whether standardized urns were, in fact, necessary. Some politicians argued that the Rickert law had in fact diminished electoral secrecy (*Stenographische Berichte des Deutschen Reichstages* February 25, 1907). Siegfried, an advocate of the adoption of uniform urns, argued that "the adoption of ballot envelopes had contributed to a significant deterioration of the protection of voting secrecy" (Bundesarchiv Berlin

Lichtenberg R1501/114695: 735). After the introduction of ballot envelopes, some urns became too narrow, which lead to the stacking of ballots: "The stacking of ballots goes hand-in-hand with the creation of a counter-list (*Gegenlist*) that records the order in which the voters have voted. Once the stack of ballots is reversed, it is very easy to determine how each individual voted with the use of this list" (Bundesarchiv Berlin Lichtenberg R1501/114695: 735). On the floor of the Reichstag, a number of opposition politicians shared Siegfried's concern about the continuing efforts to control voters through counter-lists that recorded the order of votes. A politician representing the Guelphs in Hannover's tenth district reported a conversation with an election official who asserted that his ability to control how voters cast their ballots had improved since the adoption of the Rickert law (*Stenographische Berichte des Deutschen Reichstages* March 27, 1908).

Siegfried was a manufacturer of urns who had his eye on a possible lucrative deal with the Ministry of the Interior, so one can suspect bias in his account of the worsening electoral conditions. Conservative politicians and members of the Ministry of the Interior took the opposite position, arguing that critics vastly exaggerated the number of irregularities that were attributable to the imperfect design of the urns. To support this argument, Ministry of the Interior officials conducted a comprehensive study of the electoral irregularities during the 1903 and 1907 elections (Bundesarchiv Berlin Lichtenberg R1501/114475, Wahlurnen). This study investigated the types of urns that had been used in more than 60,000 electoral precincts during these two elections. The election commission considered 156 cases of irregularities involving complaints about the stacking of ballots, but it concluded that irregularities had affected the outcomes of the elections in only two cases, both of which occurred in 1903 (Bundesarchiv Berlin Lichtenberg R1501/114475, Wahlurnen).

Bureaucratic opposition by the Ministry of the Interior succeeded in delaying urn reform. Bassermann, one of the politicians who had cosponsored legislation mandating the adoption of uniform urns, argued that the political delays were caused by the "shameful dependence of the government on the Prussian Ministry of the Interior" and by the resistance of Prussian Minister of the Interior von Dallwitz to the introduction of urns (*Stenographische Berichte des Deutschen Reichstages* April 16, 1913). The strategy of using delays and procrastination succeeded in forestalling the adoption of a final set of provisions protecting voters against intimidation: legislation adopting a uniform design of the urn was not adopted until 1914.

The remainder of this chapter develops and tests a number of hypotheses about the determinants of the support of changes in electoral institutions to better protect voting secrecy. Who were the politicians that demanded greater guarantees of the secrecy of the ballot? What economic and political factors explain their willingness to push for greater electoral reforms? How can we account for the political cleavages and coalitions that emerged during the reform process?

6.6. THE ECONOMIC AND POLITICAL DETERMINANTS OF ELECTORAL REFORM

Previous chapters shown that the incentives for public election officials and private actors to engage in electoral intimidation varied systematically across districts and over time. In Chapter 2, I developed a number of hypotheses about the economic and political conditions that increased or reduced the costs of electoral intimidation, thereby predicting the incidence of electoral irregularities across German districts. In Chapters 3 through 5, I provided a variety of qualitative and quantitative tests of these hypotheses using information from the reports on electoral irregularities.

The central hypothesis of this chapter is that the demand for electoral reform originated with politicians who could not take advantage of the opportunities for intimidation in the existing electoral system. As hypothesized in Chapter 2, politicians' calculations were affected by a combination of partisan considerations and specific conditions in their districts. My overarching hypothesis is that demand for electoral reform was higher among politicians lacking opportunities to engage in systematic electoral intimidation. By contrast, politicians able to take advantage of the imperfections of the existing electoral rules were likely to support the political status quo.

Consider first the partisan conceptions of the advantages and disadvantages of the electoral status quo. As the presentation of the parliamentary debates about the adoption of these electoral reforms in the previous three sections has demonstrated, one finds strong partisan cleavage over electoral reforms. Partisan positions on the reforms of electoral institutions can be, in part, endogenized by considering those politicians' ties to the economic and political actors that possessed the means to engage in electoral intimidation. This implies that the costs of electoral intimidation are likely to vary systematically across parties and not just across politicians of the same party. In Imperial Germany, the *Kartellparteien* – the National Liberal Party, Conservative party, and Imperial Party – had the closest political connections to industrial and agricultural "bread lords" and to state employees such as the *Landräte*. These ties remained relatively stable throughout the Imperial Period. The cartel parties faced relatively lower costs of electoral repression and were more likely to support the status quo of electoral design. By contrast, Free Liberals and Social Democrats lacked these ties and had fewer political opportunities to engage in electoral repression. Because of this differential access to the means of repression, I expect the latter parties to show stronger support for changes in electoral institutions that protected electoral secrecy.

My hypotheses about the district-level factors affecting the political demand for electoral reforms follow from the analysis formulated in the previous chapters of this book. My main hypothesis is that politicians facing low costs of electoral repression in their districts were likely to support the status quo. The same district-level conditions that predict the incidence of electoral intimidation are likely to predict the demand for electoral reform, but the sign of these variables is likely to be reversed. Consider one example: economic concentration reduces the costs of electoral intimidation for employers and increases the probability of the incidence of electoral fraud. By contrast, I expect to find a negative relationship between economic concentration and support for electoral reforms, as politicians from districts with low levels of economic concentration were more likely to find the political status quo unattractive.

In Chapter 2, I formulated at greater length my hypotheses about the relationship between district-level conditions, the costs of electoral intimidation, and support for electoral reforms. I posit hypotheses linking three district-level variables with support for reforms. First, I conjecture that demand for electoral reforms should be higher in districts with lower levels of economic concentration. Second, politicians in districts with a higher share of skilled employees are also hypothesized to encounter higher costs of electoral intimidation and are thus more likely to support electoral reforms. Finally, I conjecture that politicians from districts characterized by high levels of electoral fragmentation among right-wing parties who won during runoffs faced higher political costs of electoral intimidation. As such, I expect politicians from districts with a fragmented political right who won during runoffs to be more supportive of electoral reforms.

The theoretical hypotheses about the effects of other dimensions of electoral competition on the demand for electoral secrecy are less clear. Consider the relationship between the competitiveness of a race and the demand for the adoption of electoral reforms. If one assumes risk aversion, politicians who were elected in tight races would be more likely to support the status quo in the design of voting technology. But if politicians viewed the tightness of their races as being the result of the use of electoral intimidation by their political opponents, they would be more likely to support reforms that protect electoral secrecy.

In addition to these factors, my empirical analysis includes a range of variables that test hypotheses from two leading perspectives on democratization. First, in order to examine the hypothesis that inequality in landholding depresses the demand for democratic reforms (Acemoglu and Robinson 2000; Boix 2003), I include a measure of landholding inequality. In this chapter, I test this proposition using the standard measure of rural inequality used in contemporary scholarship: inequality in the distribution of farms. In Chapter 7, which examines the determinants of electoral reforms in Prussia, I further disaggregate rural inequality and consider the consequences of inequalities in the distribution of land and inequalities in the distribution of employment on the demand for electoral reform.

Second, I also examine hypotheses from the literature on endogenous democratization, which conjectures that economic development increases demand for electoral reforms (Przeworski et al. 2000; Boix and Stokes 2003). To test these

TABLE 6.1. *Summary of Hypotheses about Determinants of Political Support for Greater Protection against Electoral Intimidation*

Determinants of Political Support	Variable	Predicted Relationship with Support for Electoral Reforms
Partisan-Level Factors	Politicians with ties to economic and political actors who could engage in intimidation (*Kartellparteien*)	−
	Politicians from "outsider" parties (Free Liberals, Social Democrats, Zentrum members, minorities)	+
District-Level Economic Conditions	Occupational heterogeneity	−
	Skill level of the labor force	+
	Rural inequality	−
	Economic development	+
District-Level Political Conditions	Right-wing electoral fragmentation∗Runoffs	−
	Margin	?

hypotheses, I include both a measure of the economic development of a district and a measure of economic growth.

Table 6.1 summarizes the hypotheses about support for changes in electoral institutions that would protect voters against electoral intimidation. Although my main hypothesis is that politicians lacking opportunities for intimidation under existing electoral rules supported changes in the political status quo, I further conjecture that these considerations about the undesirability of the status quo can be disaggregated into partisan concerns and district-level concerns. Politicians from parties lacking ties to actors who had the means to engage in electoral intimidation were more likely to support electoral reforms. Moreover, politicians facing relatively high costs of electoral intimidation were also likely to support the adoption of electoral reforms.

6.7. EMPIRICAL ANALYSIS

The dependent variable in this chapter includes all bills submitted to the Reichstag during the period between 1870 and 1912 that were aimed at improving the protection of electoral secrecy. Table 6.2 presents the full list of legislative proposals, the date of each's submission, and the name of the politician (or group of politicians) initiating the proposal, along with a brief discussion about the main area of reform under discussion. Proposals recommending improvements in electoral technology were on the agenda of the Reichstag during eight of the thirteen legislative sessions during the Imperial Period.

TABLE 6.2. *Proposals for Electoral Reforms to Protect the Autonomy of Voters Submitted to the German Reichstag between 1870 and 1912*

Year	Document No.	Proposal for Reform	Initiating Politician
1875	52	Electoral list	Voelk (NL)
1878	66	Ballot envelopes	Blos and Most (SPD)
1878	119	Ballot envelopes	Liebknecht (SPD)
1881	66	Ballot design	Woelfel (NL)
1889	26	Ballot design and ballot envelopes	Barth (DFP) and Rickert (FVP)
1890	139	Ballot design	Gröber (Z)
1892	30	Ballot envelopes	Barth (DFP) and Rickert (FVP)
1892	35	Ballot envelopes	Gröber (Z)
1894	20	Ballot envelopes and secret urn	Gröber, von Heereman, Lieber, Rinteln, Schädler, Spahn, and Wenzel (Z)
1894	21	Ballot envelopes	Rickert (FVP)
1895	25	Ballot design and secret urn	Rickert (FVP)
1899	22	Ballot design and secret urn	Rickert (FVP)
1900	33	Ballot envelopes and secret urn	Gröber (Z)
1907	112	Electoral urn	Hompesch, Schädler, and Spahn (Z)
1909	47	Protection of electoral secrecy	Ablass (FVP)
1909	91	Electoral urn	Bassermann (NL)
1910	214	Electoral urn	von Hertling (Z)
1911	816	Electoral urn	Ablass (FVP)

Source: Stenographische Berichte des Deutschen Reichstages various years.

As the analysis of the parliamentary debates in the Reichstag illustrates, the content of these reforms varied systematically over time. During the earlier legislative periods, the main objectives of the reforms were the adoption of ballot envelopes and isolating spaces. Following the adoption of the Rickert law in 1903, the objectives of reformers turned to the design of the urns.

6.7.1. Explanatory Variables

To estimate the determinants of political support for electoral reforms, I use many of the economic and political variables that were also used in Chapter 5. I refer the reader to that chapter for a discussion of the construction of these variables.

6.7.1.1. Economic Variables

ECONOMIC CONCENTRATION: This variable is a Herfindahl-Hirschman Index of occupational fragmentation. The Herfindahl-Hirschman Index is constructed as the sum of the squares of employment shares of all occupations. Higher values of this variable indicate more concentrated economic districts. The source of this variable is the information from the German occupational censuses from 1895 and 1905.

ECONOMIC CONCENTRATION WITH AGRICULTURE: As discussed in Chapter 5, the German occupational census does not include information about the employment shares of all categories of agricultural workers in both the 1895 and 1905 censuses. Only the 1895 census includes information about all workers employed in agriculture. This measure of occupational heterogeneity provides a more accurate characterization of the occupational makeup at the time. Its drawback is that it is not time varying. I use this measure to test the robustness of the earlier results.

SKILL INDUSTRY: Using statistical information from the two waves of the German occupational census, this variable is computed as the ratio of skilled workers to unskilled workers for 200 occupations. The denominator in this measure is the number of all workers employed in industry.

SKILL ALL: This measure of the skill composition of the labor force differs from the previous measure in its denominator. Its denominator is the total number of employees in a district, including the workers in all agricultural occupations.

ECONOMIC DEVELOPMENT: I measure economic development using the share of the population that was not employed in agriculture. The source of this variable is Carl Wilhelm Reibel (2007). I use a flat-steep-flat method of interpolation for missing years.

LANDHOLDING INEQUALITY: This measure uses the Gini of landholding inequality computed by Daniel Ziblatt (2008), which was based on information from the 1895 agricultural census.

CATHOLICS: A measure of the share of the Catholic population in a district based on the ICPSR (1984).

6.7.1.2. Political and Partisan Controls

MARGIN OF VICTORY: Margin is computed as the difference in vote share between the winner and the runner-up in the decisive electoral round. Source: ICPSR 1984.

SECOND ROUND: This variable takes the value of 1 if the outcome of the election was determined in the second round. Source: ICPSR 1984.

EFFECTIVE NUMBER OF RIGHT-WING PARTIES (ENRP): This variable is computed as the squared sum of votes received by the various candidates on the right during the first electoral round. Source: ICPSR 1984.

ENRP*SECOND: This is an interaction of the measure of the effective number of right parties and runoffs.

OUTSIDER PARTIES: I model partisanship by including a variable that takes the value of zero for the *Kartellparteien* – the parties on the political right that had the means to engage in economic or political repression – and the value of 1 for all the other parties in the Reichstag. I refer to the non-*Kartellparteien* also as "outsider parties," because they were removed from the main centers of political power in Imperial Germany. I hypothesize that politicians from these outsider parties were more likely to support electoral reforms.

6.8. RESULTS

The outcome variable in the empirical analysis is whether a member of the Reichstag was a cosigner of a proposal recommending changes to the electoral law. The models estimate whether the variables of interest increased or decreased the probability for a politician from a certain district to cosign an electoral reform bill. Because we have unobserved heterogeneity over various legislative proposals, I estimate a non-nested binary model in which I incorporate random effects (Gelman and Hill 2007). To control for potential unobserved regional effects, I add fixed effects for all of the major regions in Imperial Germany (denoted β_0).

I estimate the following model and include random effects for each proposal (α_i):

$$P(y_i = 1) = logit^{-1}[\beta_0 + X_i'\beta + \alpha_i]$$

$$\alpha_i = N(0, \sigma_i)$$

In Tables 6.3 and 6.4, I present estimation results that use different measures of economic heterogeneity, the crucial economic variable in a district that is hypothesized to affect the costs of electoral repression and also political support for electoral reforms. As mentioned in the previous section, when measuring the occupational heterogeneity of a district, we encounter a trade-off between temporal and occupational coverage. The time-varying measure of economic heterogeneity excludes some categories of agricultural workers. We can construct a measure of economic concentration that includes all of the employed people in a district (and thus all agricultural workers) only for the 1895 census. To overcome this constraint of data availability, I present models that include both the time-varying and time-invariant measures of occupational heterogeneity. The models presented in Table 6.3 use the time-varying measure of occupational heterogeneity (ECONOMIC CONCENTRATION), whereas the models presented in Table 6.4 use the time-invariant measure that has broader occupational coverage (ECONOMIC CONCENTRATION WITH AGRICULTURE). The models presented in Tables 6.3 and 6.4 also differ in their measure of the skill composition of the labor force in a district.

TABLE 6.3. *Determinants of Political Support for Legislation That Protected Voters against Intimidation*

		Model 1	Model 2	Model 3	Model 4	Model 5	Model 6
Economic Conditions in Districts	Economic Concentration	-5.166***		-4.849***	-6.301***	-6.353***	-6.022***
		(1.593)		(1.568)	(1.653)	(1.659)	(1.637)
	Skill Industry	2.442***		1.965***	2.090***	2.109***	2.134***
		(0.393)		(0.383)	(0.430)	(0.432)	(0.430)
Political Conditions in Districts	ENRP	-0.000*		-0.000**	-0.000**	-0.000**	-0.000**
		(0.000)		(0.000)	(0.000)	(0.000)	(0.000)
	ENRP*Second	0.000*		0.000**	0.000*	0.000*	0.000*
		(0.000)		(0.000)	(0.000)	(0.000)	(0.000)
	Margin				-0.150	-0.153	-1.257***
					(0.202)	(0.202)	(0.474)
	Second	-0.024		0.077	0.215**	0.214**	0.182*
		0.089		0.090	(0.105)	(0.105)	(0.106)
Partisanship	Outsider Parties		0.848***	0.829***	0.567***	0.567***	0.291**
			(0.092)	(0.093)	(0.106)	(0.106)	(0.144)
	Outsider Parties*Margin						1.381***
							(0.517)

(continued)

145

TABLE 6.3 *(continued)*

	Model 1	Model 2	Model 3	Model 4	Model 5	Model 6
Controls						
Rural Inequality				−1.229**	−1.221**	−1.166**
				(0.493)	(0.493)	(0.494)
Economic Development				0.009***	0.008**	0.008**
				(0.003)	(0.004)	(0.003)
Catholics				0.007***	0.007***	0.005***
				(0.002)	(0.002)	(0.002)
Economic Change					0.010	
					(0.023)	
Constant	−3.262***	−2.997***	−3.642***	−3.331***	−3.317***	−3.064***
	(0.274)	(0.223)	(0.277)	(0.474)	(0.475)	(0.483)
Fixed Effects for Regions?	Y	Y	Y	Y	Y	Y
Observations	7,129	7,146	7,129	7,129	7,129	7,129
Number of Groups	18	18	18	18	18	18
Ll	−2,220	−2,204	−2,177	−2,159	−2,159	−2,156
χ^2	100.1	129.6	173.5	199.3	199.3	198.7

Notes: Standard errors are in parentheses; *** $p<0.01$; ** $p<0.05$; * $p<0.10$.

TABLE 6.4. *Determinants of Support for Legislation Providing Better Protection of Electoral Secrecy Using Alternative District-Level Variables*

		Model 1	Model 2	Model 3	Model 4	Model 5	Model 6
Economic Conditions in Districts	Economic Concentration All		−1.878***	−1.613***	−1.358***	−1.359***	−1.303***
			(0.411)	(0.418)	(0.428)	(0.429)	(0.429)
	Skill All		−0.571	−0.815	−0.207	−0.212	−0.109
			(0.539)	(0.550)	(0.574)	(0.576)	(0.576)
Political Conditions in Districts	ENRP		−0.000**	−0.000**	−0.000**	−0.000**	−0.000**
			(0.000)	(0.000)	(0.000)	(0.000)	(0.000)
	ENRP*Second		0.000**	0.000**	0.000*	0.000**	0.000**
			(0.000)	(0.000)	(0.000)	(0.000)	(0.000)
	Margin				−0.054	−0.053	−1.164**
					(0.202)	(0.202)	(0.472)
	Second		−0.082	0.047	0.179*	0.179*	0.149
			(0.091)	(0.092)	(0.106)	(0.106)	(0.107)
Partisanship	Outsider Parties	0.848***		0.815***	0.599***	0.599***	0.319**
		(0.092)		(0.094)	(0.106)	(0.106)	(0.145)
	Outsider Parties*Margin						1.381***
							(0.513)

(continued)

TABLE 6.4 (continued)

		Model 1	Model 2	Model 3	Model 4	Model 5	Model 6
Controls	Rural Inequality				-1.273**	-1.277**	-1.229**
					(0.514)	(0.514)	(0.516)
	Economic Development				0.006	0.007	0.005
					(0.004)	(0.004)	(0.004)
	Catholics				0.005***	0.005***	0.004**
					(0.002)	(0.002)	(0.002)
	Economic Change					-0.006	
						(0.023)	
	Constant	-1.719***	-2.997***	-2.272***	-2.046***	-2.057***	-1.793***
		(0.363)	(0.223)	(0.370)	(0.562)	(0.563)	(0.570)
Fixed Effects for Regions?		Y	Y	Y	Y	Y	Y
Observations		7,129	7,146	7,129	7,129	7,129	7,129
Number of Groups		18	18	18	18	18	18
Ll		-2,224	-2,204	-2,183	-2,171	-2,171	-2,167
χ^2		91.08	129.6	159.2	176.3	176.4	175.6

Notes: Standard errors are in parentheses; *** $p<0.01$; ** $p<0.05$; * $p<0.10$.

In all of the models in Table 6.3, I use a measure of vocational skills that measures the skill composition of the industrial labor force (SKILLED INDUSTRY). The measure is constructed by dividing the number of skilled workers in a district by the number of workers employed in industry. In the models presented in Table 6.4, I use a measure of skills in which the denominator is the total workforce in a district, including all agricultural employees (SKILLED ALL). Given that we have district-level measures of all employees in each district only for the 1895 census, this measure is time invariant.

In Model 1, I begin by examining the relationship between district-level covariates that are hypothesized to affect the costs of electoral intimidation and the probability of the cosponsorship of legislation that provided better protection for electoral secrecy. Consistent with my theoretical prediction, I find that politicians from districts with higher occupational heterogeneity were more likely to support the adoption of this legislation. As discussed in previous chapters, employers in districts with higher occupational heterogeneity were likely to face relatively higher costs of intimidation. As such, politicians in these districts were unable to rely on private actors as agents of intimidation and were likely to support electoral reform in order to equalize the electoral playing field for all candidates competing for a seat in the Reichstag. I also find that politicians from districts with a more skilled industrial labor force were more likely to support electoral reforms. One possible interpretation of this finding is that these politicians were also more constrained from using economic intimidation and electoral layoffs than those in districts with lower levels of skills. Although these results are consistent with the predictions made the variety of capitalism literature, I do not share with that literature the assumption of cooperative labor market relations between employers and employees; rather, I interpret high levels of skills as one of the constraints encountered by otherwise repressive employers. Finally, I find modest support for my hypothesis about district-level political determinants of support for electoral reforms. As hypothesized, politicians from districts with a divided political right who won during runoffs were more likely to face high costs of electoral repression than those from districts without a divided political right. As such, I hypothesize that these politicians were more supportive of electoral reforms. The interaction term between right-wing political fragmentation and the existence of a second round has the predicted positive sign, but the substantive effect of this variable is small in magnitude.

Model 2 considers only the partisan determinants of support for electoral reforms. As predicted, I find that politicians from outsider parties that lacked ties to actors that had the means to engage in political or economic intimidation were more likely to support the adoption of electoral reforms. Members of the Zentrum, Free Liberals, Social Democrats, and minority parties were more likely to support the adoption of ballot secrecy than were politicians from the *Kartellparteien*. Model 3 includes a combination of the variables from the previous two models that test the main theoretical hypotheses. The results remain unchanged.

Models 4 to 6 add a number of additional variables that examine predictions from additional theoretical perspectives and subject these results to additional robustness checks. In Model 4, I include a battery of economic and political controls at the district level. Consistent with the predictions made by alternative theories of democratization, I find a positive relationship between the level of economic development in a district and support for electoral reforms, as well as a negative relationship between landholding inequality and support for electoral reforms. As discussed in Section 6.7, I did not have an unambiguous theoretical prediction about the relationship between the margin of victory for the politician and support for electoral reforms. I find no significant relationship between the tightness of a race and support for electoral reforms in this specification. In Model 5, I include an additional test for the economic modernization hypothesis, which examines the relationship between economic changes (measured as changes in the share of the population employed in agriculture) and support for electoral reforms. Although the sign of this variable is positive and is thus consistent with the predictions made by the modernization literature, the variable does not reach statistical significance at conventional levels.

The final model reported in Table 6.3 includes an interaction term between the partisanship of the politician and the political competition in a district. The sign of this interaction (OUTSIDER PARTIES*MARGIN) is positive, suggesting that politicians from parties lacking ties to actors able to engage in repression and who won narrowly were more likely to support electoral reforms. All of the additional results remain unchanged after the inclusion of this variable.

In Table 6.4, I present similar specifications to those reported in Table 6.3, but I use different measures for two of the district-level economic variables. Here, I use the time-invariant measure of occupational heterogeneity that includes all agricultural employees in a district (ECONOMIC CONCENTRATION ALL). I also use a measure of vocational skills that computes the ratio of skilled workers to the total number of employees in a district (SKILLS ALL). The results for the main theoretical hypotheses remain, largely, unchanged. The only change comes with respect to the relationship between the skill composition of a district and support for electoral reforms. Using this alternative measure of skills, I no longer find a positive relationship between skills and democratic reforms.

6.9. CONCLUSION

Electoral reforms that improve the protection of voter secrecy and remove opportunities for intimidation at the moment of voting were an important dimension of the process of democratization. These reforms involved changes in electoral technology, such as the design of the ballot, its shape and color, the size of the urns, and their location in electoral precincts. These micro-level details about the organization of the voting process were the object of intense political contestation in Imperial Germany. These details were highly salient for politicians because they affected their ability to conduct campaigns and win offices by monitoring how their loyal supporters and potential dissenters cast their ballots.

In this chapter, I explored the economic and political determinants of demand for the adoption of reforms ensuring better protection for the secrecy of the vote. Using a novel dataset on the cosponsorship of political proposals that recommended changes in electoral secrecy, I showed that political demand for electoral secrecy originated with politicians who faced higher relative costs of electoral intimidation and who could not take advantage of opportunities for electoral intimidation. I have unpacked theoretically and empirically the latter variable, showing how partisan and district-level factors affected politicians' calculations about the desirability of these electoral reforms.

The demand for electoral reforms originated with politicians whose parties lacked opportunities to engage in political intimidation. Representatives from two parties that lacked ties to agents of electoral intimidation, the Zentrum and Free Liberals, were among the most active proponents of legislation protecting electoral secrecy. Although representatives of the National Liberal Party were initially divided over the advantages of this legislation, over time, this party also joined the pro-reform coalition. The temporal growth in the size of the coalition supporting electoral reforms can thus be explained by the growth in political strength in the Reichstag of parties lacking ties to actors that could engage in electoral intimidation.

In addition to these partisan factors, I have shown that demand for electoral reforms was also affected by the economic factors in a district. I have shown that politicians who encountered higher relative costs of electoral repression were more likely to demand electoral reforms. In particular, I found that two such economic factors affected the demand for electoral reforms: the economic heterogeneity of a district and the skill profile of the labor force. Politicians from districts with high levels of economic heterogeneity and a more skilled labor force were more likely to support the adoption of electoral reforms because of the relatively higher costs of electoral intimidation in their districts.

The empirical tests of two alternative theories of democratization stressing the importance of rural inequality and economic development, respectively, yield more mixed results. These results are supportive of a longstanding hypothesis linking landholding inequality and opposition to electoral reforms. In Chapter 7, which analyzes political support for the introduction of electoral reforms in Prussia, Germany's largest state, I subject this explanation emphasizing the importance of landholding inequality to a number of additional tests. I disaggregate rural inequality, distinguishing between inequality in the distribution of land and inequality the distribution of employment across farms. To anticipate the results, I show that inequality in landholding did *not* translate into the higher capacity of rural landlords to mobilize rural workers, seeing as large farms in districts with high levels of rural inequality were often unpopulated. Landholding inequality as such was unrelated to support for electoral reforms because it did not confer significant electoral advantages to politicians, once we control for the other labor market characteristics of a district.

Finally, the findings of this chapter also have interesting implications for prominent arguments in the literature on democratization, which highlight the consequences of modernization on democratic transitions. I do not find a relationship between either the level of economic development of a district or its level of growth and support for electoral reforms. However, I do find a strong and robust relationship between the occupational fragmentation of a district and support for electoral reforms. Economic development can lead to both economic concentration and economic diversification, as Gary Herrigel (1996) has persuasively demonstrated. Although economic concentration is conducive to electoral repression by private actors and inimical to demands for electoral reforms, economic diversification by contrast reduces employers' ability to engage in electoral repression and increases the demand for electoral reforms. Economic development is associated with higher demand for democratic reforms only through the intervening mechanism of economic diversification.

7

Labor Scarcity, Rural Inequality, and Electoral Reforms

The Determinants of Electoral Reform in the Prussian Electoral System

Efforts to reform electoral institutions and reduce opportunities for political intimidation were not confined to national elections only; they were also on the agenda of subnational parliaments throughout the period until World War I. Electoral rules differed significantly across German regions (Mares and Queralt 2014). Many regions had much more restrictive suffrage rules than those in place at the national level. In these electoral systems, political efforts to end opportunities for electoral intimidation and provide stronger guarantees for voters' political autonomy went hand in hand with efforts to reform other dimensions of the electoral system. These included changes in the method of voting (from secret voting to open voting) and efforts to replace indirect voting with direct voting.

In this chapter, I examine political conflicts over the adoption of electoral reforms aiming to reduce opportunities for electoral intimidation in Prussia. Prussia was the largest state of the German Empire, and it comprised nearly two-thirds of the territory of Imperial Germany. Proposals to reform the electoral system along the dimensions discussed above were on the agenda of the Prussian lower house beginning in 1872. This chapter examines a quantitative analysis of the roll call votes on a subset of such bills in order to understand the economic and political determinants of support for changes in electoral rules and the composition of the political coalitions supporting reforms.

The study of electoral reforms in Prussia provides us with an ideal opportunity to reevaluate one of the most prominent explanations of democratization, which stresses the importance of rural inequality as an obstacle to electoral reform. Beginning with Alexander Gerschenkron and Barrington Moore, accounts of Germany's *Sonderweg* have invoked rural inequality as a factor that inhibited the adoption of democratic reforms (Gerschenkron 1946; Moore 1966). This explanation dovetails with recent theoretical accounts of democratization that emphasize how inequalities in the distribution of fixed assets act as barriers to democratic reforms (Acemoglu and Robison 2000; Boix 2003). Dan Ziblatt (2008) provides a restatement of these classic hypotheses and a preliminary empirical test that reaffirms the importance of rural inequality.

In this chapter, I reexamine and challenge this explanation. The starting premise of my analysis is that rural inequality is a multidimensional concept involving inequalities in the distribution of land and employment. These two components of rural inequality may stand in a weak empirical relationship with each other and may affect political and electoral outcomes through different mechanisms. For example, whereas inequality in the distribution of land confers access to wealth and economic resources, inequality in the distribution of employment gives rural landowners access to a pool of voters that can be subjected to political control during elections. It remains an open question whether either dimension of rural inequality affects political outcomes.

I take up this empirical question in this current chapter. To examine the political implications of different dimensions of rural inequality and their effects on the demand for political reforms, I digitized and used for the first time a wealth of new statistical information about employment conditions in Prussian agriculture. As part of its agricultural census, Prussian statistical authorities collected information about the distribution of employment across farms of different sizes along with information about the sizes of different farms for all Prussian communes in both 1895 and 1905 (Königliches Preussisches Statistisches Landesamt 1895, 1907). This data allows me to compute measures of inequalities in the distribution of agricultural employment as well as inequalities in the distribution of land. In Prussia, these two measures of rural inequality are very weakly correlated, which suggests that inequalities in the distribution of land did not give landowners greater electoral control over rural workers. This low empirical correlation weakens the theoretical plausibility of a mechanism that links landholding inequality with opposition to democratic reforms in the German context. In other words, given that inequalities in the distribution of land did not confer significant political advantage to candidates during elections the mechanism by which land inequalities affect the preferences of politicians for reforms of electoral institutions remain unclearly specified.

I also challenge the assumption of immobile labor markets that is made in the current literature when examining the political consequences of rural inequality. The crucial assumption made by these studies is that capital is the only mobile factor, whereas land and labor are immobile. For some societies with very low levels of economic development, this assumption of labor immobility may be justified. Yet, as development economists argued nearly half a century ago, societies in their early stages of industrialization experience both intra-rural mobility of labor and mobility of labor from rural to urban areas (Lewis 1954; Kuznets 1955).

Building on the foundational work of Lewis, I show that productivity shocks in the countryside set in motion a transition from a state of "unlimited labor supply in the countryside" to one characterized by a wide regional heterogeneity in the supply of labor (see also Grant 2005). Whereas some localities continue to experience labor surplus, others experience labor market shortages. This chapter explores the implications of labor scarcity in rural areas on political outcomes and preferences toward political reforms. Conditions of scarcity in the supply of rural workers, I hypothesize, not only weaken the economic power of rural landlords but also contribute to changes in the "political price" that agricultural workers can extract in the electoral marketplace. In districts where labor is scarce, electoral strategies premised on intimidation and threats of layoffs in retaliation for choices made at the ballot box become costlier for rural landlords. In these districts, rural voters are more likely to use their increased economic power to take greater "electoral risks" and vote in favor of opposition candidates. In Chapter 8, I present additional empirical evidence supporting this proposition by showing that labor scarcity increased the political support for Social Democratic candidates.

The empirical analysis presented in this chapter explores the implications of these propositions for electoral reforms. I argue that labor shortage is, in itself, the source of a political cleavage over the design of electoral institutions. In labor-abundant electoral districts, local landlords face low costs of electoral repression. As a result, I hypothesize that politicians from these districts are likely to support the status quo with respect to electoral design and oppose proposals to reduce electoral intimidation. The calculations of politicians in areas that experience labor scarcity, however, are different. Labor shortages increase the costs of electoral intimidation for rural landowners, reducing their ability to use their economic power to achieve desired results at the ballot box. Politicians who face rising costs of electoral intimidation are more willing to support changes in electoral institutions and electoral reforms. I illustrate these propositions by showing that labor shortages increase the probability of support for greater electoral secrecy. My results are robust to the inclusion of a large number of factors that control for the political competition in a district, its religious and linguistic heterogeneity, and inequalities in the distribution of fixed assets and employment. Thus, the empirical analysis presented in this chapter challenges the central proposition of recent democratization literature, which argues that inequality in the distribution of fixed assets (e.g., landholding inequality) reduces support for democratic reforms.

To develop these arguments, I organize this chapter as follows. I begin in Section 7.1 with a brief overview of the political debates about reforming the Prussian electoral system. The goal of this section is to identify the main arguments in support of and in opposition to existing electoral laws. The following section, Section 7.2, characterizes the empirical variation in rural inequality in Imperial Germany and explores differences in the distribution of land and employment across electoral districts. This discussion highlights some limitations of existing approaches that focus only on inequalities in the distribution of fixed assets by illustrating that, in the Prussian context, this variable is a poor predictor of the ability of landowners to control rural voters and mobilize

them for electoral purposes. Next, in Section 7.3, I provide empirical evidence
for increases in labor scarcity across Prussian districts during this period and
develop a number of propositions about its effects on political competition in
the countryside. In Section 7.4, I develop a number of hypotheses about the
consequences of labor inequality and labor shortage on politicians' incentives
to support reforms of the electoral system. In the final section of the chapter,
Section 7.5, I test these propositions by examining the economic and political determinants of support for changes in electoral institutions that would
increase the secrecy of the vote. I examine two political votes on proposals to
replace open voting with secret voting in the Prussian lower house in 1910 and
1912.

7.1. ELECTORAL INTIMIDATION IN PRUSSIAN ELECTIONS

> You say that in elections to the Prussian lower house where there is open voting
> we make worse deals than in the elections to the Reichstag, so we should change
> the law for the former. We say the opposite, that we make better deals (*bessere
> Geschäfte*), and so we do not want to change it. (Von Rauchhaupt, *Stenographis-
> che Berichte des Preussischen Abgeordnetenhauses* December 6, 1883)

Prussia's electoral law was adopted in 1849 following the events of the March
Revolution (Rauchhaupt 1916). The electoral system by which politicians were
elected to the lower chamber of the Prussian parliament – which was decried
by many contemporaries as the *Junkersystem* – was based on indirect, public, and censitary voting. Electoral districts were divided into "subdistricts"
(*Urwahlbezirke*), which were in turn divided into three "classes." Voters were
assigned to the different classes according to income, which was assessed by the
payment of taxes. Each class of voters selected electors (*Wahlmänner*) through
public voting. The electors were then responsible for selecting the candidate
(Patemann 1964: 10). One contemporary assessed the implications of this electoral system: "[P]ublic voting served conservatives in the countryside, where
they were economically more powerful, rather well off, and [public voting]
could help them in their electoral victory" (Wulff 1922: 12).

Despite this strong difference in rules between the Prussian electoral system and the system for national elections, the two electoral systems had one
important commonality: opportunities for the electoral intimidation of voters
existed under both sets of rules. In national elections, opportunities for electoral intimidation resulted from the imperfect protection of electoral secrecy.
In Prussia, both the open method of voting and other imperfections in the electoral design – most notably, ambiguities in the procedures to be followed by
election officials – created permissive conditions for electoral intimidation. In
his pioneering work on electoral politics, Thomas Kühne (1994) documented
the electoral intimidation that took place in Prussia. This intimidation resulted
from both the actions of private economic agents and those of state employees
and election officials. Election officials were a much more powerful source of

electoral intimidation in Prussia than they were in national elections to the Reichstag.

Landräte occupied a central place in the Prussian administrative structure and played a critical role in elections (Kühne 1994: 67). *Landräte* accumulated a large number of responsibilities in the Prussian administration, including the collection of taxes and the ability to make decisions about tax exemptions, as well as decisions about military conscriptions. *Landräte* astutely used these positions of authority in their efforts to influence electoral behavior. Kühne reports threats made by the *Landräte* to voters that "whoever openly supports the liberal candidate should expect higher tax assessments during the following year" (Kühne 1994: 67). On other occasions, *Landräte* took advantage of their role in military recruitment by threatening voters with conscription should they vote for the "incorrect political candidate" (Kühne 1994: 67).

Finally, Kühne's work documents the existence of ample electoral intimidation by rural and urban employers. Among industrial employers, private economic intimidation was concentrated in the same regions as it was in national elections: the districts of the Ruhr, Saarland, and Upper Silesia. Private actors used the same repertoire of strategies that were used in national elections. These included layoffs for voting incorrectly as well as positive inducements, such as increases in wages or promotions in exchange for supporting the desired candidate (Kühne 1994). Because voting took place on workdays, employers often used their control over the workforce to deny workers the right to vote.

The second chamber of the Prussian parliament took up the question of electoral reform on multiple occasions. One of the common suggestions of the various reform proposals was to replicate the provisions of the national electoral system in Prussia. One of the first proposals of this type was submitted in 1873 by Zentrum politicians, but, like many proposals that came to the floor of the chamber, it remained unsuccessful (Wulff 1922: 15). Ten years later, a delegation of Free Liberals took up the issue of electoral reform. The proposal by the Free Liberals argued that "large segments of the electorate, in particular employees of the state and workers, were prevented from expressing their free opinions, both because of their economic dependence and also because of the public nature of voting. Voters had no other choice but to vote against their opinions or to abstain from voting altogether" (*Stenographische Berichte des Preussischen Abgeordnetenhauses* 1883/1884: no. 18).

The Free Liberals sponsored a number of other proposals for electoral reforms in 1892, 1903, and 1906. The peak of pre–World War I efforts to reform the Prussian electoral system occurred between 1910 and 1912. At that time, a political majority that was in favor of electoral reforms existed in the Prussian second chamber, and a bill that recommended the adoption of open voting was passed by the second chamber. However, the bill did not meet with the political support of the Prussian upper house and was not adopted. In Section 7.5, I provide a quantitative analysis of the votes for these reforms in the Prussian lower house in 1910 and 1912. I situate this statistical analysis in its proper historical context by reviewing the arguments formulated during these debates by both opponents and supporters of electoral reforms.

Opponents of electoral secrecy and protection against electoral intimidation used a variety of extremely sophisticated arguments to justify why the status quo should be maintained. The first type of argument was that the secret ballot was a costly and unnecessary institution unlikely to have an effect on the preferences of voters. This argument was invoked for the first time by Puttkammer, Prussia's Minister of the Interior, in 1883 and discussed repeatedly on other occasions. Puttkammer argued, for example, that believing that the open method of voting used by the Prussian lower house had any influence on electoral outcomes was "a colossal exaggeration of the importance of the enterprise" (*Stenographische Berichte des Preussischen Abgeordnetenhauses* 1883: 204). The method or technology of voting, Puttkammer argued, is epiphenomenal, and elections are determined by "the large hot issues of electoral campaigns. Majorities and the small, irrelevant electoral pressures are only small drops of water in the sea of the large electoral decision" (*Stenographische Berichte des Preussischen Abgeordnetenhauses* 1883: 189).

In a similar vein, other politicians argued that a change in the technology of voting would likely be epiphenomenal and only shift the temptation to engage in electoral intimidation to other stages of the voting process. Posadowsky-Wehner, a conservative politician, used this argument in 1883: "In my opinion, the introduction of a secret ballot would only displace the moment at which electoral intimidation takes place but change nothing else" (*Stenographische Berichte des Preussischen Abgeordnetenhauses* 1883: 200). The only people potentially helped by this change in voting technology would have been those who sought to intimidate, not the voters who were the targets of that intimidation.

Other Prussian politicians argued that modifications in voting technology could have potentially ominous consequences. In a nutshell, their argument suggested that the adoption of the secret ballot would generate "irrational processes" and higher politicization of voting. "Open voting," these politicians argued, "legalized deception [and the] negation of authority" (von Heydebrand, *Stenographische Berichte des Preussischen Abgeordnetenhauses* February 5, 1903). The introduction of changes in the method of voting, these politicians feared, could strengthen the political power of Social Democracy. Public voting was preferable because of its capacity to "depoliticize" the vote and protect political stability.

A different set of arguments raised by Prussian politicians who were opposed to changes in the voting technology was that the secret ballot could embolden workers to betray their employers and lead to dishonest voting. Consider the argument raised by Rauchhapt: "And I ask myself, which is worse: the employee of the state who votes for the candidate of the government out of an obligation to his oath or the worker who, with a covered ballot, betrays his employer in cold blood? The secret ballot legalizes the deception of employers and aggravates the breach of faith" (Von Rauchhaupt, December 16, 1883, cited in Wulff 1922: 20). Dishonest voting, opponents of the secret ballot argued, could disrupt economic relations in companies and lead to worse economic outcomes. Open voting, Rauchhaupt argued, was in fact in the best interests of workers. The existing electoral laws protected voters against the risks of falling prey to Social Democratic agitation. As Rauchhaupt stated, "one can say that it is, in principle, highly dangerous for workers to become prisoners of a vile electoral agitation that would be enhanced by the secret vote" (Von Rauchhaupt, December 16, 1883).

7.2. REFORMING THE ELECTORAL SYSTEM AND REDUCING OPPORTUNITIES FOR ELECTORAL REFORMS: A TEST OF ECONOMIC EXPLANATIONS OF DEMOCRATIZATION

This section turns to an analysis of the determinants of support for and opposition to reforms of the Prussian electoral system. Although the question of electoral reform is multidimensional, I focus on reforms that sought to adopt secret voting and reduce opportunities for intimidation. Given the importance of rural inequality as an explanatory variable of democratizing reforms, I devote particular attention to a test of this factor. Taking advantage of a wealth of new empirical data, I disaggregate the various dimensions of rural inequality and explore the mechanisms by which these dimensions of inequality affect the politicians' preferences toward electoral reforms.

7.2.1. The Multidimensionality of Rural Inequality

Imperial Germany occupies a central position in the comparative literature linking rural inequality with democratization. One line of research that goes back to the economic studies published under the auspices of the German Statistical Office beginning in the 1870s stressed the unequal character of German agriculture. The interpretation of Imperial Germany as the paradigmatic case of an economy with a highly unequal rural sector, where unreformed vestiges of a feudal past continued well into the nineteenth century, exercised a strong influence on classic accounts of comparative politics, such as Alexander Gerschenkron (1946), Barrington Moore (1966), and Dietrich Rueschemeyer et al. (1992).

Nevertheless, considerable disagreement exists about the extent of rural inequality in Imperial Germany. Classical assertions notwithstanding, more recent studies have argued that, compared to other countries with similar levels of economic development, the conditions in German agriculture were *not* particularly unequal (Prosterman and Riedinger 1987; Grant 2005). One recent study states this position:

The image of East Elbian agriculture as dominated by large estates, on the English pattern is to a large degree a false one. The typical farm in Brandenburg, Silesia, East Prussia and the Danzig region of West Prussia was more likely to be an owner-occupied holding of around 30–50 hectares. Even where larger estates predominated, they were very different from the English model: an average *Junker* estate might consist of around 250 hectares farmed "in hand"; the equivalent English aristocratic estate in the 1890s would be almost entirely let out to tenants and considerably larger. In most of Germany, especially in the west and south, large estates were a rarity. The typical farm was small, 10–20 hectares and owner-occupied. There was little employed labor. The rural sector was therefore, by the standards of contemporary European countries, a relatively egalitarian one. The low proportion of landless laborers in the rural population as a whole and the high level of owner-occupancy mean that the structure of nineteenth-century German agriculture compared well with the situation of many less-developed economies today. (Grant 2005: 53)

Some of this disagreement can be traced back to the different empirical indicators that have been used to assess rural inequality. Germany appears particularly unequal when one measures the distribution of land but less unequal if one measures the distribution of employment across different farms or landownership. Let us consider inequalities in the distribution of land first. In a recent study, Dan Ziblatt (2008) computed measures of landholding inequality using information about the number and size of German farms from the 1895 agricultural census. The measure used in this study, a Gini measure of landholding inequality, calculates the magnitude of the deviation from a perfectly equal distribution of agricultural land among landholders. Higher values of the Gini index indicate that larger farms accounted for a greater proportion of the total agricultural land, whereas smaller values indicate that the total farm acreage was relatively equally distributed among farms of different sizes. Ziblatt's study reveals considerable variation in patterns of landholding inequality but high average values of the measure of landholding inequality in Imperial Germany in 1895. Ginis of landholding inequalities varied between 0.49 and 0.94, with an average of 0.77.

Within Prussia, a large percentage of the districts with higher than average levels of rural inequality were located in East Elbian regions, such as Königsberg, Gumbinnen, Breslau, and Marienwerder. We find a considerable number of farms that were between 100 and 200 hectares in these districts, which leads to high values of landholding inequality. The box plots in Figure 7.1 help convey these regional differences. The shaded rectangle represents the interquartile range, and it contains the median, which is shown as a solid line. The dashed horizontal line represents the mean level of inequality across Prussian districts.

Ziblatt's study reflects a common practice in contemporary research: using measures of inequalities in the distribution of land as the preferred indicators of rural inequality (Vanhannen 1997; Boix 2003, Przeworski and Curvale 2005; Ansell and Samuels 2010). Although this measure has been widely used in

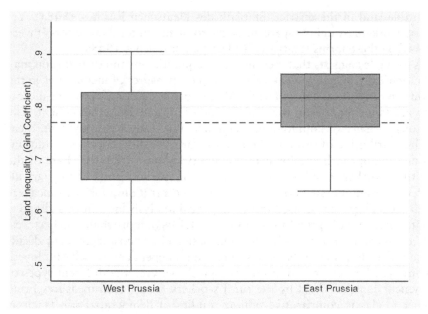

FIGURE 7.1. Mean level of landholding inequality across Prussian districts.

political science research, it is important to reflect on some of its limitations. The Gini of landholding is only an aggregate indicator of the *size* of farms in a locality, district, or country. It tells us nothing about the *ownership* of these farms. Inequalities in ownership – such as the concentration of ownership among a select group of owners or the lack of property owned by large groups of peasants – are not captured by any of the existing measures of landholding inequality. The Gini of landholding inequality also contains no information about the employment patterns on these farms. Two localities that have identical Ginis in the distribution of farms might have very different distributions of employment. Districts and regions with high inequality in the distribution of farms may nevertheless be characterized by high levels of equality in employment if most of the agricultural workers are employed on the smaller farms in that district or region. This can occur, for instance, if the land of a large farm has very little economic value or if a farm is not used for agricultural purposes.

Does the distribution of employment across German farms mirror the unequal distribution of land? With respect to employment, East Elbian farms differed from farms in the southern United States, Mexican *haciendas*, and the Chilean farms discussed in Baland and Robinson (2008). Large rural farms in Prussia were very sparsely populated. Memel, a district located at the most northeastern tip of Prussia (in today's Lithuania), provides a good illustration of this statement. There, the 1895 census recorded twenty-seven farms of more than 200 hectares and three farms of more than 500 hectares, which together comprised a little bit more than 10,000 hectares total, or 20 percent of the total arable land in the district (Statistik des Deutschen Reiches 1898a). Yet only 700 workers (roughly 6 percent of the total agricultural labor force) were employed on these farms (Statistik des Deutschen Reiches 1898a).

This example suggests that measures of inequalities in land distribution may stand empirically in a very weak relationship to measures of inequalities in the distribution of workers across farms. We can use a variety of different indicators to assess inequalities in the distribution of agricultural employment. The analogous measure of landholding inequality, the Gini of employment, measures the distribution of rural workers across farms of different sizes. Additionally, one can approach employment inequality by measuring the share of the agricultural workers employed in the largest or smallest units of the agricultural census using measures of employment concentration. One such measure of rural inequality (that is used in the empirical analysis later in this chapter) computes the share of agricultural workers in farms of more than 200 hectares. These measures are not entirely unproblematic. Their most significant disadvantage is that they do not distinguish between independent, or self-employed, and employed farmers; nor do they distinguish between the different types of employment contracts held by the rural workers. Thus, such measures bring us closer to classic comparative politics studies of democratization (such as Moore 1966), which argued that forms of "labor relations in the countryside" rather than inequalities in the size of farms were the key predictors of successful transitions to democracy, but they still fall short in their measures of the salient aspects of agricultural relations.

To assess the distribution of agricultural employment across farms of different sizes, I construct a Gini of agricultural employment. I use statistical information collected by the Prussian agricultural census and construct this measure for two censuses: 1895 and 1907. To illustrate how I construct this measure of landholding inequality and how it differs from a measure of the inequality of the distribution of farms, in Table 7.1, I present information about the inputs used for computing these two measures in one German commune (*Gemeinde*). The commune in this particular example is Memel, mentioned earlier in this section. The first column in the table presents information about the "bins" used by German (and Prussian) statistical authorities to group farms of different sizes. The second column presents information about the total number of farms in each bin. In the third column (Total Area) is the information that was used to compute the inequality in the distribution of land. The information in the last column (Total Employment) was used to compute the inequality in the distribution of employment. As can be seen in this particular example, the number of employed rural workers on the farms with the largest sizes is relatively low, and it is lower than the number of agricultural workers on smaller farms. The inequality in employment takes lower values than does the inequality in the distribution of land.

Figure 7.2 examines the relationship between rural inequality and the employment concentration of agricultural workers. It plots measures of

TABLE 7.1. *Two Faces of Rural Inequality: Land and Employment Inequality in One Prussian Commune*

Bins	Land Inequality		Employment Inequality	
	Total Number of Farms	Total Area	Total Number of Farms	Total Employment
Less than 0.1 acres	27,678	4,820,111	27,678	
0.1 to 50 acres	1,865,092	566,854.90	1,865,092	2,236,662
0.5 to 2 hectares	1,181,211	1,788,260	1,181,211	2,382,183
2–5 hectares	894,454	3,970,830	894,454	2,761,179
5–10 hectares	596,184	5,687,337	596,184	2,364,574
10–20 hectares	359,971	7,073,847	359,971	1,877,583
20–50 hectares	174,155	7,304,354	174,155	1,311,420
50–100 hectares	25,670	2,665,819	25,670	371,195
100–200 hectares	8,901	1,986,704	8,901	286,051
Gini of land holding inequality		0.55	Gini of inequality of employment	0.36

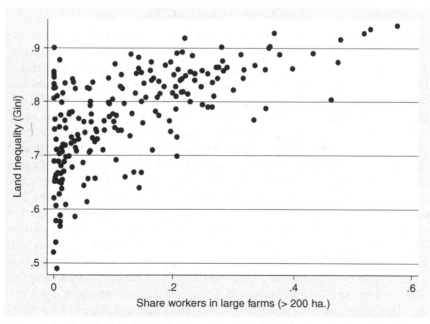

FIGURE 7.2. Landholding inequality and concentration of agricultural employment in large farms (>200 hectares).

landholding inequality against a widely used measure of the concentration of agricultural employment, the share of workers in farms of more than 200 hectares. To compute this measure of employment concentration, I use the data collected by the Prussian statistical authorities in 1907 (Königliches Preussisches Statistisches Landesamt 1907). As Figure 7.2 illustrates, most of the observations are concentrated in the upper left-hand corner of the graph. In that quadrant, inequality in the distribution of land is high, but only a very small share of workers are employed on large farms. By contrast, the upper right-hand quadrant – where both landholding inequality and the share of employment on large farms take high values – is nearly empty.

One implication of these features of German agriculture is that landholding inequality has low explanatory power in accounting for political outcomes across Prussian districts. High levels of rural inequality did not translate into a greater ability of rural employers to control their workers during elections. Before examining the consequences of landholding inequality for political reforms, let me examine another complicating factor for explanations stressing rural inequality: this complication arises from the unevenness in labor supply across Prussian districts.

7.3. LABOR SCARCITY IN GERMAN AGRICULTURE

Agricultural workers were not firmly tied to their employers; rather, they found themselves in constant flux throughout the period. As Werner Sombart notes, the German labor market in the late nineteenth century resembled an "anthill in which a hiker stuck a cane" (Sombart 1927: 408). The central economic problem experienced by German agriculture during the Imperial Period was *Landflucht*, or migration from the countryside (Quante 1933; Quante 1959; Bade 1980). As early as 1890, a statistical study commissioned by the Prussian Ministry of the Interior concluded that the "labor shortage that affected the Eastern regions of the Prussian monarchy could lead to the death (*Lebensunfähigkeit*) of German agriculture" (Bade 1980: 280). Migration intensified in the following decades. Between 1895 and 1905, several districts in East Prussia – such as Gumbinnen, Allenstein, and Posen – experienced migration rates that exceeded 10 percent of the population (Brösicke 1907). Migration severely transformed employment relations in the countryside. Regions that only a few decades earlier had enjoyed relative surpluses in the supply of available rural workers experienced "labor shortage" (*Leutenot*) (*Stenographischer Bericht über die Verhandlungen der 24. Generalversammlung der Vereinigung der Steuer und Wirtschaftsreformer zu Berlin am 14.–15. February 1899*: 5; Rieger 1914). Contemporary accounts decried labor shortage as the "main calamity (*Hauptkalamität*) of their locality, because it pushed up the wages in agriculture and contributed to the economic collapse of many farms" (Kehri 1908). In a number of articles published on the eve of World War I,

Arthur Schulz, the leading expert on rural inequality in Germany's Social Democratic Party, argued that agricultural labor shortage affected the largest farms (of more than 500 hectares) particularly strongly because it contributed to their fragmentation and the reduction of their numbers (Schulz 1912: 426). Schulz shows that over time the number of farms of more than 500 hectares declined significantly in seven East Prussian provinces, and he attributes this decline to labor scarcity.

Intense labor mobility is a reality common to all economies undergoing economic development, and the study of its implications has been at the center of development economics nearly half a century ago (Lewis 1954; Kuznets 1955; Fei and Ranis 1964; Ranis 2004; Grant 2005). In his seminal study of economic development, William Lewis explores the distributional tensions arising in developing economies when they transition from a state of "unlimited supply of labor in the countryside" to a context where rural and urban employers compete for a limited or constrained pool of workers (Lewis 1954). Incipient industrialization sets in motion a process of migration from the countryside to urban centers but also a process of intra-rural movement by agricultural workers toward areas that expand the arable land. As long as labor surplus persists, the growth of real wages is constrained and the producer surplus is captured entirely by owners of land or capital. Once the surplus of rural labor is exhausted – at a point referred to by Lewis, Ranis, and other development economists as the "economic turning point" – wages begin to rise and follow the growth in productivity (Lewis 1954). The process of migration creates large regional imbalances in the supply of agricultural workers. Some rural areas remain largely unaffected by labor mobility, whereas others that had previously been "reservoirs of nearly unlimited labor surplus" (to use Lewis's phrase) experience shortages of rural workers. In a recent study, Oliver Grant assesses the effects of labor mobility on a range of economic outcomes in Germany and argues that the empirical predictions of the Lewis and Kuznets models are borne out by the German case (Grant 2005).

From the perspective of the Lewis model, the most salient economic implication of labor mobility is the imbalance in the supply of agricultural workers and the rise of labor scarcity in some rural areas. To assess the incidence of labor shortage across agricultural districts, I rely on a panel of data on rural wages across all Prussian communes. These data have been collected – and generously shared with me – by Oliver Grant. I leave the detailed discussion of the methodology used by Grant to measure the wage rates in rural localities to the footnotes.[1] Using the rural wage data for each locality, I created a labor

---

[1] The study of the rural migration from East Prussian regions and of the resulting labor shortage of East Prussia has been has been a central theme of the study of the economic and political developments in Imperial Germany, going back to the work of Max Weber. In recent econometric work, Oliver Grant explores the effects of labor mobility for a variety of economic and demographic outcomes. I am extremely grateful to Oliver Grant for sharing the data on rural agricultural

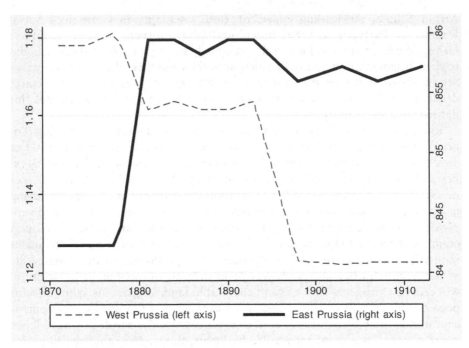

FIGURE 7.3. Rural wages versus average wage ratio.

shortage variable defined as the ratio between the real wage of the locality and the average agricultural wage for all localities. Higher values of this measure proxy for a relative labor shortage of agricultural workers in a district, whereas lower values proxy for a relative labor surplus.[2] I then match these localities to Prussian districts, using the correspondence rules between localities and communes presented in Kühne (1994). Figure 7.3 presents descriptive information of this variable, by contrasting the temporal changes in rural wages across East and West Prussia. This data lends empirical support to the discussion of the

wages in Prussian localities for 1892 and 1901. The source for the agricultural wage data is the *Zeitschrift des Königlich Preußischen Statistischen Bureaus* 1904: 320–328. I augmented these data with a measure of rural wages for 1914 that was reported in Königliches Preussisches Statistisches Landesamt 1914: 187–195. Grant's dataset for rural wages in Prussia is constructed with the goals of separating "rural" and "urban" wages and exploring the economic consequences of intra-urban and intra-rural wage inequality separately. This separation is possible because many localities in Prussia are separated based on "urban" (*Landkreis*) and "rural" (*Stadtkreis*) districts. Using the Grant dataset, I restrict the analysis to the local wage rate in rural localities and use the ratio between this local wage and the wage rate of all rural localities in the dataset as a measure of labor shortage. By excluding urban wage rates from this measure, I only examine the political consequences emanating from imbalances in the rural labor market.

[2] Because we have three data points per locality, in the empirical analysis, I assign the 1892 data to the elections up to 1890, the 1901 data to the elections up to 1903, and the 1914 data to the remaining elections.

pressures on wages of agricultural workers in East Prussia, a leitmotif in the economic and political publications of the period.

This discussion raises a number of issues that inform my analysis of the effects of rural inequality and labor shortage on the demand for electoral reform. First, I have shown that rural inequality is a multidimensional concept whose dimensions are not always correlated. The correlation between inequality in landholding and inequality in employment is 0.27. To emphasize this point more strongly, measuring inequalities in the distribution of land conveys information about the sizes of farms but *not* about the distribution of agricultural workers across farms. The distribution in landholding may be highly unequal, but it may also reflect a high number of empty parcels of land, marshes, and so on. In the Prussian context, because of the weak correlation between land-based and employment-based measures of rural inequality, inequalities in the distribution of land were unlikely to guarantee politicians control over a large pool of voters. Second, the discussion has also highlighted the acuteness of the problem of labor shortage in German agriculture during the final decades of the previous century. The following section formulates a range of hypotheses about the political consequences of landholding and employment inequality on political outcomes and on the demand for electoral reforms within the Prussian electoral system.

7.4. THE POLITICAL CONSEQUENCES OF RURAL INEQUALITY AND LABOR SCARCITY

To understand the consequences of rural inequality and labor scarcity on the demand for electoral reforms, we need to understand their effects on political competition. Political considerations, in turn, affect demand for electoral reform. Different forms of inequality, I hypothesize, affect the calculations of *economic* agents (in this case, rural landlords) to engage in electoral repression. Both inequality and the relative labor scarcity in a district also affect the economic bargaining power of rural workers and their willingness to withstand electoral pressures and take political risks at the ballot box.

As discussed in Section 7.1, private actors played a predominant role as agents of electoral intimidation in both national and Prussian elections. At the time of elections, landlords either provided political and organizational support to political candidates or became political candidates themselves, especially conservative candidates. Descriptive statistics on the social backgrounds of politicians from the German Conservative Party (DKP) who were elected to the second chamber of the Prussian Assembly reveal that 65 percent of conservative politicians were landowners (Retallack 1988: 234). This overrepresentation of landowners among DKP politicians remained very high and did not decline during the Imperial Period (Retallack 1988: 234–235).

If landlords were not the candidate and instead chose to support a particular politician, such strategies came in a variety of forms, which are discussed in

Chapters 2 and 4. Landlords could prevent undesired candidates from campaigning, distribute the "correct" electoral information to their voters, mobilize voters and bring them to the polls, and oversee the choices made by those voters. As Nipperdey has argued, "in East Prussia, landlords used their authority as a source of 'electoral terror' supplementing the absence of organization on the part of conservatives" (Nipperdey 1961: 241).

In this political context, where local competition in a district depended on the power of landlords, economic conditions were likely to affect electoral outcomes through two interrelated pathways. First, landlords weighed the optimal level of economic repression against potential economic costs. Second, labor market conditions also affected the calculations made by voters and their willingness to support political candidates from parties that were branded as official enemies of the Reich. The effect of economic conditions such as rural inequality and labor shortage on political outcomes were mediated by the political calculations made by landlords and voters, respectively.

The two different forms of rural inequality – landholding and employment – affected political outcomes through different mechanisms. Inequality of employment affected the supply of rural voters that could be pressured during elections and mobilized politically. In districts characterized by higher levels of landholding inequality (and where a higher share of rural workers were found on large farms), employers were able to "control" the supply of voters relatively easily and engage in strategies of electoral repression. By contrast, inequality in the distribution of farms affected political outcomes only indirectly, through access to economic resources rather than to voters. Cross-national research examining the political consequences of rural inequality has privileged the importance of inequalities in the distribution of fixed assets as a predictor of resistance to democratization. By contrast, I hypothesize that this dimension of inequality had a much weaker effect on electoral outcomes and, consequently, on preferences toward political reform.

Whereas inequality in landholding affects the *supply* of voters that can be subjected to electoral manipulation, labor scarcity affects the *price* of electoral intimidation. In districts where agricultural workers are relatively abundant, electoral intimidation costs less politically. In conditions of labor surplus, the bargaining power tilts toward employers. In these districts, the threat of electoral layoffs is relatively powerful and voters are therefore less willing to support opposition political candidates. By contrast, a shortage of agricultural workers constrains the economic power of local landlords, thus raising the costs of electoral intimidation. One contemporary account discussed the implications of labor scarcity for electoral politics in rural districts:

In early times, the electoral pressures of landowners on rural workers were certainly not small. In later periods, landowners had to use this means of power (*Machtmittel*) very carefully because of the labor shortage that existed in the countryside. One was happy if one could keep one's employees and one was careful to not antagonize the employees through electoral harassments and to not drive them to the cities. (Wulff 1922: 13)

TABLE 7.2. *Hypothesized Relationship between Economic Conditions and Political Outcomes*

Economic Variables	Mechanism	Indicator	Effects of an Increase in the Value of This Variable on Support for Electoral Reforms
Landholding Inequality	Affects concentration of financial resources but not access to voters	Landholding Gini coefficient	Effect unclear
Employment Inequality	Affects supply of voters that can be subjected to electoral manipulation	Workers in farms of >200 hectares; agricultural employment Gini	Opposition
Labor shortage	Affects "price" of rural workers and economic costs of electoral repression	Wage in district i as ratio of average real wage in all districts	Support

In a final step of the analysis, let me examine the consequences of these economic conditions for politicians' preferences toward electoral reforms. How did these forms of inequality affect electoral outcomes? Inequality in landholding, I hypothesize, was unlikely to affect the preferences of politicians toward electoral reforms reducing opportunities for electoral intimidation. By contrast, I hypothesize that inequalities in employment were likely to affect preferences toward electoral reforms. I expect that politicians from districts characterized by high levels of landholding inequality were more opposed to electoral reforms that sought to bring about an increase in the secrecy of the vote. Thus, I expect a negative relationship between landholding inequality and support for electoral reforms. Finally, I hypothesize that labor scarcity increased support for electoral reforms. As discussed in Section 7.3, I hypothesize that landlords in areas that experienced labor scarcity were likely to encounter higher costs of electoral intimidation. Consequently, these politicians were likely to find the electoral status quo less attractive and were more likely to support changes in electoral institutions reducing opportunities for electoral intimidation. Table 7.2 summarizes these hypotheses.

7.5. THE ECONOMIC AND POLITICAL DETERMINANTS OF ELECTORAL REFORMS IN PRUSSIA

I turn now to a test of my hypotheses by examining the effects of these economic variables on the proposals to reform the Prussian electoral system. In Chapter 6, I analyzed all of the bills promoting the protection of voter secrecy in national elections. In this chapter, I take a more modest approach by focusing on only two roll call votes in the Prussian lower house that considered the introduction of electoral secrecy in Prussia.[3] These two votes were taken in 1910 and 1912, respectively, at a time when labor scarcity in the Prussian countryside was severely pronounced. They provide us with an ideal opportunity to test the more novel theoretical conjecture advanced in this chapter, which hypothesizes that labor scarcity had a positive effect on the support for electoral reforms.

Conservative politicians opposed electoral secrecy for elections to the Prussian legislature beginning in the early 1880s, when the first proposals to introduce the secret ballot were placed on the agenda of the Prussian lower chamber. Their opposition to electoral secrecy was premised on three interrelated arguments. First, invoking the example of German national elections – where secret voting was nominally guaranteed – they argued that the secret ballot would not reduce the pressure exerted by the powerful economic actors in a district. After all, they argued, electoral pressure in the national elections was much higher than it was in the Prussian elections, which was based on public voting. The secret ballot was nothing than a "means of deception (*Täuschungsmittel*), an instrument that legalized dire deception by employers and exacerbated betrayal by workers. The secret ballot allowed workers to hide their true positions toward their employer and to double-cross employers in cold blood, despite the social welfare provided by the latter. It allowed workers to vote for candidates who were determined to undermine the very existence of the employers" (*Stenographische Berichte des Preussischen Hauses der Abgeordneten* December 16, 1883). Second, conservative politicians argued that "the secret ballot was not reconcilable with the three class system – because the voters could not determine whether the elector (*Wahlmann*)" for whom they voted would support a party representing their interests. By contrast, when elections were public, such control was possible. Third, conservatives expressed the fear that "if one removes one element from the Prussian electoral system, then the entire edifice will collapse on its own" (*Stenographische Berichte des Preussischen Hauses der Abgeordneten* December 5, 1883).

Political efforts to reform the Prussian electoral system intensified after the turn of the century (Wulff 1922). At the time, the heterogeneity in the preferences of politicians representing rural districts increased, as illustrated by intense disagreement "among conservative members of parliament, provincial spokesmen and newspaper editors about the need to accept any reform at all" (Retallack 1988: 164). Retallack summarizes the factors that contributed to this increased divergence in opinions:

---

[3] Given that my current measure of wages includes only rural wages, urban districts are excluded from the analysis. I leave the study of other dimensions of electoral reform in which the urban-rural cleavage is more pronounced for future research. The most direct expression of the urban-rural cleavage during proposals for electoral reform involved the allocation of voters to different "electoral classes" following the tax reforms of the early 1890s.

It had recently become apparent that the Conservatives' intimidation of voters in the rural districts of the East was more than matched by the SPD intimidation of shopkeepers, artisans and non-Socialist voters in the cities of the West. In the end, conservative leaders had come to the conclusion that the secret *Landtag* franchise could be a benefit to them. (Retallack 1988: 164)

At the opening of the 1908 session of the Prussian chamber of parliament, Wilhelm II signaled the support of the monarchy for a reform of Prussia's electoral system that should "correspond to economic development, the diffusion of education, and political understanding," which nudged a divided Conservative Party toward electoral reform (Wilhelm's throne speech, cited in Wulff 1922: 101). Following this announcement, Chancellor Theobald von Bethmann-Hollweg introduced a proposal to reform the Prussian electoral system. In Bethmann-Hollweg's own words, the motivation for this proposal was to help "conservatives regain touch with the mood of the people" after their unpopular behavior during the finance reform struggle of 1909 (Retallack 1988: 164). The proposal recommended the wholesale transformation of Prussia's electoral system, including: 1) a replacement of indirect elections with direct elections; 2) an increase in the size of the districts; 3) the determination of the winner on the basis of the proportional method of representation; and 4) allowing better-educated citizens, such as civil servants (*Beamte*), academics, and officers, to vote in the higher income category. The proposal left two aspects of the Prussian electoral system unchanged: public voting and the *Klassenwahlrecht*.

This bold proposal experienced a dramatic change in the commission of the Prussian lower house (*Drucksachen des Preussischen Abgeordnetentages*: *Schriftlicher Bericht der Komission über ihre Beratungen* 1910: no. 157; *Mündlicher Bericht der Komission über ihre Beratungen durch ihren Berichterstatter Dr. Bell* March 9, 1910). A "black-blue" compromise between conservatives and representatives of the Catholic Party recommended an alternative proposal of electoral reform, one that maintained indirect elections to the Prussian lower house but also introduced voter secrecy. As one contemporary conservative publication reflected on this compromise, "despite our serious reservations, this is less dangerous than the proposal of the government to introduce direct elections and a highly dubious proportional representation" (Konservative Partei 1910: 11).

In the empirical analysis that follows, I concentrate on two votes. The first vote was taken on March 10, 1910, in the lower house of deputies of the Prussian parliament. This was a vote on a proposal to change the Prussian electoral system to a direct electoral system with secret ballots.[4] This proposal to reform

---

[4] The specific wording of the proposal was as follows: "Soll der Antrag der Abgeordneten Aronsohn und Genossen zur zweiten Beratung der Wahlgesetznovelle (Drucksache Nr. 172) und zwar der zweite Satz des vorgeschlagenen Paragraph 4 folgenden Wortlauts: Die Abgeordneten werden von den stimmberechtigten Wählern des Wahlbezirks mittels verdeckter Stimmzettel unmittelbar gewählt."

the Prussian electoral system was ultimately defeated because of the inability of the two houses of the Prussian parliament to reach a compromise and because of the unwillingness of the Prussian government to step in and resolve this disagreement (Wulff 1922: 170). Although an agreement between the two houses of parliament over the introduction of secret elections was reached, the proposals ultimately foundered over other minor details of electoral design, such as the income thresholds that would be used to assign voters to different electoral classes (the so-called *Maximierung*) (Wulff 1922: 175). The proposal to adopt the secret ballot came on the agenda of the Prussian lower house one additional time prior to World War I on May 20, 1912. This is the second vote analyzed in this chapter. In a recent paper, Ziblatt (2008) argues that inequality in landholding is a robust predictor of opposition to this May 20, 1912, vote. By contrast, I hypothesize that labor market conditions in a district – especially labor market scarcity – affect in direct and immediate ways electoral competition and, thus, demand for electoral secrecy. In addition to testing for the effects of a shortage of rural voters, my analysis differs from the analysis presented by Ziblatt in several respects. First, I make use of *all* roll call votes recorded at that time (rather than a subset of the votes). As a result, the number of observations reported in my analysis is twice as large as the number of observations reported by Ziblatt. I also use measures of political competition for each politician (MARGIN) and a measure of the political fragmentation in a district. A final point of contrast is that I also report models controlling for the partisan affiliation of the politician.

My working hypothesis is that politicians in districts that experience labor market shortages are less likely to support the electoral status quo than are politicians from labor abundant districts. This difference in the preferences of politicians from labor scarce and labor abundant districts could be attributed to their different costs of labor repression. Politicians in labor scarce districts are less likely to owe their political victory to electoral intimidation. I empirically explore the consequences of labor shortages alongside political competition in a district to explain the variation in support for electoral institutions.

Because the unit of analysis is now the Prussian electoral district (whose geographic boundaries differed from the boundaries of the electoral districts to the national parliament), I have recalculated all economic and social covariates at the level of the Prussian district, using the correspondence tables mapping localities into districts that are presented in Kühne (1994). Table 7.3 presents descriptive information about the values of the variables for Prussian electoral districts. Because of significant gerrymandering that occurred in the drawing of the boundaries of Prussian districts, the maximum values of rural inequality are higher in the Prussian electoral districts than they are in the districts that were used for German national elections. I supplement the existing variables with two additional measures of political competition at the district level. First, to measure the electoral vulnerability of different politicians, I include a measure

TABLE 7.3. *Description of the Main Explanatory Variables Used in the Analysis*

Variable	Obs	Mean	Std. Dev.	Min.	Max.	Source
Labor Shortage	372	1.00	0.19	0.60	1.52	Grant 2005*
Gini of Agricultural Employment	480	0.56	0.07	0.00	0.71	Königliches Preussisches Statistisches Landesamt 1907
Gini of Landholding Inequality	483	0.77	0.09	0.49	0.94	Ziblatt 2008**
Workers on Farms of >200 hectares (%)	453	0.99	1.42	0.00	11.08	Königliches Preussisches Statistisches Landesamt 1907
Linguistic Fractionalization	453	0.12	0.18	0.00	0.69	Königliches Preussisches Statistisches Landesamt 1900
Economic Development	453	0.60	9.38	13.87	99.56	ICPSR 1984
Catholics (%)	485	36.80	36.51	0.00	100.00	Hohls and Kaelble 1989
Margin	476	60.18	34.49	0.60	100.00	ICPSR 1984
Divided	472	0.11	0.32	0.00	1.00	

Notes: * Based on *Zeitschrift des Preussischen Statistischen Bureaus* 1904; ** Based on *Statistik des Deutschen Reiches* 1898.

for their margin of victory. I code this variable according to the historical information reported by Kühne (1994), who presents information about the vote share received by each politician elected to the Prussian lower house and that of each runner-up. I find wide variability in the electoral vulnerability of politicians across Prussian districts. The variable MARGIN takes values between 0.60 and 100.00, with an average of 60.10 and a standard deviation of 34.48. I expect a negative relationship between margin and the support for the secrecy of the ballot. Because some of the Prussian electoral districts were multimember districts, I compute a measure of the political fragmentation in each district. The variable DIVIDED takes the value of 1 if the district was represented by politicians from different political parties and the value of 0 otherwise. Finally, I add dummies for the parties with the largest legislative contingent: the Free Conservative Party, National Liberal Party, Zentrum, and Social Democrat Party (with Conservatives being omitted).

The specifications reported also include a range of additional economic and political controls. To control for the level of economic development of a district, I include a measure of the percentage of the population employed in industry and services (ECONOMIC DEVELOPMENT). I also use two additional controls for the religious and linguistic fragmentation of a district. The first variable (CATHOLICS) measures the percentage of the Catholics in a district (ICPSR 1984). The second variable (LINGUISTIC FRACTIONAL-IZATION) measures the linguistic fragmentation of a district. To compute this measure, I take advantage of information collected by the Prussian Statistical Office in 1900 on the mother tongue spoken in each locality (*Gemeinde*) within Prussia (Königliches Preussisches Statistisches Landesamt 1900). The list of language communities within Prussia is rather large and includes twenty possible "mother tongues." In addition to Polish, Danish, and Lithuanian – which were the largest non–German-speaking minorities – other language communities in Prussia included speakers of West Slavic dialects, such as Masurian and Kasubian (*Kaschubisch*) (Königliches Preussisches Statistisches Landesamt 1900). Using this information, I compute a measure of linguistic fractionalization as 1 minus the Herfindahl Index of ethnolinguistic group shares. I find significant variation in the linguistic heterogeneity across Prussian districts. The measure of linguistic fragmentation takes values between a minimum of 0.01 and a maximum of 0.68, with a mean of 0.12.

For each vote, I code the dependent variable (vote for reform) in three ways: first, I compare "yes" to other types of votes (abstentions and "nos"); second, I exclude abstentions from the analysis and only concentrate on the "yes" and "no" votes; and finally, I follow the ordinal ranking proposed by Ziblatt and treat "yes" votes as 2, abstentions as 1, and "no" votes as 0. Table 7.4 presents results for each of these models, with and without partisan controls, respectively. The first four models are estimated as probit models, whereas the last two models are estimated as ordered probit.

It is interesting to note that regardless of the coding of the dependent variable, proposal, and inclusion of party identification dummies, the variable proxying for labor market conditions is the measure of rural inequality that consistently affects elite incentives to support electoral reform. In particular, the reported marginal effects suggest that politicians from districts experiencing labor shortage were more likely to approve both bills. These effects are sizable considering the sample probability of voting for reform in each year (see the last row in Table 7.4). Building from the coefficients of Models 1 and 3, Figure 7.4 simulates the probability of supporting both bills across the full range of labor shortage proxy while holding the rest of the variables at their mean or modal values. A one–standard deviation change in labor shortage is associated with an increase in the probability of support of electoral reform from 61 percent to 81 percent in 1910 and from 45 percent to 51 percent in 1912.

Among other findings, the electoral vulnerability of each politician also shapes the incentives to support electoral reform, with politicians in tighter races favoring greater electoral secrecy, although the effect of this variable is relatively small. By contrast, the level of partisan fragmentation in Prussia's

TABLE 7.4. *Marginal Effects after Probit: Parliamentary Votes on Electoral Reforms (March 11, 1910, and May 20, 1912)*

	Yes vs. Others				Excluding Abstentions				Ordinal Ranking			
	1910		1912		1910		1912		1910		1912	
Labor Shortage	0.617***	0.354***	0.492***	0.329*	0.739***	0.361*	0.905***	0.633**	0.508***	0.235**	0.429***	0.254*
	(0.125)	(0.130)	(0.165)	(0.191)	(0.148)	(0.189)	(0.258)	(0.272)	(0.111)	(0.108)	(0.136)	(0.140)
Gini of Landholding Inequality	0.306	0.255	−0.224	−0.152	0.346	0.777*	−0.205	0.383	0.233	0.167	0.082	0.271
	(0.280)	(0.280)	(0.383)	(0.443)	(0.332)	(0.414)	(0.564)	(0.585)	(0.241)	(0.229)	(0.329)	(0.342)
Workers on Farms of >200 hectares (%)	−0.009	0.000	−0.035	−0.029	−0.017	−0.013	−0.087	−0.042	−0.023	−0.011	−0.069**	−0.049**
	(0.017)	(0.014)	(0.031)	(0.031)	(0.021)	(0.023)	(0.053)	(0.045)	(0.018)	(0.014)	(0.029)	(0.025)
Economic Development	0.041	0.049	0.108**	0.116**	0.051	0.046	0.215***	0.219***	0.018	0.027	0.093**	0.079*
	(0.040)	(0.035)	(0.052)	(0.061)	(0.046)	(0.051)	(0.071)	(0.075)	(0.037)	(0.031)	(0.043)	(0.045)
Linguistic Fractionalization	0.285**	0.192*	−0.198	−0.305	0.362***	0.242	−0.071	0.282	0.266**	0.169*	−0.055	−0.042
	(0.118)	(0.114)	(0.183)	(0.213)	(0.132)	(0.165)	(0.222)	(0.231)	(0.107)	(0.101)	(0.142)	(0.142)
Catholics (%)	−0.001*	0.001	0.003***	0.004**	−0.001*	0.002	0.009***	0.005***	−0.001*	0.001	0.005***	0.003***
	(0.001)	(0.001)	(0.001)	(0.001)	(0.001)	(0.001)	(0.001)	(0.002)	(0.001)	(0.001)	(0.001)	(0.001)
Margin	−0.003***	−0.002***	−0.002**	−0.002**	−0.003***	−0.003***	−0.001	−0.002*	−0.003***	−0.002***	−0.001	−0.001
	(0.001)	(0.001)	(0.001)	(0.001)	(0.001)	(0.001)	(0.001)	(0.001)	(0.001)	(0.001)	(0.001)	(0.001)
Divided	0.102	0.040	0.090	0.104	0.106	0.001	0.006	−0.017	0.065	0.022	0.004	0.002
	(0.078)	(0.067)	(0.089)	(0.105)	(0.086)	(0.079)	(0.108)	(0.109)	(0.069)	(0.059)	(0.075)	(0.075)
Free Conservative Party		−0.066				−0.090*				−0.092***		−0.151***
		(0.041)				(0.052)				(0.033)		(0.046)
National Liberal Party		0.460***		0.222**		0.906***		0.646***		0.557***		0.324***
		(0.093)		(0.099)		(0.030)		(0.099)		(0.068)		(0.088)
Zentrum		−0.126***		0.028		−0.122*				−0.107**		0.210**
		(0.047)		(0.122)		(0.069)				(0.046)		(0.102)
Social Democratic Party										0.876		0.779***
										(.)		(0.026)
Observation	347	346	364	303	306	305	287	200	347	347	364	347
Prob(y = 1)	0.151	0.121	0.262	0.298	0.171	0.148	0.349	0.246	0.162	0.127	0.249	0.226

Notes: Robust standard errors are in brackets; *** $p<0.01$; ** $p<0.05$; * $p<0.10$.

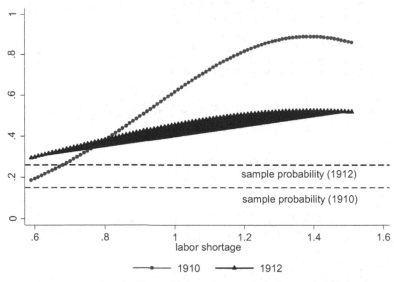

FIGURE 7.4. Simulated effect of labor shortage on the probability of support for electoral reforms.

multimember districts has no effect on the probability of support for reforms. Among the partisan variables, the Social Democrats and National Liberals have strong, positive effects in support of reforms.

As a final robustness check, Table 7.5 reports results from an IV approach, in which I assess the effects of labor market conditions on the probability of electoral reform using the productivity and outflow variables as instruments for labor shortage, along with several IV diagnostics. With one exception, the IV coefficients behave in the expected direction and reach standard levels of statistical significance. It is important to note that the two instruments are indeed relevant: the correlations between labor shortage, productivity, and migration are 0.14 and −0.55 respectively, and both are statistically significant at the 1 percent level. Additionally, note that the Wald F-statistics for the first stage regressions are well above the critical values identified by Stock and Yogo 2005: 80–105) as indicating a problem with weak instruments. Additionally, because the model is overidentified, I can test whether the instruments are exogenous. The usual econometric approach to this identification question is to run a test of overidentification. The results of these tests fail to reject the null hypothesis that the IVs are uncorrelated with the structural error (exclusion restriction). Finally, the test of exogeneity (Durbin-Wu-Hausman test) does not lead me to conclude that the labor shortage proxy is an endogenous variable. Because 2SLS can yield inefficient estimates when endogeneity is not significant, I am confident that the results presented in the previous tables do not suffer from a consistency problem.

TABLE 7.5. *Parliamentary Vote on Electoral Reforms: IV Estimates*

	Yes vs. Others		Excluding Abstentions		Ordinal Ranking	
	1910 IV-2SLS	1912 IV-2SLS	1910 IV-2SLS	1912 IV-2SLS	1910 IV-Ordered Probit	1912 IV-Ordered Probit
Labor Shortage	0.658**	0.390	0.690**	0.954***	1.457**	1.304**
	(0.293)	(0.294)	(0.292)	(0.322)	(0.700)	(0.591)
Gini of Landholding Inequality	0.247	−0.691	0.138	−0.526	1.048	0.596
	(0.360)	(0.423)	(0.413)	(0.439)	(1.059)	(1.088)
Workers on farms of >200 hectares (%)	−0.007	−0.007	−0.007	−0.013	−0.111	−0.311***
	(0.012)	(0.014)	(0.012)	(0.014)	(0.086)	(0.107)
Economic Development	0.006	0.061	0.006	0.099*	0.105	0.242*
	(0.053)	(0.054)	(0.060)	(0.058)	(0.134)	(0.133)
Linguistic Fractionalization	0.385**	−0.063	0.447**	0.166	1.012**	−0.112
	(0.174)	(0.190)	(0.177)	(0.169)	(0.475)	(0.426)
Catholics (%)	−0.001	0.003***	−0.001	0.007***	−0.004	0.015***
	(0.001)	(0.001)	(0.001)	(0.001)	(0.002)	(0.002)
Margin	−0.003***	−0.002*	−0.003***	−0.001	−0.011***	−0.003
	(0.001)	(0.001)	(0.001)	(0.001)	(0.002)	(0.002)
Divided	0.112	0.038	0.104	−0.043	0.238	0.059
	(0.089)	(0.090)	(0.096)	(0.104)	(0.223)	(0.213)
Constant	−0.567	−0.220	−0.455	−1.363		
	(0.837)	(0.862)	(0.886)	(0.885)		
Observations	298	314	261	244	368	368
Wald F-Statistic (First Stage)	24.32	39.76	24.18	31.22		
DWH Test P-Value	0.94	0.48	0.94	0.32		
Overidentification Test P-Value						
Hansen J-Statistic	0.352	0.106	0.385	0.229		

Notes: Robust standard errors are in parentheses; *** p<0.01; ** p<0.05; * p<0.10.

7.6. CONCLUSION

The findings of this chapter about the political implications of labor shortages in countries with high inequality in the distribution of fixed assets open up a range of additional implications for the comparative literature that examines the economic preconditions of democratization. First, they suggest that theoretical accounts of democratization need to examine the consequences of labor mobility on electoral politics in societies where electoral systems generate significant opportunities for electoral intimidation. Labor mobility creates regional inequalities in the abundance or shortage of agricultural workers. I showed that the relative shortage in the supply of rural workers opened up a political cleavage among politicians from rural areas over the desirability of electoral reforms. Because of the relatively higher costs of economic repression there, politicians from areas that experienced labor shortages were more likely to support changes in electoral institutions and reforms of electoral secrecy than were politicians in areas with a relative abundance of agricultural workers.

This chapter generates a number of implications that can be tested in a broad comparative framework. First, economic shocks that generate intra-regional differences in the costs of "electoral intimidation" precede and spur changes in political institutions. Democratizing reforms are less likely to happen in economies experiencing an "unlimited supply of workers," to use Lewis's (1954) term. Second, labor shortage during the early onset of democratic transitions lowers the electoral strength of actors who owed their victories to the ample intimidation of voters. Labor scarcity, I showed, is likely to change the composition of the political coalition that supports changes in electoral institutions. Because of the high costs of strategies aimed at electoral intimidation, politicians from labor scarce areas may join the political coalition supporting change in electoral institutions. By contrast, rural politicians from labor abundant areas are likely to persist in their support of existing electoral rules. Political cleavages and coalitions over electoral reforms are predicted by relative labor shortages and not by inequalities in the distribution of land.

8

Voting for Opposition Candidates

Economic Concentration, Skills, and Political Support for Social Democracy

The literature on the origin and development of the German Social Democratic Party (SPD) is vast. The puzzle about the steady increase in electoral strength of a party whose voters were subjected to systematic harassment and intimidation throughout the political history of the Empire has fueled the imaginations of every generation of historians and political scientists. What explains the rise in electoral strength of the SPD, and how did it become the largest political party in the Reich? I draw on a wealth of new economic data unavailable to previous scholars in order to reexamine this classic research question in comparative politics.

An analysis of the cross-sectional and temporal variation in the electoral strength of the SPD allows me to test a range of additional observable implications of the theoretical framework developed in this book. The first part of the book (Chapters 1–4) developed a number of hypotheses about the relationship between economic and political conditions in German districts and the "costs of electoral repression" encountered by private actors. I showed that the costs were higher in districts characterized by high levels of economic heterogeneity. The costs of electoral intimidation for state employees – such as policemen and tax collectors – also varied significantly across districts and were higher in districts characterized by high levels of political fragmentation among right-wing parties, where the outcome of a race was determined in runoffs. This chapter explores an additional observable implication of this analysis: I examine the factors that affected the variation in the willingness of voters to take political and economic risks by supporting opposition candidates. The corollary of the empirical findings presented in the first part of this book is that political support for Social Democratic candidates should be higher in districts where state employees and private actors faced higher relative costs of electoral intimidation. In districts where private actors faced higher costs of electoral repression, voters were more likely to take risks and support opposition candidates, because the threat of post-electoral punishment by employers was less credible. Similarly, if candidates and employees of the state were constrained in their use of electoral repression (by political considerations about the possible adverse effects of the use of intimidation on the willingness of other candidates on the right to form electoral coalitions), then this again created a political opportunity for the electoral mobilization of opposition candidates. In Chapter 2, I conjectured that regional and temporal variation in electoral support for opposition candidates can be predicted by variation in the cost of electoral intimidation.

The empirical analysis in this chapter also examines the influence of the legislation adopted in 1903 – which mandated the introduction of ballot envelopes and isolating spaces – on the willingness of voters to support opposition candidates. The 1903 election represented a turning point in the political history of German Social Democracy. During the 1898 election, the number of voters cast for Social Democratic candidates stood at 2.1 million. By 1903, the number of Social Democratic votes exceeded 3 million. In this chapter, I explore the political consequences of the legislation protecting voter secrecy for the subsequent temporal and cross-sectional variation in the electoral strength of Social Democracy.

The chapter is organized as follows. I begin in Section 8.1 by outlining additional observable implications of the analysis developed in the first part of the book on voters' willingness to support opposition candidates. One interesting and novel empirical implication is that the economic heterogeneity of a district likely affected the electoral strength of Social Democracy. I hypothesize that the strength of Social Democracy was higher in economically heterogeneous districts where employers faced a higher cost of electoral repression. To my knowledge, this is the first study that demonstrates empirically the existence of a strong and robust relationship between the economic heterogeneity of a district and the political strength of Social Democracy. In Section 8.2, I provide a brief overview of the temporal and regional variation in the political strategies that employees of the state and employers used in the electoral intimidation of Social Democratic voters. The systematic harassment of ballot conveyors and other electoral agents who mobilized on behalf of Social Democratic candidates and of voters expressing political allegiances for the SPD did not end with the lifting of the anti-socialist legislation but rather continued during subsequent decades. Drawing on a combination of historical sources, I discuss the strategies of electoral repression directed against Social Democratic candidates during the decades following the abolition of the anti-socialist law. In Section 8.3, I provide an empirical test of the hypothesis that the level of political support for Social Democratic candidates was higher in districts where private actors and public election officials faced higher costs of electoral intimidation. The empirical tests presented in this section examine distinct factors that affected the magnitude of the costs of electoral intimidation. In the first set of models, I examine the effects of the economic and political conditions in German districts on electoral support for Social Democratic candidates. In the second set of empirical tests, I examine the effects of the scarcity of agricultural labor on the political strength of Social Democratic candidates in a district. Because of the absence of measures of rural labor scarcity for the entire Empire, these empirical models are restricted to Prussian districts only. In my final set of models, I examine the effects of the legislation adopted in 1903 on electoral support for Social Democracy. The chapter concludes by showing how regional differences in the history of the intimidation and harassment of Social Democratic candidates caused variation in the political strategies used by Social Democratic candidates. I reexamine a political hypothesis formulated by Gregory Luebbert (1991) in his study *Liberalism, Fascism, or Social Democracy.* Luebbert suggests that the absence of "Lib-Lab" electoral alliances between Social Democratic candidates and liberal candidates accounts for Germany's non-democratic political trajectory during the interwar period. By taking advantage of fine-grained district-level information about electoral alliances formed in German elections, I show that the probability of the formation of Lib-Lab electoral alliances varied significantly across German districts. I argue that the history of electoral intimidation in a district predicts the probability of the formation of Lib-Lab electoral coalitions.

8.1. TAKING RISKS: ELECTORAL INTIMIDATION AND ELECTORAL SUPPORT FOR SOCIAL DEMOCRATIC CANDIDATES

German voters who contemplated casting their ballot in favor of Social Democratic candidates faced a barrage of electoral pressures, ranging from political harassment by policemen or *Landräte* to threats of layoffs by private economic actors. As the previous chapters demonstrated, the intensity of these political and economic threats varied significantly across districts. I hypothesize that voters encountered spaces of political freedom allowing them to cast their ballots in support of opposition candidates in districts where private economic actors and employees of the state faced higher costs of electoral intimidation.

As the previous chapters demonstrated, supporting Social Democratic candidates carried potential economic costs for voters. The highest economic cost was being dismissed from their jobs for their political choices. An analysis of the variation in the electoral strength of Social Democracy needs to uncover the factors that facilitated risk-taking by voters. In Chapter 2, I formulated a number of hypotheses about the determinants of electoral support for opposition candidates before and after the adoption of the Rickert law. I only briefly discuss those hypotheses here. As discussed in that chapter, one simple way to analyze the calculations made by a voter who considered casting his ballot in favor of a Social Democratic candidate is to assess the relative magnitude of three components of his utility. The first was a net gain in utility that encompassed the expected gains from electing a representative who could advocate for policies closer to those preferred by voters. In the case of Social Democratic candidates, such policies included tax reforms lowering the regressive burden of indirect taxes and trade reforms that lowered the price of bread. Voters were likely to weigh these potential gains in utility against likely losses. The second term in the utility of voters was an estimation of the punishment that could be imposed by an employer if the latter identified voters' choices. This punishment was affected by the probability of an employer being able to detect the political choices of its employees. Finally, voters assessed the probability of being reemployed if their employers punished them for supporting a Social Democratic candidate by laying them off.

In contrast to standard models of electoral choice, I hypothesize that voters weighed the net expected gain in utility they derived from supporting a Social Democratic candidate against the likely loss in income they would face if their employers identified their vote choice and punished them for their political decisions. These additional assumptions about the utility of voters are justified because of the existence of ample evidence of voters having been subjected to economic punishments by their employers in the German political context. The expectations of economic losses by voters were, in turn, affected by a number of additional factors. The first was the probability that their opposition vote would be detected. One important determinant of this probability was voting technology. Improvements in voting technology were likely to reduce the probability of detection and reduce the fear of economic reprisals by employers. In conditions in which the secrecy of the vote was perfectly protected, voters' expected loss of income as a result of punishment by employers was likely to approach zero.

In conditions in which ballot secrecy was imperfectly protected, the probability of detection was affected by the decisions of state employees and private actors to monitor voters' choices. The amount of effort devoted by these actors to the monitoring of voters' choices was in turn affected by a range of additional political and economic conditions. Repression by employees of the state was likely to be higher in conditions of right-wing political coordination and to decline as right-wing fragmentation increased. The monitoring costs for private actors were likely to be lower in districts with high economic concentration and to increase as the heterogeneity of a district increased.

The magnitude of the economic loss experienced by Social Democratic voters whose choices were identified by employers was also likely to vary across districts. The factors affecting the willingness of employers to punish workers who had "dangerous" political views varied systematically across districts, and the factors affecting this variation have been analyzed on repeated occasions throughout this book. The punishment of subversive voters, I hypothesize, was more likely in concentrated economic districts and in conditions of labor surplus. Firms were also more likely to lay off unskilled employees as opposed to skilled employees.

Finally, voters' decisions to take "political risks" and support opposition candidates were also affected by their ability to find other employment if they were laid off. These opportunities for reemployment were higher in conditions of labor scarcity than they were in conditions of labor abundance. I also conjecture that these opportunities for reemployment were higher in districts with high occupational heterogeneity because of the presence of other firms with similar production profiles. It is ex ante unclear whether the opportunities for reemployment for high skilled or low skilled workers were higher. Voters with higher reemployment opportunities were more likely to support Social Democratic candidates than were voters with fewer reemployment opportunities.

8.2. THE ECONOMIC AND POLITICAL DETERMINANTS OF ELECTORAL SUPPORT FOR SOCIAL DEMOCRATIC CANDIDATES

The abolition of anti-socialist legislation did not end the electoral repression of Social Democratic candidates. An internal memorandum of the Prussian Ministry of the Interior from July 1890 summarized the new approach of bureaucratic officials toward the SPD after anti-socialist laws were abolished (Wittwer 1983: 93; Kupfer 2003: 288). Lower-level bureaucratic officials were urged to exploit every legally permissible means to prevent Social Democratic candidates from organizing politically. After the abolition of the anti-socialist law, Prussian bureaucratic officials relied primarily on other laws – such as the law on associations and the law governing the freedom of the press – to prevent Social Democratic candidates from competing in a district.

Under the provisions of the anti-socialist law, policemen could close Social Democratic meetings (para. 9, sec. 2). Although such unmediated strategies were no longer available after 1890, bureaucratic officials in the Prussian Ministry of the Interior recommended that policemen continue to monitor Social Democratic electoral meetings, submit detailed reports of all the statements made at these meetings, and note any possible violations of the provisions of the 1850 Prussian law of associations. Any action that could "pose dangers for public safety" created a legal pretext for intervention by policemen and cancellation of the meeting. As a result, Prussian Ministry of the Interior officials urged policemen to exercise rigorous surveillance during meetings and immediately intervene if speakers made statements that could be prosecuted under the provisions of the 1850 law. Policemen were also urged to contact military personnel if they anticipated a disruption of the public order.

In the same memorandum, officials of the Prussian Ministry of the Interior noted that the number of Social Democratic publications was likely to increase following the abolition of the anti-socialist law. This included both partisan newspapers and also other electoral material. The law of the press from 1874 defined politically permissible statements. If violations of this law occurred, policemen were instructed to intervene swiftly and confiscate the materials.

The most pervasive strategy used by policemen and *Landräte* to preempt Social Democratic mobilization was to allege violations of the law of associations. Wide discrepancy existed in the ways in which local policemen interpreted the existing legislation. Kupfer notes a high level of arbitrariness in the actions of low-level state employees immediately after the abolition of anti-socialist laws. Low-level officials "ended up creating their own legislation. This was especially true with respect to the application of association law in rural areas" (Kupfer 2003: 100). Social Democratic candidates could contest obvious abuses in courts. However, this strategy was also fraught with danger, seeing as courts were themselves erratic and interpreted law in diametrically opposed ways (Schultze 1973).

Finally, policemen and other employees of the state could hinder Social Democratic candidates from organizing by turning a blind eye to incidents of electoral violence directed against the latter. In Bielefeld in 1891, in an event that was later known as the Battle of Spenge (*die Schlacht von Spenge*), a local priest and supporter of the Anti-Semitic Party led a mob of 1,500 peasants in an attack on a Social Democratic meeting (Kranzmann 1981: 79). The 500 "red voters" asked for electoral support from the local policemen, but the latter refused to intervene. The passivity of the law enforcers allowed the peasants to expel the "reds" from the village. This incident had lasting political consequences for the electoral strategy used by the SPD in the countryside: the party shifted its strategy toward "silent rural agitation" (Kupfer 2003: 104).

On numerous occasions, employees of the Prussian administration shared information with prominent local employers about voters who showed political sympathy with Social Democratic candidates. The sources of this sensitive information were the records of military recruitment, where detailed information about partisan affiliation was collected. *Landräte* urged employers to lay off workers with such sympathies and force them to leave the locality and the region (Kupfer 2003: 98). Consider the following examples, which illustrate the type of political and economic intimidation that was pervasive in the years following the abolition of anti-socialist laws. In 1891, the *Landrat* in Goarshausen, a locality in Wiesbaden, asked local employers to lay off a number of workers who had migrated to the district and who were believed to support the SPD. The employers complied, and the *Landräte* reported that "absolute peace" returned to the district (Kupfer 2003: 98). The same report noted that Höchste Farbwerke, a company in Wiesbaden, initially resisted pressure by local officials. One year later, workers in that company tried to mobilize support for the Social Democratic candidate in the company, and Höchste Farbwerke laid them off (Kupfer 2003: 98).

Electoral layoffs were also reported in other localities. In Arnsberg, people with Social Democratic loyalties experienced difficulty finding employment in the local mines. In the Saar region, a region that was also referred to as "Kingdom Stumm," firms were reported to have "coordinated" by refusing to re-hire workers who had been laid off by another company for supporting

Social Democratic candidates. The dismissal slips given to workers contained a variety of signals by which firms obliquely communicated politically motivated dismissals. Similar reports of "economic coordination" to prevent Social Democratic supporters from finding jobs were reported in Düsseldorf. There, a local glass manufacturer, the Gerresheimer Glasfabrik, coordinated local firms to not rehire workers with known Social Democratic political sympathies.

The combination of political pressures by state employees and economic pressures by employers had consequences for the mobilizational capacity of Social Democratic candidates. Numerous studies on the political history of German Social Democracy share this observation. Kupfer argues:

The material livelihood of workers was threatened by the fact that employers worked hand in hand with policemen in many localities. The fear of potential members of the Social Democratic Party that the membership list would be conveyed by policemen to local employers delayed the formation of a number of Social Democratic organizations and limited the membership growth among the existing organizations. (Kupfer 2003: 140)

8.3. EMPIRICAL ANALYSIS

This section tests the hypotheses outlined in the previous sections by analyzing variation in the electoral strength of the SPD. I begin by analyzing the determinants of electoral strength of Social Democratic candidates during the period before the 1903 election. The central dependent variable of the analysis is the electoral vote share of the SPD across the 397 electoral districts of the German Empire. Then, I estimate a range of models examining the implications of the legislation that introduced ballot envelopes and electoral support for Social Democratic candidates.

Chapter 5 discusses at greater length the construction of the main variables used in the empirical analysis. Here I keep the presentation of these variables concise.

ECONOMIC CONCENTRATION: Time-varying Herfindahl-Hirschman Index of economic concentration. Source: Statistisches Reichsamt 1898a, 1898b, 1909a, 1909b.

SKILL INDUSTRY: Measure of skilled workers as a share of the labor force employed in industry.

SKILL ALL: Measure of skilled workers as a share of all workers in the district. This measure is time invariant (measured in 1895 only) because of the absence of a disaggregated measure of all agricultural workers in the 1905 census.

ENRP (EFFECTIVE NUMBER OF RIGHT-WING PARTIES): Measure of right-wing political fragmentation in the district calculated as the sum of squares of the votes received by all parties on the political right. Source: ICPSR 1984.

TABLE 8.1. *The Economic and Political Correlates of Social Democratic Support Prior to the Adoption of Rickert Law*

	Variables	Model 1	Model 2	Model 3	Model 4	Model 5
Economic Factors	Occupational Heterogeneity	−0.22*** (0.05)	−0.18*** (0.05)		−0.23*** (0.05)	−0.20*** (0.05)
	Skill Industry	0.42*** (0.02)			0.38*** (0.02)	
	Skill All		0.30*** (0.02)			0.28*** (0.02)
Political Factors	ENRP			−0.00 (0.01)	−0.00 (0.01)	−0.00 (0.01)
	Second			0.11*** (0.02)	0.08*** (0.02)	0.10*** (0.02)
	ENRP*Second			−0.02*** (0.00)	−0.02*** (0.00)	−0.02*** (0.00)
Controls	Catholics	−0.00*** (0.00)	−0.00*** (0.00)	−0.00*** (0.00)	−0.00*** (0.00)	−0.00*** (0.00)
	Economic Development	−0.00 (0.00)	0.00*** (0.00)	0.00*** (0.00)	−0.00 (0.00)	0.00*** (0.00)
	Rural Inequality	−0.03* (0.02)	−0.03* (0.02)	0.04* (0.02)	−0.03 (0.02)	−0.03 (0.02)
	Population	1.37*** (0.07)	1.47*** (0.08)	1.56*** (0.08) (0.02)	1.26*** (0.07)	1.34*** (0.08) (0.02)
	Constant	−0.14*** (0.02)	−0.17*** (0.02)	−0.18*** (0.02)	−0.11*** (0.02)	−0.13*** (0.02)
	Fixed Effects for Regions?	Y	Y	Y	Y	Y
	Observations	3,937	3,937	3,543	3,543	3,543
	R-Squared	0.56	0.53	0.57	0.62	0.60
	Ll	3,453	3,326	3,072	3,298	3,210

Notes: Robust standard errors are in parentheses; *** $p<0.01$; ** $p<0.05$; * $p<0.10$.

SECOND: Variable that takes a value of 1 if the outcome of the race was determined during a runoff.

ECONOMIC DEVELOPMENT: The percentage of the labor force in agriculture. Source: Reibel 2007.

LANDHOLDING INEQUALITY: A Gini measure of landholding inequality. Source: Ziblatt 2008.

CATHOLICS: The percentage of Catholics in a district. Source: ICPSR 1984.

POPULATION: The population of a district. Source: ICPSR 1984.

Table 8.1 presents the results of the analysis of electoral support for Social Democratic candidates during the period prior to 1903, the year when

Germany adopted ballot envelopes and isolating spaces. The dependent variable is the vote share for Social Democratic candidates. All specifications include fixed effects for different German provinces. Models 1 and 2 report the results of reduced-form "economic models" that examine the relationship between the economic conditions in a district and electoral support for Social Democratic candidates. The main difference between the two models is the measure of skill, with Model 1 using SKILL INDUSTRY and Model 2 using SKILL ALL. Consistent with the main theoretical hypothesis, I find that the Social Democratic vote share is higher in districts with higher levels of occupational heterogeneity. I also find a positive relationship between the skill intensity of the labor force in a district and the Social Democratic vote share there. One possible interpretation of this finding is that more highly skilled workers were more likely to defy pressure from employers, take political risks, and support opposition candidates.

Model 3 is a reduced-form political model that examines the relationship between district-level political variables and the political strength of Social Democracy. This model examines whether particular political conditions in a district that are hypothesized to have increased the costs of political intimidation also affected the strength of Social Democracy. As hypothesized in Chapter 2, candidates that competed in districts with a fragmented political right where the race was decided in a runoff were likely to face high costs of political intimidation. That was likely to deter them from using the state apparatus against their political opponents. As such, I hypothesize that the constraint on the ability of these candidates to use the resources of the state during elections was likely associated with higher levels of political strength of Social Democracy. The empirical results do not confirm this hypothesis. I find that the Social Democratic vote share was lower in districts with a fragmented right and in races that were won during runoffs.

Models 4 and 5 present specifications that include all of the economic and political factors hypothesized to have affected the political strength of Social Democracy in a district by incentivizing economic and political actors to engage in electoral intimidation. The basic results of the previous models remain unchanged. I find support for the economic hypotheses about the determinants of the vote share of Social Democracy but not for the political hypotheses. The economic factors in a district that were conducive to voters' greater willingness to take political risks and support Social Democratic candidates include the district's economic heterogeneity and the skill profile of its labor force. The results on other control variables are consistent with previous findings: I find higher Social Democratic strength in more populous and economically more developed districts, as well as in districts with a lower Catholic population. There was no robust relationship between the level of landholding inequality and Social Democratic vote share prior to the adoption of the Rickert law.

Figure 8.1 plots the predicted relationship between the skill composition of the labor force and the political strength of Social Democracy. Although

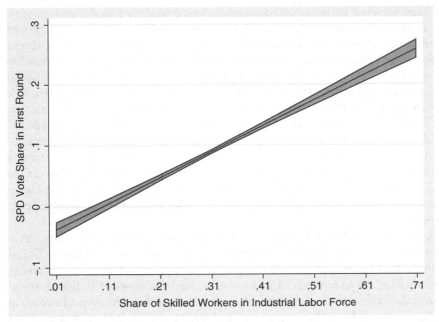

FIGURE 8.1. Predicted relationship between the share of skilled workers in the industrial labor force and political support for Social Democracy prior to 1903.

a vast amount of the historical literature on the political origins of the SPD has conjectured that political support for Social Democracy came primarily from skilled workers, this study presents for the first time systematic evidence to support this conjecture. Chapter 2 discussed possible mechanisms by which the skill level of a worker affected his political calculations at the ballot box and his willingness to take electoral risks and support opposition candidates. Given that firms incurred higher costs to train skilled workers, it is likely that they would be more reluctant to lay off these workers on account of their political views. Anticipating these constrains of firms, higher workers were more willing to take risks in the political marketplace, defy the pressures of their employers and support Social Democratic candidates even in conditions where voting secrecy was not entirely protected.

How did the changes in electoral rules adopted in 1903 affect the willingness of voters to support Social Democratic candidates? The Rickert law, which mandated the introduction of ballot envelopes and isolating spaces, created a space of political freedom that gave voters the ability to cast their ballots unencumbered by the political pressure that came from the presence of representatives of the company at the voting place. The goal of the Rickert law was to enhance the autonomy of voters at the ballot box. The net effect of this change in electoral rules was that the credibility of employers' threats of post-electoral punishments declined. If the law was effective in creating this space of political autonomy, one would expect to find a weaker relationship between the economic conditions in a district and political support for Social Democratic candidates after 1903.

The models presented in Table 8.2 examine these questions. In all of the specifications presented in Table 8.2, I interact a variable (POST-1903) that takes the value of 1 during the period after 1903 with the salient economic and political variables that affected the costs of electoral repression during the period before 1903. I interact post-1903 with occupational heterogeneity, skills, and the interaction term of right-wing political fragmentation and runoffs. Models 1 and 2 are reduced-form economic models (that use different measures of the skill composition of a district), whereas Models 3 and 4 include both economic and political variables.

The first finding of the results reported in Table 8.2 is that the Rickert law had a strong positive effect on the political strength of the SPD. In all of the specifications presented in this table, I find a positive relationship between the post-1903 variable and political support for the SPD. In addition, I find some indirect evidence that the adoption of the Rickert law changed the willingness of voters to support opposition candidates. Given that employers' threats of post-electoral punishments were lower after the adoption of the Rickert law, one expects that lower-skilled voters would have been more willing to take electoral risks and support opposition candidates in the aftermath of its adoption. The results support this hypothesis. Figure 8.2 displays visually the results for the marginal effect of the skill profile of the labor force on the electoral strength of Social Democratic candidates in a district following the adoption of the Rickert law. As can be seen in the figure, the slope of the relationship between the skill profile of the labor force and the Social Democratic vote share in a district was steeper during the period after 1903. This is consistent with the finding that lower-skilled workers were more willing to take political risks and support opposition candidates in the period after 1903, because the probability of economic reprisals for their political choices became lower during that period. The significant inroad of the German SPD among low-skilled workers during the final elections of the Imperial Period can be, to a large extent, attributed to the Rickert law. With respect to economic heterogeneity, I find no change in the direction of the relationship between the economic concentration of a district and the strength of Social Democracy there during the period after 1903. The political strength of Social Democracy continued to be higher in regions with high levels of economic heterogeneity even after 1903. Similarly, the adoption of the Rickert law did not modify the relationship between the political conditions in a district and the strength of Social Democracy there.

TABLE 8.2. *Consequences of Rickert Law for Social Democratic Political Support*

Variables	Model 1	Model 2	Model 3	Model 4
Post-1903	0.23***	0.10***	0.22***	0.09***
	(0.05)	(0.01)	(0.06)	(0.02)
Occupational Heterogeneity	−0.18***	−0.16***	−0.19***	−0.17***
	(0.04)	(0.04)	(0.05)	(0.04)
Occupational Heterogeneity*Post-1903	−0.65***	−0.70***	−0.60***	−0.65***
	(0.18)	(0.16)	(0.18)	(0.16)
Skill Industry	0.36***	0.32***		
	(0.02)	(0.02)		
Skill Agri		0.33***		0.31***
		(0.02)		(0.02)
Skill*Post-1903	−0.31***	0.15***	−0.27***	0.17***
	(0.09)	(0.03)	(0.09)	(0.04)
ENRP*Second			−0.00	−0.01
			(0.01)	(0.01)
Post-1903*ENRP*Second			−0.02	−0.00
			(0.02)	(0.02)
ENRP			−0.02***	−0.01***
			(0.00)	(0.00)
Post-1903*ENRP			−0.01	−0.00
			(0.01)	(0.01)
Second			0.08***	0.10***
			(0.02)	(0.02)
Post-1903*Second			0.04	−0.00
			(0.03)	(0.03)
Catholics	−0.00***	−0.00***	−0.00***	−0.00***
	(0.00)	(0.00)	(0.00)	(0.00)
Economic Development	0.00***	0.00***	0.00***	0.00***
	(0.00)	(0.00)	(0.00)	(0.00)
Rural Inequality	0.05**	0.01	0.05***	0.01
	(0.02)	(0.02)	(0.02)	(0.02)
Population	0.94***	0.78***	0.92***	0.75***
	(0.09)	(0.08)	(0.08)	(0.07)
Constant	−0.20***	−0.16***	−0.18***	−0.13***
	(0.02)	(0.02)	(0.02)	(0.02)
Fixed Effects for Regions?	Y	Y	Y	Y
Observations	5,128	5,128	4,734	4,734
R-Squared	0.60	0.61	0.65	0.66
Ll	4,062	4,128	3,961	4,066

Notes: Robust standard errors are in parentheses; *** p<0.01; ** p<0.05; * p<0.10.

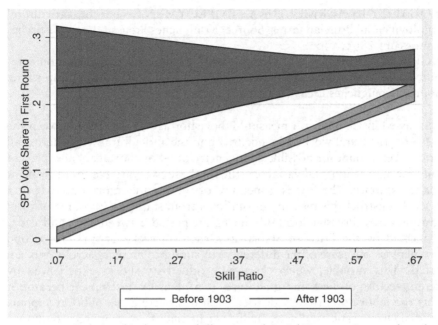

FIGURE 8.2. Relationship between skill ratio and Social Democratic vote share before and after 1903.

8.4. LABOR SCARCITY AND THE SOURCES OF POLITICAL SUPPORT FOR SOCIAL DEMOCRACY IN RURAL PRUSSIAN DISTRICTS

In Chapter 7, I hypothesized that the labor scarcity of a district is an important determinant of the economic costs of electoral repression encountered by private actors. Labor scarcity, I hypothesize, changes the economic bargaining power between employers and workers and increases the bargaining power of the latter (Ardanaz and Mares 2014). As a result, one expects that the willingness of voters to take electoral risks and support Social Democratic candidates was higher in districts characterized by higher levels of labor scarcity. This implies that one expects to find a positive correlation between the labor scarcity in a district and the level of electoral strength of the SPD there.

To examine the economic determinants of Social Democratic support in the countryside, I use a number of additional variables that were also used in the analysis in Chapter 7. I refer the reader to that chapter for more details about the construction of these measures.

LABOR SCARCITY: Measure constructed as the ratio between the agricultural wages in a district and the average agricultural wages across Prussian localities. Source: Grant 2005.

INEQUALITY IN AGRICULTURAL EMPLOYMENT. Gini of agricultural employment in Prussian farms. Source: Königliches Preussisches Statistisches Landesamt 1895, 1907.

LINGUISTIC HETEROGENEITY: Measure of linguistic fragmentation computed as 1 minus the Herfindahl Index of the ethnolinguistic group share. Source: Königliches Preussisches Statistisches Landesamt 1900.

As discussed in Chapter 7, I measure labor shortage as the ratio between the wages of agricultural workers in a district and the agricultural wages across all districts. To account for possible endogeneity of labor shortage, I also present results for an instrumental variable estimate. I use two variables to instrument for labor scarcity. The first is a measure of the net migratory outflows of a district. I construct this measure of outflows from statistical accounts of rural migration across Prussian localities during the period between 1895 and 1905, as collected by the Prussian Statistical Office (Brösicke 1907). The second instrument is a measure of the differences in rural productivity across Prussian districts. This variable, which captures productivity shocks experienced by different sectors of German agriculture, is a plausible instrument because it affects the labor scarcity of a district without affecting the political support for Social Democratic candidates. In his recent analysis of economic conditions in the Prussian countryside, Grant computes new and precise time-varying estimates of productivity differences for Prussian agriculture. The measures used in my analysis are based on Grant (2002: appendix B).

The results reported in Table 8.3 present both OLS and IV estimates of the relationship between labor scarcity and electoral support for Social Democratic candidates in Prussian rural districts during the period prior to the adoption of the Rickert law. Across all specifications, I find a positive relationship between the level of rural scarcity and the vote share of Social Democratic candidates. Depending on the model used, change in labor shortage by one standard deviation boosts the electoral gains of SPD candidates by up to 2.5 percentage points, which represents a 22 percent increase with respect to the mean level of support. Model 1 is a baseline model that includes controls for the ethnic and linguistic fragmentation of the district, as well as variables that control for the inequalities in the distribution of land and employment, in addition to the measure of labor shortage. Political support for Social Democratic candidates is lower in districts with higher levels of ethnic and linguistic fractionalization. The findings about the relationship between the different measures of rural inequality and political support for Social Democratic candidates are also interesting. The two dimensions of rural inequality stand in different relationships with Social Democracy's level of political strength. I find a negative correlation between the Gini of inequality in employment and the political strength of Social Democracy. By contrast, I find a positive relationship between inequality in landholding and electoral support for Social Democracy. This finding is consistent with a range of additional results presented in the earlier chapters

TABLE 8.3. *Relationship between Labor Scarcity and Electoral Support of Social Democracy before 1903*

	OLS Estimates			IV Estimates		
	Model 1	Model 2	Model 3	Model 4	Model 5	Model 6
Labor Shortage	0.030**	0.0213*	0.0231*	0.36***	0.32***	0.32***
	(0.012)	(0.0129)	(0.0128)	(0.126)	(0.114)	(0.117)
Occupational		−0.157*	−0.152*		−0.368*	−0.368*
Heterogeneity		(0.0834)	(0.0818)		(0.208)	(0.212)
Skill All		0.208***	0.205***		0.0496	0.0478
		(0.0235)	(0.0227)		(0.064)	(0.0654)
Linguistic	−0.06**	−0.06***	−0.07***	−0.0153	−0.0174	−0.0196
Heterogeneity	(0.010)	(0.0110)	(0.0110)	(0.045)	(0.044)	(0.0454)
Catholics	−0.0007	−0.00***	−0.00***	−0.0003*	−0.0003*	−0.00032
	(0.00)	(0.00)	(0.00)	(0.000)	(0.000)	(0.0002)
ENRP			0.022***			0.00691
			(0.0050)			(0.0042)
Economic	0.001***	0.0006***	0.0006***	−0.0007	−0.0006	−0.0006
Development	(0.000)	(0.0001)	(0.000)	(0.000)	(0.0007)	(0.0007)
Rural Inequality	0.0706**	0.0477	0.0653**	0.155*	0.129	0.135
	(0.0293)	(0.0292)	(0.0286)	(0.0880)	(0.0869)	(0.0887)
Employment	−0.107*	−0.141**	−0.133**	0.0595	0.0315	0.0393
Inequality	(0.0640)	(0.0617)	(0.0619)	(0.166)	(0.160)	(0.164)
Population	1.56***	1.387***	1.363***	2.34***	2.34***	2.35***
	(0.111)	(0.101)	(0.0986)	(0.121)	(0.119)	(0.119)
Constant	−0.1***	−0.13***	−0.19***	−0.6***	−0.5***	−0.6***
	(0.036)	(0.036)	(0.038)	(0.194)	(0.178)	(0.182)
Observations	1,840	1,840	1,840	1,790	1,790	1,790
R-squared	0.298	0.339	0.349			

Notes: Robust standard errors are in parentheses; *** $p<0.01$; ** $p<0.05$; * $p<0.10$.

of this book. It reinforces the argument that inequalities in the distribution of land were not easily fungible into political resources that could be used by rural landlords or politicians in their efforts to deter voters from supporting opposition candidates.

The additional models presented in Table 8.3 add economic and political controls to this baseline specification. The inclusion of these variables does not modify the sign or the statistical significance of the relationship between labor shortage and electoral support for Social Democracy. In Model 2, I include controls for the economic heterogeneity of a district. The variable has the predicted negative sign and is statistically significant at conventional levels. I also find a positive relationship between the skill composition of a district and the political support for Social Democracy. The skill variable fails, however, to reach statistical significance at conventional levels in Models 5 and 6, where the measure of labor shortage is instrumented. In Model, I include a control for the skill level of the labor force. Similar to the empirical specifications presented in Table 7.2, the coefficient of this variable is positive and statistically significant. In Model 3, the coefficient for the measure of economic heterogeneity also reaches statistical significance at conventional levels. In Model 3, I include an additional control that measures the political fragmentation among right-wing parties. The sign of this variable is positive and significant at conventional levels in Model 3 but loses statistical significance in the model where I instrument the measure of labor shortage.

The models presented in Table 8.4 examine the consequences of the adoption of legislation that protected electoral secrecy for the political strength of the SPD. In contrast to the models presented in Table 8.3, I restrict the analysis to Prussian rural districts for which I can construct measures of labor scarcity. Similar to the specification presented in Table 8.3, I interact a variable that takes the value of 1 after 1903 with the salient economic and political variables affecting the costs of electoral repression during the period before 1903. Table 8.4 presents three different specifications. Model 1 is a reduced-form economic model that includes measures of labor scarcity and the skill composition of a district, interactions of these variables with the post-1903 dummy, and other economic controls. In Model 2, I add a control for the economic heterogeneity of the district (and an interaction between this variable and the post-1903 dummy). Finally, in the third model, I examine the relationship between right-wing political fragmentation in a district and political support for Social Democracy in the period after 1903.

Several interesting findings emerge. First, labor scarcity was no longer a significant predictor of the political support for Social Democratic candidates. In Models 2 and 3, neither the measure of labor scarcity nor its interaction with the post-1903 dummy variable reach statistical significance at conventional levels. By contrast, we find a statistically significant relationship between the interaction of the post-1903 dummy with the other relevant covariates in a district and the political strength of Social Democracy there. Although the interaction between occupational heterogeneity and the post-1903 variable is statistically significant at conventional levels, the sign of the relationship does not change across periods. Both in the pre- and post-1903 periods, I find a negative relationship between the occupational heterogeneity of a district and the political support for Social Democracy. Similarly, the relationship between right-wing political fragmentation and the political strength of Social Democracy did not change over time. Figure 8.3 plots the marginal effects of the skill level of the labor force on political support for Social Democracy before and after the adoption of the Rickert law. I find a striking reversal in the relationship between the skill composition of a district and political support for Social Democratic candidates in the period following the adoption of the ballot envelopes. This suggests that the adoption of ballot envelopes increased the political freedom of low-skilled workers to support opposition candidates.

TABLE 8.4. *Consequences of Legislation Protecting Electoral Secrecy in Rural Prussian Districts*

Variables	Model 1	Model 2	Model 3
Post-1903	0.290***	0.308***	0.269***
	(0.0734)	(0.0749)	(0.0779)
Labor Shortage	−0.0221*	−0.0200	−0.0182
	(0.0128)	(0.0129)	(0.0128)
Labor Shortage*Post-1903	0.0442	0.0496	0.0425
	(0.0309)	(0.0311)	(0.0307)
Skill_All	0.360***	0.370***	0.362***
	(0.0307)	(0.0312)	(0.0311)
Skill_All*Post-1903	−0.571***	−0.582***	−0.569***
	(0.122)	(0.124)	(0.123)
Occupational Heterogeneity		−0.163**	−0.157**
		(0.0790)	(0.0786)
Occupational Heterogeneity*Post-1903		−0.502*	−0.510*
		(0.260)	(0.263)
Linguistic Fractionalization	−0.050***	−0.042***	−0.050***
	(0.0109)	(0.0112)	(0.011)
Catholics	−0.001***	−0.001***	−0.0009***
	(0.00)	(0.00)	(0.00)
ENRP			0.00869*
			(0.00512)
ENRP*Post-1903			0.0208**
			(0.00952)
Economic Development	0.0009***	0.001***	0.001***
	(0.0001)	(0.0001)	(0.0001)
Rural Inequality	0.0706**	0.0668**	0.0828***
	(0.0282)	(0.0284)	(0.0283)
Gini of Agricultural Employment	−0.0428	−0.0322	−0.0262
	(0.0570)	(0.0563)	(0.0567)
Population	0.752***	0.782***	0.772***
	(0.129)	(0.143)	(0.142)
Constant	−0.151***	−0.158***	−0.191***
	(0.0342)	(0.0338)	(0.0378)
Observations	2,408	2,408	2,408
R-Squared	0.484	0.488	0.492

Notes: Robust standard errors are in parentheses; *** $p<0.01$; ** $p<0.05$; * $p<0.10$.

8.5. THE CONSEQUENCES OF ECONOMIC AND POLITICAL REPRESSION: THE FORMATION OF LIB-LAB ALLIANCES

Did the history of sustained economic and political repression in a district affect both the strength of Social Democratic candidates as well as their radicalism? An important theme in existing research on German Social

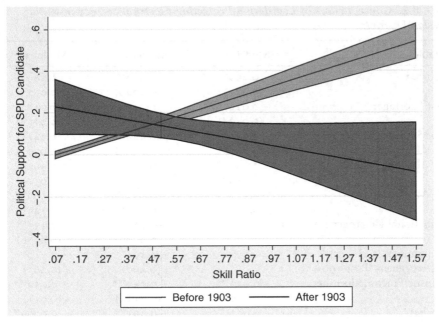

FIGURE 8.3. Relationship between skill level and SPD vote share in Prussian rural districts.

Democracy is the existence of political cleavage within the movement between radical and accommodationist Social Democratic candidates. Whereas the former rejected any accommodation with parties on the right, the latter were willing to engage in electoral cooperation with some candidates on the right.

One observable indicator of this distinction between militant and accommodating Social Democratic candidates is whether candidates were willing to form electoral alliances during runoffs with candidates who represented other political parties on the right. Given the increase in the political fragmentation of the German party system, electoral alliances among right-wing candidates were common, and they increased in importance during the final elections of the period. A recent groundbreaking study published by the German Historical Commission sheds new light on the patterns of political competition in German elections by documenting all of the different forms of electoral coordination that formed among candidates. Reibel (2007) conducts painstaking research on announcements by political candidates and parties in local newspapers across all 397 German districts to document the successful (and failed) electoral coalitions in all of the elections between 1890 and 1912. One interesting finding that emerges from Reibel's data is that electoral coalitions between Social Democratic candidates and other right-wing candidates were not uncommon during the period. This finding contradicts the conjecture made by Luebbert (1991) that Lib-Lab alliances were absent from Germany.

Consider some examples of these Lib-Lab alliances. Such district-level coalitions were relatively rare in Prussian districts. One exception was the 1890 election in Zauch-Belzig, Potsdam, where a coalition between Free Liberals and Social Democrats formed during runoffs in opposition to a conservative candidate (Reibel 2007: 171). In Danzig's first district, a Lib-Lab alliance formed between the Free Liberal Party and the Social Democrat candidate during the runoff in the 1907 election (Reibel 2007: 63). Outside of Prussia, though, Lib-Lab alliances between local Free Liberal and SPD organizations were relatively common. Consider just a few examples of these alliances. In Brackenheim-Heilbronn, a district in Württemberg, the SPD recommended that their supporters should vote for the candidate of the German People's Party (*Deutsche Volkspartei*) during the runoff in the 1893 election (Reibel 2007: 310). In Freudenstadt Oberndorf, another district in Württemberg, SPD leaders recommended that their supporters should vote for the Free Liberal candidate, who competed during runoffs against a candidate from the Zentrum (Reibel 2007: 1231). In Dessau-Zerbst, a district in Anhalt, an electoral coalition formed between a candidate of the Demokratische Vereinigung and a Social Democratic candidate (Reibel 2007: 1449). In Erbach Bensheim, Hessen's sixth district, the Social Democratic candidate formed an electoral alliance with the Progressive People's Party (*Fortschrittliche Volkspartei*) against a candidate of the Christian Social Party (Reibel 2007: 1341). In Friedberg-Budingen, another district in Hessen, Social Democrats and Free Liberals (*Fortschrittliche Volkspartei*) formed an electoral coalition during runoffs to oppose a National Liberal candidate (Reibel 2007: 1325). During the 1912 election in Augsburg, an electoral coalition was formed during runoffs and included representatives of all of the liberal parties and the SPD to oppose the representative of the Zentrum (Reibel 2007: 1105).

What explains the probability of the formation of such Lib-Lab alliances in German districts? What are the political and economic characteristics of a district that influence the likelihood of their formation? To answer these questions, I created a variable that codes all instances of district-level electoral coalitions that included a Social Democratic candidate. Most such alliances occurred during the second round, when the need for electoral coordination among candidates was more critical. The most significant coalition partners for Social Democrats were Free Liberals, followed by parties that represented ethnic minorities (such as Danes).

In Table 8.5, I examine the factors that affected the probability of the formation of such electoral alliances. The main question examined in this table is whether Lib-Lab alliances were more likely to form in districts whose economic conditions made economic intimidation less likely. A lower history of political repression, I conjecture, was more conducive to higher levels of political cooperation. I use three different dependent variables in the analysis. The first

TABLE 8.5. *The Determinants of Lib-Lab Alliances*

Coalition Partner of SPD Electoral Round	Model 1 Free Liberal 2	Model 2 Minorities 2	Model 3 Any Party 2
Occupational Heterogeneity	−1.825**	−1.901**	−2.255***
	(0.899)	(0.813)	(0.752)
Skill All	−0.029***	−0.021***	−0.020***
	(0.004)	(0.003)	(0.002)
Catholics	−1.134	−1.747	−1.882*
	(1.142)	(1.069)	(1.013)
Economic Development	0.009	0.00471	0.002
	(0.007)	(0.00704)	(0.006)
Landholding Inequality	−2.141*	−2.647***	−2.765***
	(1.127)	(0.991)	(0.928)
Population	1.979**	3.314***	3.538***
Constant	−0.920	−0.0369	0.441
	(1.111)	(0.992)	(0.926)
Constant			
Fixed Effects for Regions?	Y	Y	Y
Observations	4,805	4,818	4,818

Notes: Robust standard errors are in parentheses; *** $p<0.01$; ** $p<0.05$; * $p<0.10$.

dependent variable presented in Model 1 takes the value of 1 if a coalition between a Social Democratic candidate and a Free Liberal candidate existed in the district. The dependent variable in Model 2 takes the value of 1 if there was an alliance between a Social Democratic candidate and a minority candidate in that particular district. In Model 3, the dependent variable is an electoral alliance between a Social Democratic candidate and a candidate from any other party on the right.

The results lend support to my hypotheses and illustrate that variables making electoral repression less likely were also likely to facilitate the formation of these cooperative political alliances in a district. Lib-Lab alliances were more likely in districts with high occupational heterogeneity and low levels of landholding inequality. With respect to the skill level of the labor force, I find that Lib-Lab alliances were more likely to form in districts characterized by low skill levels. This finding runs counter to the predictions of the Varieties of Capitalism perspective, according to which vocational skills were the glue for political cooperation during this period. In Figure 8.4, I display the relationship between occupational heterogeneity and the probability of the formation of a Lib-Lab alliance between Social Democratic candidates and candidates on the right. The graph shows that such probability was higher in districts with high economic heterogeneity, but it declined as the economic concentration of a district increased.

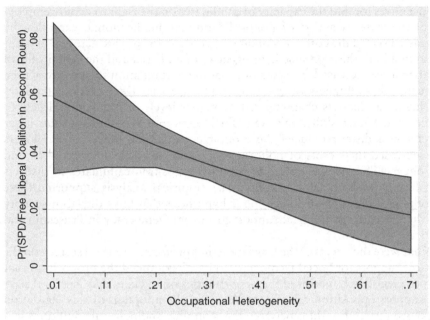

FIGURE 8.4. Relationship between economic heterogeneity of a district and the probability of formation of a Lib-Lab alliance.

8.6. CONCLUSION

The spectacular growth in political strength of the German SPD during the period prior to World War I has fascinated generations of historians and political scientists for decades. In a short time, the German SPD rose from being a party that mobilized around 6 percent of the electorate to becoming the largest political party in the German Reichstag. What makes this dramatic increase in the political strength of Social Democracy puzzling is that it took place in a political environment characterized by systematic electoral repression against Social Democratic voters perpetrated by both employees of the state and powerful German employers.

In this chapter, I formulated a set of new hypotheses that seek to explain the regional and temporal variation in the political strength of Social Democracy, and I tested these hypotheses using a wealth of new data unavailable to previous generations of scholars. I found that prior to the adoption of legislation protecting electoral secrecy, voters were more likely to take political risks and support Social Democratic candidates in districts where candidates on the political right faced relatively higher costs of economic and political repression. I disaggregated the economic and political dimensions of the determinants of the costs of electoral repression. With respect to political variables, I hypothesized that the political fragmentation among right-wing parties reduced both the incentives for and the capacity of candidates on the right to deploy employ-ees of the state as agents of political intimidation. Economic variables, by contrast, affected the costs of economic repression for private actors. I hypoth-esized that both the economic heterogeneity of a district and the skill profile of its labor force increased the costs of economic intimidation for private actors. As such, the willingness of voters to support Social Democratic candidates was higher in districts characterized by higher levels of occupational hetero-geneity and higher skill levels. One final economic hypothesis is that labor scarcity in a district reduced the economic bargaining power of employers and increased their costs of political repression. As such, I expected to find a stronger willingness of voters to support opposition candidates in districts with higher levels of labor scarcity. The empirical analysis supported these hypotheses. I tested the final economic hypothesis that links the labor scarcity in a district with the political support for Social Democracy in Prussian rural districts.

What were the effects of the legislation that protected electoral secrecy on the political support for Social Democracy? First, I examined the proposition that the 1903 legislation increased the opportunities of voters to take electoral risks and support opposition candidates. As such, the adoption of this legislation weakened the relationships between the economic and political conditions in a district and the political strength of Social Democracy that had been in place prior to the adoption of these electoral reforms. I therefore expected to find a weaker relationship between these economic and political variables and the electoral strength of Social Democracy in the period after the adoption of the Rickert law. I found mixed results for this hypothesis. Although the adop-tion of legislation protecting electoral secrecy did not modify the relationship between occupational heterogeneity and the support for Social Democracy, it did change the relationship between the skill composition of a district and Social Democratic strength. I interpret this finding as being consistent with the hypothesis that low-skilled workers were more willing to take electoral risks and defy the political pressure of their employers after the introduction of ballot envelopes.

Beyond its importance for understanding the historical origins of Social Democracy, the analysis in this chapter also has implications for a comparative analysis of the support for opposition parties in countries where elections are characterized by significant electoral intimidation and imperfect protection of electoral secrecy. Existing research on opposition parties in semicompetitive regimes examines primarily the political strategies of dominant parties and the selective use of state resources or patronage by the state as strategies to deter voters from supporting opposition candidates (Lust-Okar 2005; Mag-aloni 2006). In contrast to this explanation, this chapter directs attention to the importance of economic and labor market conditions – such as the skill composition of the workforce, the occupational heterogeneity, and the relative labor scarcity in a district – as important predictors of support for opposition candidates. In deciding to take electoral risks and support opposition candidates, voters considered the likelihood of economic punishments by employers. Because they affected voters' considerations about losing employment and being rehired by other firms, the economic conditions in a district also influenced the political strength of opposition candidates in semicompetitive electoral regimes.

9

Dilemmas on the Right and the Road to Proportional Representation

The improvement in the protection of electoral secrecy had far-reaching consequences for political competition in German elections to the Reichstag. These changes in the electoral law reduced the opportunities for electoral intimidation. By emboldening voters to take electoral risks, the Rickert law made possible the spectacular political growth of the Social Democratic Party (SPD) during the final elections of the period. These gains for Social Democrats came at the expense of parties on the right. Because of the reduction in their ability to monitor voters' choices, many candidates on the right lost districts that had previously been their electoral strongholds.

This chapter investigates the implications of the changes in electoral competition for German parties on the right. My analysis focuses on one dimension of electoral competition that was salient for parties rather than candidates: the ability of parties to translate votes into parliamentary seats. I find that the Rickert law affected parties on the right in different ways depending on the district-level distribution of their support. Those right-wing parties whose voters were concentrated in particular regions – such as the Zentrum or the Conservatives – experienced no changes in the vote-seat proportionality in the aftermath of the Rickert law. The situation was entirely different for other right-wing parties, such as the National Liberals and Free Liberals. The ability of these parties to convert their votes into parliamentary seats deteriorated dramatically during the elections that were held after the adoption of the Rickert law and the onset of World War I.

This worsening of the relationship between the votes won by individual candidates and the number of seats held by representatives of the respective parties in the Reichstag led to an intense search by politicians for a solution that could allow their parties to survive electorally in the changed electoral landscape. In the process, the positions of several parties about questions of electoral reform experienced a gradual change. Over time, these parties began to support the dramatic overhaul of the existing electoral system and its replacement with proportional representation. The eventual decision to change electoral rules, one of the last political choices made by the parliament elected in 1912, marks an important institutional turning point in Germany's political history.

The study of the changes in electoral rules and the adoption of proportional representation have been the object of intense scholarly debate in recent years. This debate has pitted various studies that revive hypotheses advanced by Stein Rokkan nearly three decades ago against alternative, "anti-Rokkanian" explanations that stress the importance of economic considerations as the determining factor that accounts for the change in electoral rules. Whereas recent studies have examined the question of changes in electoral rules by relying on an analysis of cross-national data, this chapter tests these theories by analyzing the determinants of the behavior of individual legislators.

The chapter is organized as follows. I begin in Section 9.1 with a discussion of the varied ability of different parties on the political right to translate their electoral votes into parliamentary seats during the final elections in the period prior to World War I and examine their opposition or support for changes to the electoral rules. In the next few sections, I turn to a discussion of the main hypotheses that have been formulated in existing studies about the origins of proportional representation and the limitations of empirical research that is intended to adjudicate among these competing explanations. In Sections 9.5 and 9.6, I attempt to resolve this controversy by testing whether these theories can account for the decisions of individual legislators to support the adoption of proportional representation.

9.1. DILEMMAS ON THE RIGHT: POLITICAL COMPETITION IN THE AFTERMATH OF THE RICKERT LAW

One important issue that affected the electoral success of different parties was their ability to translate the votes won across different districts into parliamentary seats, that is, their vote-seat disproportionality. On this dimension, the electoral fates of the different parties on the right competing in German elections diverged during the final three elections prior to World War I. Some parties on the right, such as the Conservatives and the Zentrum, did not experience any changes in the ratio of votes to seats during those elections. Conservatives experienced a net gain of seats of 3.6 percent during the 1903 election, 5.7 percent during the 1907 election, and 1.6 percent in 1912 (Duverger 1969: 375). The Zentrum also experienced gains in the allocation of votes to seats. During the 1903 election, the Zentrum gained a seat bonus of 5.5 percent. Its seat bonus was 7 percent during the 1907 election and 6.6 percent in 1912, Germany's final election under a majoritarian system.

The situation was entirely different for the two other parties on the right, the National Liberals and the Free Liberals. During the final elections of the period, both parties experienced losses in the allocation of votes to seats. The trend was

204 Dilemmas on the Right and the Road to Proportional Representation

less pronounced for the Free Liberal Party, which lost in the allocation of votes to seats only during the 1903 and 1907 elections. For the National Liberals, the negative trend in the deterioration of the ratio by which votes were translated into seats set in during the 1903 election. In 1903, the National Liberals experienced a 1.1 percent loss in the translation of votes to seats. In 1907, the loss was 0.8 percent, and in 1912, it was 2.6 percent (Duverger 1969: 376). The relationship between the absolute number of votes and the number of seats illustrates in a more dramatic fashion the predicament of the National Liberal Party. During the 1912 election, the Conservative Party won slightly more than 1 million votes (1,046,030 votes), which translated into forty-two seats. By contrast, National Liberals won more than 1.6 million votes (1,662,670 votes), which brought them forty-five seats. That same year, the Zentrum won more than 2 million votes (2,051,730 votes), which translated into ninety-one seats. Another way to interpret these numbers is to say that a deputy of the National Liberal Party "required" 36,948 votes to win a seat during the 1912 election. By contrast, a Conservative Party member of the Reichstag required 24,905 votes, and a deputy of the Zentrum needed 22,543 votes.

An internal document drafted by officials of the Ministry of the Interior sought to identify the factors that accounted for the fate of the National Liberals. According to that publication, the electoral difficulty of the National Liberal Party did not result from a lack for political support for their candidates. After all, the document noted, National Liberals had won 400,000 more votes in 1912 than they had in 1907 (Bundesarchiv Berlin Lichterberg R 1501: 191–198). The National Liberal predicament instead resulted from the geographic fragmentation of its vote. Officials of the Ministry of the Interior noted that the reason for the poor electoral performance by National Liberals "is that there are no regions where there are only Liberals. Rather there are regions where there are conservatives or Free Liberals or Social Democrats" (Bundesarchiv Berlin Lichtenberg R 1501: 198).

This consideration of the worsening translation of votes to seats accounted for the decision by leaders of the National Liberal Party to search for changes in electoral rules. National Liberals fared far worse in the translation of votes to seats than other parties on the right did. Graf, a National Liberal politician, was reported to have replied to Heinrich Rickert, the leader of the Free Liberals.: "Mr. Rickert knows that although our parties receive a roughly equal number of votes, our party will receive on average thirty less mandates" (quoted in Gagel 1958: 129). For these National Liberal leaders, proportional representation presented an alternative. In the National Liberal Press, one can find the earliest proposals for the adoption of proportional representation beginning in the 1890s. (This is not unsurprising, given that the 1890 election was the first election in which the National Liberal Party experienced a negative vote-seat disproportionality. The vote-seat disproportionality of the party improved in the following elections but turned negative again following the 1903 election). On March 8, 1890, the *Nationalzeitung* published an editorial recommending the adoption of proportional representation. The *Gegenwart*, another liberal publication, endorsed the adoption of proportional representation, calling it "the electoral system of reason and of the future" (Gagel 1958: 127).

National Liberal support for proportional representation grew during the first decade of the twentieth century, the period in which prominent leaders of the party begin to advocate for this change in electoral system. Gagel describes this change in political support: "[P]roportional representation acquired a special electoral importance for the National Liberals. At the time when the Free Liberals recommended the introduction of democratic reforms in the Prussian electoral law, the National Liberals objected that those reforms did not go far enough and attempted to provoke the Free Liberals to support the adoption of proportional representation" (Gagel 1958: 129).

The Free Liberals also supported the adoption of proportional representation. Two competing considerations shaped the positions of the Free Liberals on the question of electoral reforms. Like the National Liberals, the Free Liberals also worried about their inability to translate their votes into seats during a period of heightened electoral competition. Beginning in 1905, leading Free Liberal politicians, such as Friedrich von Payer, began to advocate the adoption of proportional representation in national elections (Simon 1969: 106). The position of the Free Liberals was also affected by more immediate tactical considerations. The Free Liberals competed with the Social Democrats for a similar part of the German electorate. To appeal to these voters, they advocated a proposal for electoral reform that was especially favorable to voters in large urban areas, whose representation was disfavored by existing electoral rules (Simon 1969: 106).

In contrast to the National Liberals, the Conservatives opposed the adoption of proportional representation. One can reconstruct the conservative position about the adoption of proportional representation from newspaper editorials, parliamentary deliberations, and various internal publications by officials of the Ministry of the Interior (Bundesarchiv Berlin Lichtenberg R 1501: 309–350). An internal document prepared by the Ministry entitled "Considerations about the Division (*Einteilung*) of Electoral Districts" reviewed political arguments that had been made in favor of or in opposition to proportional representation and developed interesting simulations about the likely effects of this change in electoral rules on the number of deputies representing each party. Conservatives acknowledged the existence of profound inequalities in representation in German elections. Although Germany had experienced dramatic economic changes in the decades after 1870, the electoral system had not been modified to accommodate this new demographic landscape. As a result, the ratio between voters and representatives differed significantly across Germany's electoral districts. In 1912, in Germany's most populous district, Teltow-Beeskow, 1,315,601 voters elected one representative. By contrast, Schaumburg Lippe, Germany's least populous district had only 46,652 voters electing one representative (Bundesarchiv Berlin Lichtenberg R 1501: 311).

Conservatives opposed proposals for electoral reforms that recommended either proportional representation or redistricting to create equally sized constituencies of 100,000 voters each. From their perspective, the disadvantage of redistricting was that it would increase the number of representatives elected in urban areas and therefore strengthen the electoral power of the Social Democrats in the Reichstag. Conservatives countered such proposals to create new districts on the basis of the population of a locality by proposing an alternative criterion: creating districts on the basis of territory (Bundesarchiv Berlin Lichtenberg R 1501: 322). Conservative politicians defended this territorial criterion of representation – which was known at the time as the *Flächenprinzip* – in the parliamentary debates of the Reichstag. On February 12, 1912, Graf von Posadowsky-Wehner, a conservative politician, argued:

[O]ne of Germany's most unfortunate developments is that every fifth person is now an inhabitant of a city. In answering the question of which interests have to be considered in the redistricting of districts, one has to consider not just the number of voters but also the larger interests of the entire country. To protect agriculture, one needs to consider not just the number of voters but also the size and use of the land. (*Stenographische Berichte des Reichstages* February 17, 1912)

The Conservatives also opposed the adoption of proportional representation. To preempt the adoption of these reforms, Ministry of the Interior officials invoked the practical difficulties associated with them. True proportionality, officials of the Ministry of the Interior argued, could only be achieved through the creation of a single district. Given Germany's federal structure, this was impossible (Bundesarchiv Berlin Lichtenberg R 1501: 339). Ministry of the Interior officials had a more immediate motivation to reject the adoption of proportional representation. The Conservatives knew that the number of conservative deputies elected under new electoral rules would be significantly lower than the number elected under the existing majoritarian system. Table 9.1 reproduces the results of the calculations made by Ministry of the Interior officials about the consequences of proportional representation for the different political parties represented in the Reichstag. The input for these calculations was the number of votes received by the different parties during the 1912 election. These calculations find that the adoption of proportional representation would likely result in seven fewer seats for the Conservative Party. The number of seats for the Zentrum would decline even more – by twenty-five seats.

The deliberations to modify electoral institutions intensified after the 1912 elections. The National Liberal fraction in the Reichstag declined by nine deputies, despite the fact that the party had won an equal number of votes in 1912 as it had in the 1907 election. In the aftermath of the 1912 election, the National Liberal delegation in the Reichstag submitted a proposal that recommended "correcting the inequalities of the existing electoral system" (*Stenographische Berichte des Deutschen Reichstages* 1912: no. 94). The Free

TABLE 9.1. *Expected Impact of the Adoption of Proportional Representation on the Seat Share of Different Parties in the Reichstag*

| Party | Votes Received during 1912 Election | Number of Seats under PR with D'Hondt Rule If: | | Number of Seats in 1912 | Number of Seats under PR (with Multiple Districts) Compared to the Results under Majoritarian Rules | |
		The Reich is One District	Districts Correspond to the Different States		Gains	Losses
Conservatives	1,126,270	37	38	45		7
National Liberals	1,662,670	54	48	46	2	
Free Liberals	1,497,041	49	47	42	5	
Zentrum	1,998,843	65	68	31		25
Social Democrats	4,250,401	140	142	110	32	

Source: Bundesarchiv Berlin Lichtenberg R 1501/343, Betrachtungen über die Einteilung der Reichstagswahlkreise.

Liberal delegation in the Reichstag advanced a similar bill at the same time (*Stenographische Berichte des Deutschen Reichstages* 1912: no. 71). The motivation for this change in electoral rules advocated by the Free Liberals was that the "proportional representation system could eliminate the inequalities created by the existing electoral system" and "provide better protection for minorities" (*Stenographische Berichte des Deutschen Reichstages* 1912: no. 71). In addition to the two liberal parties, the Social Democrats supported proportional representation and submitted a draft bill recommending the change in electoral rules (*Stenographische Berichte des Deutschen Reichstages* 1912: no. 69). For Social Democrats, this recommendation did not represent a change in political strategy but rather a reiteration of a demand that the party had already made on many previous occasions.

The Reichstag delegated the discussion of these reforms to a constitutional committee (*Verfassungsausschuss*) that included representatives of all of the political parties. The committee published its first (and only report) on July 4, 1917 (*Stenographische Berichte des Deutschen Reichstages*, 1917: no. 985).

9.2. THE ADOPTION OF PROPORTIONAL REPRESENTATION: A TEST OF THREE THEORETICAL PERSPECTIVES

This section considers three competing explanations that have been advanced to explain the adoption of proportional representation. Questions about the determinants of the reform of electoral institutions and the adoption of proportional representation have been the object of intense theoretical and empirical controversy in recent years (Boix 1999; Benoit 2004; Blais et al. 2005; Colomer 2005; Cusack et al. 2010; Ahmed 2012). Yet although these studies have advanced a wide range of competing explanations about the economic and political determinants of electoral reforms, their empirical tests to adjudicate among these competing explanations have been inadequate. This empirical deficit has arisen because the core theoretical concepts of the literature either have not been measured at the correct level of aggregation or have not been measured at all.

The dominant empirical strategy used in contemporary research, which is premised on the quantitative analysis of variation between just a few countries, is severely constrained by the small number of observations in the sample. The number of observations in cross-national studies is relatively low, ranging from twenty-four countries in Carles Boix's (1999) original paper to twelve countries in some of the specifications presented by Thomas Cusack et al. (2007). Because of the small number of cases and the high multicollinearity among competing variables, we cannot assess the relative importance of competing explanations. Due to this limitation, scholars have therefore been unable to test *all* of the explanations for the adoption of proportional representation. Often, the debate has taken the form of a horse race between two competing explanations that leaves out other alternatives.

The empirical approach adopted in this chapter builds on Leemann and Mares (2014) and seeks to remedy the empirical deficit of the existing literature. Although many of the persistent disagreements cannot be resolved with existing cross-national data, additional leverage can be gained by shifting to a lower level of aggregation – the individual politician. This move to a lower level of aggregation is desirable for two reasons. First, although existing explanations are framed at a theoretical level that is quite abstract, ultimately they seek to explain choices made by individual legislators. Second, by testing existing explanations about the adoption of proportional representation at the level of the individual politician, we can examine how electoral competition at the district level, partisan considerations, and economic conditions each affect the votes of legislators.

Stein Rokkan's shadow looms over much of the contemporary research seeking to explain the adoption of proportional representation in Europe during the first decades of the twentieth century (Rokkan 1970). Two of the dominant hypotheses concerning the adoption of proportional representation can be traced back to his work. The first argues that incumbent elites supported the adoption of proportional representation to avoid a complete disaster in the face of Social Democratic mobilization. Boix takes up this hypothesis and argues that if parties on the right are equally balanced in electoral strength but unable to coordinate on a common candidate (either at the level of the constituency or nationally), then those parties are likely to support the adoption of proportional representation. By contrast, the incentive to adopt changes in electoral institutions is weaker if one party dominates the electoral arena (Boix 1999: 612).

Rokkan's second hypothesis – which is taken up in current research by Ernesto Calvo (2009) – attempts to specify the conditions under which incumbent parties on the right favored changes to the electoral institutions even in the absence of Social Democratic threats. This hypothesis suggests that parties with a geographically disperse distribution of votes also had incentives to demand changes in electoral institutions, because multi-party competition increased the vote-seat disproportionality of the electoral results. According to this logic, proportional representation was a mechanism that reduced the "severity of the partisan bias and of electoral regimes to districting problems" (Calvo 2009: 256). This hypothesis is sometimes alternatively labeled the "minority representation thesis" (Caramani 2004) or the "electoral geography thesis" (Norris 1997).

In Rokkan's original study, the two political hypotheses acted as substitutes. Rokkan conjectured that in some countries – such as Germany, Norway, and Sweden – socialist mobilization played a significant role in the adoption of proportional representation, whereas in other countries – such as Belgium, Denmark, and Switzerland – considerations about the disproportionality of the translation of votes to seats were the primary motivation for politicians to adopt changes in electoral institutions (Rokkan 1970: 157). This chapter argues that the two political hypotheses can complement rather than exclude one another. Both explanations can operate within the same case by capturing constraints on the activity of legislators that operate at different levels. The first political explanation (Rokkan I) locates the salient constraint at the level of the electoral district in the district-specific electoral vulnerabilities encountered by candidates on the political right who faced Social Democratic challengers. By contrast, the second Rokkanian explanation (Rokkan II) locates the salient constraint at the level of the party. An important part of my analysis that seeks to understand the determinants of political support for the adoption of proportional representation involves identifying the relative influence of district-specific vulnerabilities and partisan variables on legislators' preferences about changes in the design of electoral institutions.

These Rokkanian hypotheses differ in the relative importance that each places on the Social Democratic threat. Both stress, however, that the "electoral coordination" (or the failure thereof) by incumbent parties was a critical variable that influenced the decisions of incumbents to support or oppose changes in electoral rules. Critics have noted that the notion of electoral coordination is theoretically unclear and poorly operationalized empirically. Cusack et al. (2007: 375) note two limitations of the test of electoral coordination presented by Boix (1999). First, Boix's studies fail to take account of the opportunities for coordination that were created in electoral systems that used runoffs. Runoffs allowed parties on the political right that had competed in the first round to form electoral alliances in the second round in order to oppose a Social

Democratic candidate. Cusack et al. note some limitations of the empirical test of the Rokkanian notion of electoral coordination employed by Boix. They argue that the variable used by Boix, the effective number of parties, fails to distinguish between cases in which one party on the right was dominant and cases where the parties on the right were equally sized (Cusack et al. 2007: 375). Blais and Indriadson (2005) present a similar critique. They argue that the incentives of all parties to switch to proportional representation were stronger in countries that required a majority of votes, rather than just a plurality of votes, to win a district.

Although they raise criticisms, Cusack et al. do not propose a superior empirical solution. It is impossible to measure district-level electoral competition using cross-national data. Using aggregate data, we cannot learn whether parties on the right coordinated with each other. Clearly, runoffs could have alleviated potential coordination problems among parties on the right. But although runoffs created some incentives for electoral coordination during the second round, they did not necessarily produce coordination among right-wing parties as Cusack et al. argue (Bertram 1964; Fairbairn 1990; Reibel 2007). Parties on the political right could use a range of possible strategies during runoffs. These included forming pre-electoral coalitions restricted to right-wing parties, supporting the left-wing candidate over the ring-wing opponent (in districts where a candidate on the right encountered a candidate on the left during runoffs), recommending that voters abstain during the second round, and refusing to endorse any of the remaining candidates.

To illustrate how recommendations to abstain made by one of the parties on the right contributed to victories by Social Democratic candidates, consider the following examples (from the 1912 election). In Potsdam-Osthavelland Spandau, the candidates in the runoff were a representative of the Imperial Party and a representative of the SPD. The Free Liberal Party, whose candidate had received 24 percent of the votes in the first round, recommended their voters to abstain, which led to the victory of the Social Democratic candidate (Reibel 2007: 163). In Heiligenstadt Worbis, a Free Liberal candidate encountered a Social Democrat candidate during runoffs. In this case, an electoral committee of the United Conservative Parties (*Vereinigte Rechtsstehende Parteien*), which included National Liberals, Conservatives, and the Economic Union, told their voters to abstain during runoffs. This led to the victory of the Social Democratic candidate, Cohn (Reibel 2007: 540).

This within-country variation in electoral strategies during runoffs reflects distinct distributions of voter preferences across districts, previous patterns of electoral competition, and so on. One specific form of failed coordination occurred when a right-wing party recommended abstention in the second round and supported neither candidate. This "failed coordination" was most severe if one of the two candidates was a Social Democrat. During the 1912 election, one can identify at least thirteen districts in which a non-socialist party recommended abstention and the Social Democrats eventually won the district in the runoff. Although runoffs offered the *opportunity* to coordinate, the presence of a runoff was not sufficient to assure coordination.

In recent years, Cusack et al. have formulated an alternative economic perspective about the origin of proportional representation. According to this approach, "the choice of electoral systems is endogenous to the structure of economic interests" (Cusack et al. 2007: 388). The key structural economic conditions that are hypothesized to generate variation in electoral outcomes – in other words, the adoption or non-adoption of electoral representation – are the presence of "co-specific assets," or investments in human capital that are jointly made by employers and workers. These authors hypothesize that in economies characterized by "consensual labor relations" and high levels of co-specific assets, economic actors consider majoritarian electoral rules to be potentially detrimental to their long-term economic interests. First-past-the-post electoral systems allow groups with a narrow geographic base to capture political power and enact legislation that could potentially harm actors that had made long-term economic investments. In the presence of significant investments in skills, Cusack et al. predict that the most significant interest groups and the political parties to which those groups are tied will demand the adoption of proportional representation. By contrast, majoritarian institutions persist in economies that have lower levels of co-specific assets. In contrast to the Rokkanian explanations, economic hypotheses about the adoption of proportional representation derive their political predictions about the demand for changes in electoral institutions from the distribution of economic endowments and not from partisan or electoral considerations. Cusack et al. formulate their hypothesis, which links specific assets with proportional representation as follows:

Two broad alternative patterns of labor and skill regulation in industry can be found at this critical period in the early twentieth century. They relate to the question of the control of skill formation and the content of skilled jobs. The first possible alternative, which we find subsequently in each of the PR adopters, was some form of cooperative agreement between business and unions: in exchange for collective bargaining rights and monitoring of skill formation, business would have managerial control of the shop floor and determine training levels. This alternative had major implications for the politics of regulation because skills in this system are co-specific assets. . . . Unions and employers become vulnerable to opportunism and holdup and they consequently need credible long-run guarantees which include an appropriate framework agreement at the political level to underwrite the relevant labor market and social security institutions and rules. The political system has to be such that the agreement cannot be changed by a change of government without the consent of other groups. This requires not just a system of proportional representation to enable the different groups to be represented through parties, but also a political system that allows for consensus decision making in the regulatory areas that concern them. (Cusack et al. 2007: 328)

I interpret this argument as generating two testable empirical implications. First, in countries and regions where investments in specific skills are higher, economic actors seek to establish proportional systems of representation either independently or through their partisan representatives. By contrast, the demand for proportional representation is lower in regions that have lower levels of co-specific assets. Second, regions characterized by higher levels of investment in skills also experience more consensual relations in the industrial sphere and among parties.

Yet despite the straightforward nature of these empirical implications, Cusack et al. have not yet provided a direct empirical test of their theory. In their cross-national analysis, the variable they use to test the importance of co-specific assets is a composite variable that includes measures of the strength of employer associations and the existence of rural cooperatives and preexisting guilds. The other indicator – the strength of employer associations – is a problematic empirical measure. As Kuo (2010) illustrates, most of the employer associations that existed in Europe prior to World War I (and thus prior to the adoption of proportional representation) were established with the explicit goal of repressing labor movements. The existence of a coordinated employer association is not a proxy for harmonious labor relations and co-specific investments, the critical variables of this theory.

Chapters 4 and 5 provided empirical evidence that the presence of co-specific investments was not conducive to cooperative political relations. Significant employer intimidation existed in areas with highly skilled workers. Moreover, the quantitative analysis presented in Chapter 5 suggests that the presence of skills does not reduce the probability of the incidence of electoral fraud.

In a more recent paper, Cusack et al. restated their explanation that links investments in specific assets with the adoption of proportional representation (Cusack et al. 2010). In this paper, Cusack et al. seek to explain subnational variation in the adoption of proportional representation across German regions. Saxony, Württemberg, and Baden are used interchangeably because they are presumably cases of similarly high endowments of human capital. However, Cusack et al. provide no empirical evidence to support this conjecture. At the turn of the century, Baden and Württemberg were relatively underdeveloped regions of the German Empire, and they displayed levels of agricultural employment that were higher than the average levels in the Reich (Hohls and Kälble 1989: 167–187). In 1895, the share of the labor force employed in agriculture in Baden and Württemberg stood at 44 and 45 percent, respectively. The share of agricultural employment for the entire Reich stood at 37 percent. By contrast, Saxony's share of agricultural employment stood at 17 percent. These relative differences in economic development did not change much until around 1905. Similarly, Baden, Württemberg, and Saxony were also quite dissimilar with respect to the endowment in skills in each region. The share of skilled workers in the industrial labor force stood at 36.2 percent for the national level. Although Saxony reached 54 percent, Baden was at 37 percent and Württemberg was slightly below the national average at 36 percent. Thus, the characterizations of nineteenth-century economic realities (based on twentieth-century outcomes) provided by Cusack et al. turn out to be inaccurate. The core explanatory variable (the distribution of asset-specific investments) takes different values across these regions. As such, it cannot serve as the common explanation for subnational electoral reforms.

   Although the debate between economic and political explanations of the adoption of proportional representation has occupied a visible place in prominent publications, it has not yet been resolved. Quite the contrary. This inconclusiveness has several causes. The link between the theoretical concepts and the data has been tenuous. Significant ambiguity exists about what constitutes electoral coordination and how it should be operationalized. Many of the existing tests of the first Rokkanian hypothesis have only assessed the effects of variation in national-level competitiveness on the probability of the transition to proportional representation. This remains an imperfect assessment of the first Rokkanian hypothesis, which must be tested using more disaggregated subnational and district-level measures. Similarly, existing studies have not yet assessed whether the presence of co-specific assets affects the probability of support for proportional representation.

9.3. A THEORETICAL REFORMULATION OF THE ROKKANIAN HYPOTHESES

The two Rokkanian hypotheses locate the prime determinant of legislators' calculations about the attractiveness of different electoral systems at different levels of analysis: the individual district versus the party. The first hypothesis highlights electoral vulnerabilities at the level of the district. In this hypothesis, the general contestation in a race, the availability or absence of coalition partners, the strength of the contender on the left, and the potentially scarring experience of a runoff are more likely to affect the decision of a politician about whether or not to support changes in electoral institutions. By contrast, the second political hypothesis locates the important determinants at the level of the party. Partisan preferences about the desirability of different electoral rules are influenced by the attractiveness (or unattractiveness) of the way in which the policy status quo allocates votes to seats. In their calculations about the relative attractiveness of different electoral rules, politicians are constrained both by district-specific factors and by the general beliefs held by their party. The partisan and district-level incentives can reinforce each other to support a particular electoral rule, or they can come into conflict. Consider the case of a politician representing a right-wing party who experiences an unfavorable distribution of votes to seats and who has been elected by a narrow margin in a runoff against a Social Democratic opponent. For this particular politician, the constituency-level incentives and the partisan incentives reinforce each other, and one expects the politician to support the adoption of proportional representation. Partisan and district-specific electoral incentives may, however, come into conflict. Consider a politician from the same party who is elected by a large margin without facing any significant competition from the left. In this case, the district-level incentives push the politician toward supporting the policy status quo, whereas the partisan incentives push the politician toward supporting changes in electoral institutions.

By hypothesizing that the two political explanations about the origins of proportional representation highlight political incentives located at different levels of analysis, I challenge a number of statements made by Rokkan. Instead of viewing the two political hypotheses as separate roads to proportional representation that were undertaken by different countries, I hypothesize that both can be present within the same country. The two hypotheses specify different constraints on the behavior of legislators. To put this point more starkly, contra Rokkan, I argue that there are not two roads to proportional representation; rather, there are two distinct sets of political constraints on the behavior of politicians that operate at the level of the district and the level of the party, respectively. A legislator-based account of the origins of proportional representation allows us to disentangle the relative effects of these two constraints.

To test the implications of the first Rokkanian hypothesis, I examine the consequences of district-specific factors on the support for the adoption of proportional representation. I hypothesize that three variables that were linked to the contestability of a race were likely to affect the legislator's support for changes in electoral institutions. The first is whether the politician was elected in the first round or in runoffs. All other things being equal, I hypothesize that politicians who were elected in runoffs were more vulnerable than politicians who were elected during the first round. Runoffs are themselves an indicator of coordination difficulties among parties on the right. As such, I hypothesize that politicians on the right who were elected during runoffs were more likely to support changes in electoral institutions than were politicians who were elected during the first round. A second district-specific factor that was likely to affect preferences toward electoral institutions is the margin of victory. All other things being equal, I hypothesize that politicians who were elected in races with larger margins were more likely to support the policy status quo than were politicians who were elected in races with narrower margins. A final prediction of the first Rokkanian hypothesis is that the magnitude of the threat of the Social Democratic Party (as measured by the vote share of the Social Democratic candidate during the first round) was likely to increase support for changes in electoral institutions.

I include three variables to test for these hypotheses that seek to examine the relationship between the electoral vulnerability in a district and support for changes in electoral institutions. The first variable takes the value of 1 if the politician was elected during runoffs (SECOND). The second variable (MARGIN) is a measure of the margin of victory during the decisive electoral round. Finally, I control for the vote share of the Social Democratic candidate.

When combined, these variables allow me to capture only the theoretical expectations laid out by the first Rokkanian hypothesis: they capture

TABLE 9.2. *Vote-Seat Disproportionality for the Largest Parties in the Reichstag during the 1912 Election*

Party	Vote Share	Seat Share	Disproportionality	Prediction of Rokkan II
SPD	34.8	27.7	−7.1	Support of PR
Zentrum	16.8	22.9	6.1	Opposition to PR
National Liberals	13.6	11.3	−2.3	Support of PR
Conservatives	11.6	14.1	2.5	Opposition to PR
Free Liberals	13.1	10.6	−2.5	Support of PR
Minorities	4.5	8.3	3.8	Opposition to PR

Sources: Reibel (2007) and www.wahlen-in-deutschland.de.

district-specific electoral constrains. But they remain insufficient for capturing the full set of political constraints on and considerations of the politician. To understand the latter, we need to examine partisan considerations about the effect of the electoral formula on the political fate of the party. I turn to a discussion of these considerations in the next section.

9.4. PARTISAN PREFERENCES ABOUT CHANGES IN ELECTORAL RULES

The predictions of Rokkan's second political hypothesis occur at the level of the party. In this hypothesis, the key variable likely to affect the preferences of parties about the adoption of proportional representation was the disproportionality in the allocation of votes to seats under existing electoral rules. The hypothesis is straightforward: parties that benefited from the current allocation of votes to seats (by obtaining a higher seat share than vote share) were likely to favor the policy status quo. By contrast, parties that lost from the allocation of votes to seats were likely to favor changes in electoral institutions and the adoption of proportional representation.

Table 9.2 presents descriptive information about the effects of the vote-seat disproportionality for the major political parties during the 1912 elections to the Reichstag. Deputies elected at this time adopted legislation that introduced proportional representation. Table 9.2 groups existing deputies into six partisan families, which include Social Democrats (who at the time were the largest parliamentary group in the Reichstag), the Zentrum, National Liberals, Free Liberals, Conservatives, and parties representing minorities (such as Poles or Alsace independents). Column 2 presents information about the number of votes cast for these candidates, and Column 3 includes information about the number of seats held by that respective party during the final session of the Reichstag. Column 4 presents the measure of vote-seat disproportionality, and Column 5 lists the prediction about that party's willingness to support changes in electoral institutions.

As Table 9.2 illustrates, the SPD experienced the most unfavorable ratio in the allocation of votes to seats. Industrialization, which led to the concentration of voters in urban areas, aggravated the disproportionality experienced by the Social Democratic Party (Duverger 1963: 375;). The disproportionality worsened from −2.6 percent in 1871 to −7.1 percent in 1912. As a result, the SPD became the staunchest advocate for the introduction of proportional representation. During the period leading up to World War I, Social Democratic candidates cosponsored legislation that recommended the introduction of proportional representation in national elections to the Reichstag and actively advanced similar proposals during discussions of electoral reforms for the subnational parliaments. Many studies of the adoption of proportional representation have assumed that the SPD was a priori supportive of changes in electoral rules, an assumption that has been criticized by Penades (2008) and Ahmed (2010). Taking the vote-seat disproportionality into account allows us to theoretically derive the preferences of the Social Democrats.

As discussed in Section 9.1, the Free Liberals and the National Liberals were the two parties on the right that had experienced the most significant losses in the allocation of votes to seats during the final elections of the Reich. During the 1912 election, the disproportionality index for the Free Liberal Party was −2.5 percent, and for the National Liberals it was −2.3 percent. In contrast to the Social Democrats, who had been disfavored by the allocation of votes to seats during every election in the period, the negative vote-seat disproportionality was a more recent phenomenon for the two liberal parities. Section 9.1 discussed how the leaders of these two parties embraced the proposal for changes in electoral rules much later than the Social Democrats. The question about the advantages of electoral reforms remained the subject of significant intra-party disagreement (Gagel 1958: 125–141). For Free Liberals, the push for the adoption of proportional representation originated with party leaders from southern German states, where the presence of Catholic minorities in some districts could lead to the waste of Free Liberal votes under the existing single-member electoral system (Simon 1969).

The two large political parties on the right that gained from the allocation of votes to seats were the Zentrum and the Conservatives. Leaders from both parties understood the electoral advantages of existing electoral institutions and rejected the introduction of proposals calling for the adoption of proportional representation (on the Zentrum, see Penades 2011; on the Conservatives, see Kühne 1994). This opposition to any reform of the electoral system was one of the issues that led these two parties – which had been bitter enemies during the *Kulturkampf* – to create the "black-blue" electoral alliance during the 1912 election (Bertram 1964; Reibel 2007).

An internal report commissioned by the German Ministry of the Interior in the immediate aftermath of the 1912 election noted the varied rates of success that different parties on the right had in the translation of their votes into seats. The report observed that whereas the "Liberal Party obtained more than

3 million votes in 1912, it was able to obtain only 4 seats in the first round, [and] the Zentrum obtained more than 80 seats with only 2 million votes. The explanation for this fact," the report noted, "is that there are no areas where there are only Liberals; rather, there are areas where there are Liberals and either Conservatives or Zentrum or Social Democrats" (Bundesarchiv Berlin Lichterfeld R 1501: 192–193). Prominent liberal politicians also noted the worsening vote-seat disproportionality encountered by their parties and began to advocate the adoption of proportional representation (Brandenburg 1917: 30; Gagel 1958: 128).

The Social Democrats had militated for changes in electoral institutions beginning with the 1891 Erfurt Congress. By contrast, Free Liberal and National Liberal politicians only began to advocate the adoption of proportional representation much later (Gagel 1958). This shift in position on the desirability of electoral reforms by these two parties on the right guaranteed the formation of an encompassing political coalition in support of the adoption of proportional representation. The political factor that motivated this change in strategy by these two parties on the right was the worsening of their vote-seat disproportionality.

The predictions of the second Rokkanian hypothesis for the preferences toward the reform of electoral institutions are supported by information from the party manifestoes. Parties that lost from the allocation of votes to seats (Social Democrats, National Liberals, and Free Liberals) supported the adoption of proportional representation. By contrast, parties that gained from vote-seat disproportionality (Conservatives and the Zentrum) opposed it. How constraining were these desiderata of party leaders on the decisions made by individual legislators during the actual vote for electoral reforms? My empirical analysis allows me to examine whether individual legislators internalized the needs of their respective parties or whether their calculations were affected by district-specific vulnerabilities. To test how the disproportionality in the allocation of votes to seats affected the preferences of legislators, I include a measure of vote-seat disproportionality (SEAT VOTE DISPR.) as an additional control in the analysis of legislators' choices.

9.5. A TEST OF THE ECONOMIC HYPOTHESIS: THE DISTRIBUTION OF "ASSET-SPECIFIC" INVESTMENTS AND SUPPORT FOR PROPORTIONAL REPRESENTATION

Both Rokkanian explanations are political explanations. They locate the source of the demand for changes to electoral institutions in either electoral vulnerabilities at the district level or in partisan calculations. The causal chain presupposed by these hypotheses is relatively short: politicians, it is hypothesized, respond either to their increased electoral vulnerability or to calculations about the translation of votes into seats. By contrast, anti-Rokkanian explanations locate the source of the political demand for electoral change in economic conditions at the district level. The causal chain that links these economic factors with the actions of legislators is long and tenuous. In this alternative explanation, politicians favor the adoption of proportional representation not because it serves an immediate political need but because they expect that proportional representation will produce more favorable labor regulation that will protect the "asset-specific investments" made by employers in their districts (Cusack et al. 2007, 2010). Let us suspend possible questions about the farsightedness of politicians and assume (following Cusack et al.) that this logic captures some plausible political constraint on the activity of legislators. The empirical question that I seek to answer is whether structural conditions at the district level affect the political choices made by legislators once we control for all of the other relevant political factors (Rokkan I and Rokkan II) that presuppose a much shorter causal chain.

Section 9.2 noted that non-Rokkanian approaches have not yet tested the core element of their explanation – which hypothesizes that support for proportional representation can be predicted by high levels of asset-specific investment. We seek to remedy these shortcomings by replacing the imprecise characterizations of variation in co-specific assets with actual measures of human capital development across German electoral districts. For these, I use the measures of skills that are discussed extensively in other sections of the book. In Chapter 5, I construct two measures of the share of skilled workers to industrial workers (SKILL INDUSTRY) and the share of skilled workers to the entire labor force in the district (SKILL ALL). Finally, I also use a measure of skills aggregated at a higher level, which corresponds to the subnational political units of Imperial Germany (SKILL REGION).

9.6. EMPIRICAL ANALYSIS: EXPLAINING INDIVIDUAL-LEVEL SUPPORT FOR THE ADOPTION OF PROPORTIONAL REPRESENTATION

The dependent variable for analysis is the support for the adoption of a bill that recommended proportional representation and "the creation of larger electoral districts" (*Stenographische Berichte des Deutschen Reichstages* 1918: 5962–5964). The bill was approved by a rather narrow political margin of 10 percent of the votes, with 55 percent of deputies voting in favor of it, 42 percent opposing it, and 3 percent casting invalid ballots. The vote in the Reichstag represented the endpoint of an intense (but relatively short) period of parliamentary negotiations over changes to electoral rules for the second chamber of the national parliament. I conducted an extensive search of all legislative bills that recommended the introduction of proportional representation throughout the thirteen legislative sessions of the Reichstag during the period between 1870 and 1912, but I only found such legislative initiatives during the thirteenth Reichstag, which was elected in 1912.

I attempt to solve the puzzle presented by the existing literature about the origins of proportional representation: competing explanations of this political choice differ widely in their postulated causal mechanisms. The test presented in this chapter is decisive in adjudicating among these competing explanations for a number of reasons.

First, it has the crucial advantage of being carried out at the lowest possible level of analysis – the individual level. Subsequently, one can also move further up and aggregate at a higher level of analysis. This allows the researcher to test which level is the salient level of analysis rather than presupposing it. Because the decision to change an electoral system is made by a politician who represents a district, we should be relying on district-specific measures; with this test, one can use the margin of victory in a district instead of relying on a country-wide average to gauge the closeness of vote outcomes. Secondly, it allows us to test for a range of additional factors – most notably, partisan concerns about disproportionality – that have not yet been incorporated into economic models that purport to explain electoral system change. Finally, the measures of the theoretical concepts invoked by various explanations (such as asset-specific investments) are, I believe, more precise than the existing indicators of coordination used in cross-national research. The latter measures are both quite distant from the core variables hypothesized to affect the outcomes ("skills") and also susceptible to measurement error (Kreuzer 2010).

I carry out a full test that includes the salient variables in each of the main hypotheses in the literature, including the second Rokkanian hypothesis. I use predictors originating from all three political explanations: district-specific vulnerabilities and socialist threats (Rokkan I), vote-seat disproportionalities (Rokkan II), and the levels of skills acquired through the vocational training system (Cusack et al. 2010). This is not only the first test that includes all of these variables, but also the first time that these hypotheses have been tested at the district level, the regional level, and the partisan level.

The models presented in Tables 9.3 and 9.4 operationalize all three hypotheses. The test of the second Rokkanian hypothesis is the degree of disproportionality in the translation of votes to seats. I use the dataset on electoral politics in Imperial Germany (ICPSR 1984), which I cross-checked with Reibel (2007), to determine the partisanship of the winning politician in each district.

The measure of disproportionality (SEAT VOTE DISPR.) takes higher values if the share of seats held by each party was higher than its share of votes. Thus, a positive number reflects a party that gained from the existing electoral arrangement. Negative numbers indicate parties whose fortunes might have improved under proportional representation (see Table 9.2). I use three variables to test for the effects of the district-specific uncertainties postulated by the first Rokkanian hypothesis on the decisions of legislators to support proportional representation: a measure of the strength of the SPD in a district (SOCIALVOTE), a measure of the decisive electoral round, which takes the

TABLE 9.3. *Probit Models of the Determinants of Support for Proportional Representation*

Level	Variable	Model 1	Model 2	Model 3	Model 4
Partisan	Seat Vote Dispr.	−0.301***	−0.391***	−0.406***	−0.414***
		(0.307)	(0.056)	(0.058)	(0.061)
District	Social Vote	0.026**	0.026**	0.111**	0.100**
		(0.011)	(0.013)	(0.044)	(0.047)
District	Second*SocialVote			−0.095**	−0.093**
				(0.039)	(0.043)
District	Right Margin* SocialVote			−0.001	−0.001*
				(0.001)	(0.001)
District	Right Margin		−0.003	0.015	0.021
			(0.009)	(0.015)	(0.016)
District	Second		−0.507	1.149	1.197
			(0.469)	(0.822)	(0.862)
Economic	Skill	−3.719	−2.773	−2.487	−3.803
		(3.244)	(3.596)	(3.680)	(4.328)
Control	Catholics		0.008	0.005	0.001
			(0.005)	(0.006)	(0.006)
Control	Non-Agricultural		0.025**	0.024*	0.027*
			(0.012)	(0.013)	(0.015)
	Constant	1.769	−0.079	1.367	0.983
		(1.954)	(2.348)	(2.523)	(2.943)
	Regional Fixed Effects	X	X	X	√
	R^2	0.690	0.713	0.729	0.766
	CPC	95.07%	94.72%	94.72%	96.48%
	N	284	284	284	284
	Ll	−60.555	−56.082	52.871	−45.789
	$p(\chi^2)$	0.000	0.000	0.000	0.000
	BIC	143.706	157.356	162.232	176.313

Notes: Standard errors are in parentheses; *** $p<0.01$; ** $p<0.05$; * $p<0.10$; R^2: McFadden's R^2; CPC: correctly predicted cases; baseline 55.28%.

value of 1 if the politician was elected during the second round (SECOND), and a measure of the closeness of the race between non-socialist parties in the first round (RIGHT MARGIN).

Three additional explanatory variables model differences in economic and social conditions across districts. I use the skill measure (SKILL) to account for the consequences of different investments in co-specific assets, the critical explanatory variable proposed by Cusack et al. The measure of differences in economic development is a variable that captures the share of the labor force not employed in agriculture (NON-AGRICULTURAL). I also measure the share of Catholics (CATHOLICS) in a district to account for the possible

TABLE 9.4. *Hierarchical Probit Models for the Adoption of Proportional Representation*

Level	Variable	Model 5	Model 6	Model 7	Model 8
Partisan	Seat Vote Dispr.	−0.317***	−0.362***	−0.381***	−0.393***
		(0.102)	(0.112)	(0.107)	(0.106)
District	SocialVote	0.033***	0.035**	0.087*	0.088*
		(0.013)	(0.015)	(0.048)	(0.053)
District	Second*SocialVote			−0.072	−0.079
				(0.045)	(0.049)
District	Right Margin* SocialVote			−0.000	−0.001
				(0.001)	(0.001)
District	Right Margin		−0.004	0.006	0.016
			(0.010)	(0.017)	(0.018)
District	Second		−0.965	0.475	0.724
			(0.616)	(1.001)	(1.048)
Economic	Skill	−2.965	−2.774	−2.351	−2.643
		(3.780)	(4.338)	(4.403)	(5.040)
Control	Catholics		−0.001	−0.004	−0.008
			(0.008)	(0.008)	(0.009)
Control	Non-agricultural		0.021	0.020	0.021
			(0.013)	(0.013)	(0.016)
	Constant	1.001	0.306	−0.609	0.978
		(2.299)	(2.920)	(3.026)	(3.366)
	$(\ln \sigma_j^2)$	0.007	0.089	−0.070	−0.169
		(0.856)	(0.851)	(0.870)	(0.930)
	Regional Fixed Effects	X	X	X	√
	CPC	95.07%	95.07%	95.07%	96.13%
	N	284	284	284	284
	Ll	−50.375	−47.643	−45.907	−40.987
	$p(\chi^2)$	0.000	0.003	0.003	0.007
	BIC	128.995	146.127	153.951	172.358

Notes: Standard errors are in parentheses; *** $p<0.01$; ** $p<0.05$; * $p<0.10$; R^2: McFadden's R^2; CPC: correctly predicted cases, baseline 55.28%.

effects of religious heterogeneity. This measure is consistent with cross-national analyses of the effects of religious fragmentation on the probability of adopting proportional representation (Boix 1999).

I estimate four different model specifications. In all of the models, the outcome is whether a member of the Reichstag voted "yes" or "no" on the proposal to introduce proportional representation. All four models are presented in Table 9.3 The first specification, Model 1, is a probit model that includes variables relating to the three theoretically interesting concepts: the vote-seat disproportionality, the strength of left parties, and the average skill level in a district. The second specification, Model 2, adds a number of controls for the tightness of the election in a district (RIGHT MARGIN, SECOND) as well as the controls for the Catholic population (CATHOLICS) and for the share of the labor force not employed in agriculture (NON-AGRICULTURAL). The third model also includes two interactions, one between SOCIALVOTE and SECOND and one between RIGHT MARGIN and SOCIALVOTE. These interactions reflect the theoretical argument that when politicians are elected in a second round, their district is already competitive. The strength of the left parties or the right margin should therefore add less to their propensity to support proportional representation than it would have if they had been elected in the first round. Finally, in Model 4, I also include regional fixed effects as an illustration of the robustness of the results.

As hypothesized, one finds a negative effect for vote-seat disproportionality across all specifications. The more disadvantageous the vote-seat ratio under majoritarian elections was for a party, the more likely it was that its members would support the adoption of proportional representation (Rokkan II). An increase in the strength of left parties in a district increased the likelihood that the politician would support a change in electoral rules (Rokkan I). Finally, the average skill level in a district had no effect on the willingness of the representative to support changes in electoral institutions. A comparison of the estimates from Model 2 (without interactions) and Model 3 (with interactions) shows how the size of the coefficient for SOCIALVOTE more than triples, whereas the interaction with SECOND is negative and significant. The explanation for the increase in the size of the coefficient for SOCIALVOTE is that we now allow the model to have two different effects for SOCIALVOTE: one for those politicians elected in the first round and one for those politicians elected in the second round. The left threat exerted an effect for politicians who were elected in the first round, whereas those representatives who had to face a runoff were already in competitive districts and the left threat should have affected them less. The change in SOCIALVOTE from Model 2 to Model 3 is consistent with the theoretical predictions of the first Rokkanian hypothesis. Finally, adding fixed effects does not change the estimates in any meaningful way, with the exception of the interaction between RIGHT MARGIN and SOCIALVOTE which achieves statistical significance. A χ^2 test of whether SECOND and SECOND*SOCIALVOTE are significant predictors or not yields a test statistic of 13.38 and a p-value of 0.001 based on Model 3 (for Model 4, χ^2 is 10.24 and yields a p-value of 0.005).

To fully illustrate these effects, I present a graph of predicted probabilities to clarify the interaction effect. Figure 9.1 plots the predicted probabilities for two hypothetical cases where the only difference is that one legislator was elected in the first round and the other was elected in a runoff. Simulation results rest on estimates from Model 3, and the predicted probabilities are displayed with a one standard deviation. The marginal effect of the strength of the SPD in a district is positive and significant. In addition, the magnitude

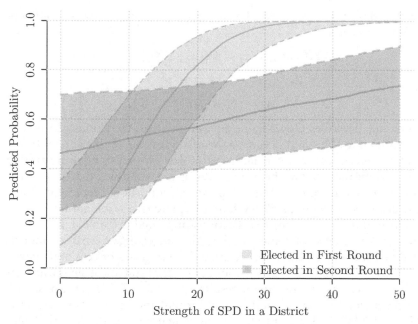

FIGURE 9.1. Support for the adoption of proportional representation.

of the effect is stronger in those districts which did not require a runoff election.

Finally, I turn to the economic predictors. In all specifications, I find that the average skill ratio of a district had no significant influence on the probability of a legislator to vote in favor of proportional representation. Although I find an effect for economic modernization, this effect is not robust and disappears in alternative model specifications. The non-finding for SKILL does not depend on the inclusion of NON-AGRICULTURAL: all models support the null hypothesis that there is no relationship between the probability of a "yes" vote and the average skill level.

The two Rokkanian arguments do not apply to the same level of analysis. The left threat is a district-level variable, whereas the vote-seat disproportionality is a party-level variable. To take these different levels fully into account empirically, I reestimate Models 1 through 4 with new specifications that take the hierarchical data structure into account (Steenbergen and Jones 2002; Gelman and Hill 2007). Table 9.4 presents the estimation results for hierarchical probit models where the first level is the district level and the second level is the partisan level.

Again, the outcome variable in both models is the vote of members of the German Reichstag. The specification is the same as in the models presented in Table 9.3, with the exception that I model the vote-seat disproportionality (SEAT VOTE DISPR.) as a level two variable and I include a random effects variable that differs across parties. Let subscript i denote legislators and subscript j denote parties:

$$\Pr(Vote_{ij} = 1) = \phi(\beta_{oj} + \beta X_{ij})$$

$$\beta_{oj} = \alpha_j + \alpha_1 SVD_j + u_j$$

$$u_j \sim (N(o, \sigma_u)$$

The first line describes the level one equation where Xij denotes the matrix of explanatory variables and β is a vector of regression coefficients with the same number of elements as explanatory variables. The substantive effects and statistical significance of the three most important variables that model the three competing explanations of the adoption of proportional representation – vote-seat disproportionality, skill level, and left strength – remain unchanged when compared to the previous specifications presented in Table 9.3.

Moreover, the effects of these variables do not change across all models presented in Table 9.4. In these specifications, the measure of economic development (NON-AGRICULTURAL) no longer reaches statistical significance at conventional levels, as opposed to the results reported in Table 9.3. The coefficients of the interactions between the second round and the Social Democratic vote (SECOND*SOCIALVOTE) and the right margin and the Social Democratic vote (RIGHT MARGIN*SOCIALVOTE) also do not reach statistical significance. These changes notwithstanding, we find that the tests of the relevant theoretical hypotheses remain unchanged. The skill level in a district had no effect on the probability of whether a legislator in the Reichstag would support a change in the electoral system. By contrast, political variables exercised considerable effect. Increases in vote-seat disproportionality and the strength of left-wing candidates competing in a district increased the probability of support for the adoption of proportional representation.

Figure 9.2 presents predicted probabilities of legislator support for changes in the electoral system. The darker curve presents the predicted probability of support for proportional representation by a legislator representing the National Liberal Party as a function of the level of electoral strength of the Social Democratic challenger (left threat). The blue curve represents similar probabilities for a candidate representing the Zentrum.

National Liberal legislators were more likely to support a change in the electoral system even when there was no left threat at all. This can be explained by the unfavorable allocation of votes to seats experienced by this party during the 1912 election. By contrast, a hypothetical legislator representing the Zentrum found the existing electoral rules more attractive. The Zentrum, a party with strong regional strongholds in Bavaria, Baden, and the Ruhr, benefited from the allocation of votes to seats under the existing electoral rules throughout the Imperial Period. During the 1912 elections, the Zentrum ended up receiving a surplus in the allocation of seats (of 6.1 percent). Despite these differences across parties, the plot reveals that an increase in the left-wing threat increased

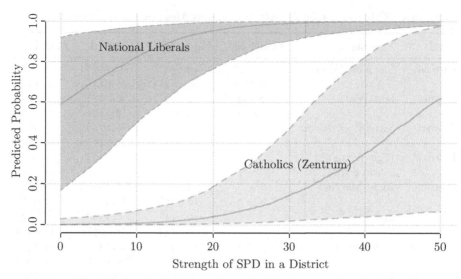

FIGURE 9.2. The relationship between district-level SPD strength and political support for proportional representation.

the probability of support for changes in electoral rules for both National Liberal and Zentrum representatives.

One might object to the operationalization of the level of skills at the district level and hypothesize instead that the effect of skills on the demand for proportional representation operated at the party level. According to that hypothesis, individual representatives might be responsive even when their own districts were not endowed with a high skill level but most of the other members of their party came from districts with above-average skill levels. In Table 9.5, I provide estimation results for an operationalization that aggregates average skill levels at the partisan level for each party (the average of the skill levels for all districts held by a party) and add this variable as a party-level variable to the hierarchical model. The results are substantively similar to the models presented in Table 9.3. There is a negative and significant effect for vote-seat disproportionality, a positive and significant effect for the strength of the left in a district, and no relationship between the skill level and the propensity to support proportional representation.

9.7. PARTY DEFECTION AND LEFT THREAT

The two political variables that influenced the political decisions of legislators – the left threat in individual districts and party interests – reinforce each other on some occasions, but on other occasions, they pull in different directions. In this section, I examine those cases in which legislators defected from their

TABLE 9.5. *Robustness Checks with Skill Levels Measured at the Party Level*

Level	Variable	Model 5d	Model 6d	Model 7d	Model 8d
Partisan	Seat Vote Dispr.	−0.291**	−0.351***	−0.358***	−0.365***
		(0.119)	(0.134)	(0.124)	(0.122)
District	SocialVote	0.034***	0.036**	0.088*	0.089*
		(0.013)	(0.015)	(0.048)	(0.053)
District	Second*SocialVote			0.074*	−0.081
				(0.045)	(0.050)
District	Right Margin* SocialVote			−0.000	−0.001
				(0.001)	(0.001)
District	Right Margin		−0.005	0.006	0.014
			(0.009)	(0.017)	(0.018)
District	Second		−0.941	0.538	0.794
			(0.614)	(1.003)	(1.059)
Economic	Skill Party Level	−33.058	−15.334	−30.286	−35.350
		(84.592)	(91.136)	(84.120)	(82.461)
Control	Catholics		0.001	−0.003	−0.006
			(0.007)	(0.007)	(0.008)
Control	Non-Agricultural		0.023*	0.021	0.021
			(0.013)	(0.013)	(0.015)
	Constant	18.849	7.646	15.857	20.308
		(50.160)	(54.107)	(49.904)	(48.898)
	$(\ln \sigma_j^2)$	−0.041	0.094	−0.101	−0.212
		(0.860)	(0.854)	(0.878)	(0.942)
	Regional Fixed Effects	X	X	X	$\checkmark$
	CPC	94.72%	94.01%	95.07%	96.13%
	N	284	284	284	284
	Ll	−50.606	−47.832	−45.984	−41.033
	$p(\chi^2)$	0.000	0.004	0.003	0.006
	BIC	129.456	146.505	154.107	172.450

Notes: *** $p<0.01$; ** $p<0.05$; * $p<0.10$; R^2: McFadden's R^2; $E(y) = 0.553$.

party position and voted against the party's interest. Can such defections be explained by district-level motivations?

To illustrate how district-level and partisan considerations can come into conflict with each other, consider the case of politicians from the two parties opposing the adoption of proportional representation – the Zentrum and the Conservative Party – who faced a strong Social Democratic threat in their district. In those cases, partisan considerations pulled the politicians toward supporting existing electoral rules, and district-level calculations pulled them in the direction of changes in the electoral system. The defection of these politicians from the position advocated by their party can be explained by district-level competition. This was the case, for example, of Eugen Schatz, a

TABLE 9.6. *Explaining Party Defection*

Variable	Model 9	Model 10	Model 11	Model 12	Model 13
Social Vote	0.092**		0.118**		0.110**
	(0.040)		(0.052)		(0.052)
Skill		−18.703		−15.080	−12.926
		(12.452)		(13.562)	(15.403)
Right Margin			0.006	−0.018	0.012
			(0.026)	(0.027)	(0.028)
Non-Agricultural			0.002	0.018	−0.009
			(0.032)	(0.030)	(0.036)
Catholics			−0.058	−0.025	−0.067
			(0.043)	(0.044)	(0.045)
Second			−3.116	−2.121	−2.747
			(1.976)	(1.769)	(1.980)
Conservative	−2.911*	−1.840	−5.336	−2.759	−5.983
	(1.599)	(1.482)	(3.549)	(3.454)	(3.922)
Constant	−3.754***	8.769	0.554	8.811	9.473
	(0.883)	(7.251)	(3.522)	(10.099)	(11.487)
N	108	108	108	108	108
Ll	−14.871	−21.940	−2.401	−9.802	−4.560
$p(\chi^2)$	0.040	0.146	0.202	0.500	0.323
BIC	43.789	57.927	37.577	52.378	46.577

Notes: Standard errors are in parentheses; *** $p<0.01$; ** $p<0.05$; * $p<0.10$; logit model with penalized maximum likelihood function, "firthlogit" (Firth 1993).

Zentrum politician from Saargemünd-Forbach, who supported the adoption of proportional representation. Schatz had won his seat with a narrow margin against a Social Democratic opponent. Albert Thumann, a politician from Gebweiler and another Zentrum politician who defected from the position of his party, also clinched victory narrowly (with a majority of 55 percent of the votes) against a Social Democratic challenger.

In Table 9.6, I present an array of five different models that explain defection from the party line for the Catholics (Zentrum) and the Conservatives. As hypothesized, the strength of the vote of the Social Democratic candidate in a district (SOCIALVOTE) can explain party defection. All specifications include the alternative explanatory variables proposed by Cusack et al. (2007, 2010), which includes a measure of skill at the district level, as well as the control variables used in previous specifications. I also add a dichotomous indicator for the Conservatives to allow for party differences. Because the variable measuring whether the politician was elected during runoffs (SECOND) causes perfect separation (it perfectly predicts the outcome; see Zorn 2005), I use a logit model based on a penalized maximum likelihood function, which is similar to a Bayesian estimation of the model (Firth 1993).

Regardless of the model specification, all of the results in Models 9 through 13 support the first Rokkanian hypothesis that legislators who faced a stronger left supported the adoption of proportional representation. Those members of the Zentrum and the Conservatives who defected from the party line faced considerably stronger left candidates in their district. Testing the difference in the means of SPD vote share, we find a test statistic of t = 2.60 and a p-value of 0.013. A non-parametric test, randomization inference, yields the same result. The average vote share of the Social Democratic candidates in the districts of politicians who deviated from the party line is significantly higher than the average SPD vote share in any random draw of the Zentrum members. A test based on 100,000 randomizations found a p-value of 0.02 (Gerber and Green 2012).

The fact that those members of the Zentrum who voted against their party line faced significantly stronger left contenders in their districts illustrates the strength of Rokkan's two hypotheses when they are allowed to jointly explain the same observations on the party level as well as on the level of an individual district. The analysis not only establishes that the two Rokkanian hypotheses can explain the overall vote outcome and the adoption of proportional representation, but it also establishes that Rokkan's first hypothesis (which highlights the Social Democratic vote share as a threat) explains the defection from the position advocated by the party by those deputies enjoying an electoral advantage because of existing electoral rules. As such, *contra* Rokkan, my analysis shows that the two explanations are not two different roads that can lead to the adoption of proportional representation; rather, they are arguments that can apply simultaneously at different levels of analysis within the same case.

9.8. CONCLUSION

This chapter presented an account of the final significant electoral reform enacted by the German parliament in 1912. This electoral change replaced the existing majoritarian electoral rules and introduced proportional representation. The narrative presented in the first part of the chapter showed that the position of some parties on the political right – such as the National Liberal Party and the Free Liberal Party – toward the question of electoral reform changed during the first decades of the twentieth century. Until 1900, only the SPD advocated for changes in electoral institutions and for the adoption of proportional representation. Over time, the National Liberal Party and the Free Liberal Party began to advocate for more far-reaching changes in electoral rules. The primary reason that accounted for the dissatisfaction of these parties with the existing electoral system was the worsening vote-seat disproportionality they experienced in the elections after the adoption of the Rickert law. The combination of a costlier control of the electoral choices made by voters (after the introduction of the Rickert law) and an increased electoral strength of the

SPD increased the difficulty of these parties to carry single-member districts. Thus, the Rickert law adopted in 1903 is an important factor that contributed to partisan realignment and to the formation of an electoral coalition in support of proportional representation.

In the central part of the chapter, I explored the determinants of political support for the adoption of proportional representation through an analysis of the roll-call vote of German legislators on the proposal to change electoral institutions. Although this question has occupied an important place in contemporary research, existing studies have examined these questions with rather blunt empirical tools. The current debate about the origins of proportional representation has been framed as a race between the first Rokkanian hypothesis and the economic arguments formulated by Cusack et al. (2007). The debate neglects alternative explanations (which are also Rokkanian in origin) that attribute an important role to partisan calculations (the exception is Calvo 2009). A notable shortcoming in existing studies is the absence of measures of the key explanatory factors hypothesized to affect the choices made in the decisive vote on proportional representation. Most notable is the absence of precise data measuring the core concept of the economic explanation for proportional representation: the co-specific assets. Finally, existing explanations have been tested at a level of aggregation that is uninformative (the national level) rather than at the salient level for electoral competition (the level of the electoral district).

This chapter attempted to resolve some of these problems that have affected the validity of the existing results by shifting the unit of the analysis from the country to the individual legislator. This legislator-centered design has several advantages. It reinstalls individual politicians as the center of the analysis and allows us to simultaneously study how electoral competition at the district level, partisan considerations, and economic conditions affected the decisions made by individual legislators. One can include variables from all of the explanatory theories that have been advanced in the past to explain the adoption of proportional representation, and one can measure them at the appropriate level where electoral competition took place: the level of the electoral district. The empirical challenge for this analysis – which this book has successfully resolved – was to compute measures of skill-specific investments at the level of the electoral district.

I found that political support for the adoption of proportional representation was affected by partisan considerations about the disproportionality in the translation of votes to seats and by the political conditions in a district. The skill composition in a district cannot explain the adoption of proportional representation, regardless of the number of alternative specifications employed. Thus, the empirical analysis presented in this chapter disconfirms the economic hypothesis of the adoption of proportional representation. But given that Germany is a hard case for Rokkanian explanations, the findings presented in this chapter also significantly weaken our confidence in the comparative explanatory power of the economic hypotheses for the adoption of proportional representation in other cases. The findings here also qualified the Rokkanian hypothesis about the importance of the Social Democratic threat as a determinant of the adoption of proportional representation in Germany. Political choices made by German legislators about the adoption of proportional representation can be explained by a combination of partisan dissatisfaction and district-level vulnerabilities. Thus, contra Rokkan, the adoption of electoral representation results from a combination of partisan and electoral considerations and not from district-level vulnerabilities to the Social Democratic threat alone.

10

From Macro- to Micro-Historical Analysis in Comparative Research

In prewar Germany, a silent process of democratization took place during the final decades of the nineteenth century. This process unfolded through a series of piecemeal reforms of the administration of elections that attempted to provide better protection of voter autonomy. Questions about the size of the ballot, the size of the urn, the location of the urn in the voting place, and whether election officials should shake urns before counting ballots carried large political weight. Both opponents and supporters of changes in electoral institutions understood that these micro-regulations in the administration of the electoral process had profound consequences not only for political competition and the relative strength of different parties, but also for more abstract ideals such as electoral freedom.

Empirically, this book examined how this process of electoral reform unfolded in Germany between 1870 and 1912. The adoption of reforms in this electoral authoritarian context resulted from the confluence of two distinct transformations. First, economic changes such as labor scarcity and increases in economic heterogeneity raised the costs of electoral intimidation for private actors. Secondly, in political terms, the rise in strength of parties that lacked access to the repressive state apparatus and to the economic actors with the means to engage in electoral intimidation contributed to an increase in the size of the electoral coalition that supported reforms. The adoption of legislation that protected electoral secrecy, I showed, had important consequences for the rise in political strength of the largest opposition party: the Social Democrats. These reforms also had more indirect consequences for different parties on the right and facilitated the formation of an electoral coalition supporting the adoption of proportional representation.

In what follows, I consider and reflect on the contributions made in this book and their consequences for other cases of democratization. I begin in Section 10.1 by discussing the broader methodological contribution of this study to comparative historical analysis. The empirical analysis presented here persuasively demonstrates the advantages of a method of research that I call micro-historical analysis. I discuss the distinct advantages of micro-historical analysis as compared to two widely used alternative approaches to comparative research: historical institutionalism and quantitative cross-national research. Section 10.2 then discusses the implications of my findings for electoral reforms in political regimes that are situated in a "foggy zone" between democracy and authoritarianism (Schedler 2002). I discuss the implications of my study for three avenues of research in the literature on electoral authoritarianism. The first, in Section 10.2.1, concerns the variety in the strategies of electoral clientelism. The study of Imperial Germany suggests that the menu of strategies used by politicians and their brokers to influence the choices of voters is broader than what is depicted by the literature on political clientelism, which has overlooked the importance of electoral intimidation by private actors. In Section 10.2.2, I next discuss the implications of this book for understanding the growth of political opposition in electoral authoritarian contexts. Finally, in Section 10.2.3, I discuss the implications of this study for the adoption of electoral reforms that reduce opportunities for vote buying and intimidation and that democratize political practices in other contexts.

10.1. MICRO-HISTORICAL ANALYSIS IN COMPARATIVE RESEARCH

In this book, I examined the economic and political determinants of reforms leading to the democratization of electoral practices by increasing the autonomy of voters. By drawing on a wealth of historical data that was previously unavailable, I examined the relative importance of economic conditions, political variables, and partisan concerns on the support of German legislators for these electoral reforms. The mode of empirical analysis proposed in this book can be referred to as "micro-historical analysis." Such an empirical analysis differs in important ways from the two dominant approaches in comparative research. These include macro-historical analysis (or historical institutionalism), on the one hand, and cross-national analysis, on the other hand. Section 10.2 discusses the unique advantages of micro-historical analysis over these alternative modes of inquiry.

The unit of analysis in micro-historical studies is the individual district, instead of larger political unit such as a country or a region. This approach incorporates a long-standing recommendation made by Maurice Duverger (1969) and, more recently, Gary Cox (1997) for district-centered empirical analysis. As these scholars persuasively argue, political competition is first and foremost a district-level variable. Shifting the analysis from the national level to the district level is desirable because it allows scholars to investigate the consequences of a variety of dimensions of electoral competition on politicians' support for particular reforms. Such dimensions of electoral competition include the margin of victory, the effective number of candidates, the strength of the opposition candidates, and so on. As this study demonstrated, these distinct dimensions of electoral competition may have different and offsetting effects on the preferences of politicians for electoral reforms. By contrast, studies that rely on a cross-national analysis of a small number of countries lack valid measures of electoral competition and as such are unable to examine a range of important questions about the relationship between political competition and electoral reforms.

Electoral considerations are, however, only one of the factors that influence the decision of a politician to support particular reforms. Politicians' calculations are also affected by the economic conditions in a district. In the case of the particular reforms that were examined in this book, the economic conditions in a district affected politicians' preferences about electoral reforms by influencing the relative costs of electoral intimidation. Macro-historical analyses have developed a number of propositions about the impact of economic conditions on the probability of a transition to democracy and have conducted empirical tests of these arguments using national-level data. Given that these studies have not examined the importance of political factors in accounting for the adoption of electoral reforms, the empirical results are only preliminary and may suffer from an omitted variable bias. Micro-historical studies have a decisive advantage over macro-historical studies, because they allow us to examine the interplay of the political and economic factors that contribute to the adoption of democratic reforms.

A third variable that influences the decisions of politicians to support particular electoral reforms is partisanship. Micro-historical analysis again has a distinct advantage over macro-historical approaches, because it allows us to assess the relative importance of partisan factors and district-level variables on the demand made by individual politicians for particular reforms. The relationship can be an interactive one, because particular political conditions in a district may amplify or offset the effects of partisan calculations. The analysis of the determinants of political support for the adoption of proportional representation presented in Chapter 9 demonstrated the advantages of such an approach. Support for changes in electoral rules, I showed, results from an interaction between district-level variables – in the case of Imperial Germany, the Social Democratic threat – and partisan considerations about the disproportional translation of votes to seats. Thus, the advantage of micro-historical analysis is that it allows us to consider the relative explanatory power of variables that operate at different levels of analysis and to take advantage of the hierarchical nature of the data.

The theoretical hypotheses formulated in comparative macro-historical scholarship operate at a very high level of abstraction and are, in fact, compatible with a wide range of mechanisms. Micro-historical studies have the unique opportunity to disaggregate the multiple mechanisms implicit in these explanations by employing empirical measures that are more closely connected to the hypothesized theoretical process. In Chapter 7, I reexamined the propositions advanced by the comparative literature on democratization, which have hypothesized that inequalities in the distribution of land predict opposition to democratic transitions. By disaggregating the various dimensions of rural inequality, I showed that inequality in the distribution of land and inequality in the distribution of employment stood only in very weak empirical correlation with each other in Prussia. Given that higher levels of inequality in the distribution of land did not translate into the political power of landowners over agricultural workers, this variable remains theoretically and empirically uncorrelated with the incidence of electoral fraud or with the preferences of politicians about political reforms. The use of fine-grained measures of different dimensions of rural inequality allowed me to examine the variety of mechanisms by which rural inequality affects support for or opposition to democratic reforms.

The hypotheses formulated by macro-historical studies often presuppose very long causal chains. Consider the theoretical conjecture of the economic (anti-Rokkanian) explanation of the adoption of proportional representation. According to this explanation, politicians from districts with higher levels of skills support the adoption of proportional representation, because they anticipate that proportional representation will result in larger welfare states, which will protect the investments of employers and workers in co-specific assets (Cusack et al. 2007, 2010). Micro-historical analyses can subject these theoretical explanations that presuppose long causal chains to more stringent tests than macro-historical research. By testing these hypotheses at the level of the individual politician – rather than at the country level – this approach can examine how individual legislators weigh these considerations about the long-term effects of proposed institutional changes against more immediate short-term calculations. To return to the example presented earlier in this paragraph, considerations about the possible long-term effects of proportional representation on investments in skills may be one possible factor among the many that a politician may consider when deciding whether to support a change in electoral rules. One needs to evaluate the importance of these considerations against a range of other factors that affect politicians' incentives in more direct and unmediated ways. These include, among other things, considerations about the likelihood of being reelected under existing electoral rules and concerns about the translation of votes into seats for their party. In Chapter 9, I showed that more immediate factors play decisive roles in accounting for the decisions of policymakers about whether to support the adoption of proportional representation and that skills – a proxy for long-term considerations – have no impact on support for electoral reforms. This empirical test, I believe, resolved an outstanding debate in the literature about the origins of proportional representation that could not be resolved with cross-national data alone.

In sum, micro-historical analysis provides numerous advantages over macro-historical research for scholars who are examining electoral reforms or other political decisions leading to changes in the design of institutions and policies. First, this method allows us to examine the interplay of political, economic, and partisan factors on the decisions of politicians. A second advantage of this method of analysis is that it allows us to disaggregate mechanisms that are often aggregated in macro-historical studies and to examine their relative importance for political outcomes. Economic inequality and modernization are multidimensional concepts that affect outcomes through a wide range of mechanisms. As the empirical analysis presented in this book demonstrated, micro-historical analysis allows us to conduct a more disaggregated analysis of the relative importance of these factors. In a number of cases, micro-historical analysis has overturned the results produced by macro-historical research.

10.2. FROM NOMINAL TO SUBSTANTIVE DEMOCRACY: IMPLICATIONS FOR REFORMS IN ELECTORAL AUTHORITARIAN REGIMES

The theoretical propositions formulated in this book inform other political contexts and speak to a range of debates concerning electoral politics in imperfect democracies. The analysis generates new implications for understanding three dimensions of political competition in electoral authoritarian contexts. First, the findings contribute to the literature on electoral clientelism by highlighting the importance of a range of political strategies that have been insufficiently examined in the literature. Secondly, the findings contribute to the understanding of the rise of political opposition in electoral authoritarian settings. Finally, the theoretical propositions in this book can be applied in other historical and contemporary political contexts, which allows us to explain the adoption of similar electoral reforms that democratized electoral practices in other places and times.

10.2.1. The Role of Economic Intimidation in the Menu of Clientelistic Strategies

This book provided a detailed account of the mix of political strategies that politicians and their agents used in their attempts to influence voters' political choices in Imperial Germany. Its findings contribute theoretically and empirically to the vast amount of literature that has explored the incidence of clientelistic practices during elections (Kitschelt and Wilkinson 2007; Stokes et al. 2014). The findings from Imperial Germany contribute to this literature by demonstrating that the range of electoral irregularities and the types of brokers deployed by politicians during elections is larger than previous studies have shown. More significantly, the literature on electoral clientelism has insufficiently examined the political importance of employers during elections.

The findings presented in the first part of this book draw attention to the importance of economic intimidation perpetuated by employers within the broader array of repressive electoral strategies. Employers can exert a remarkably strong influence over voters because of their ability to control wages and employment conditions. From the perspective of voters, the magnitude of the punishment inflicted by employers, which can come in the form of layoffs or a reduction in the future stream of income, can outweigh in importance the magnitude of the punishments imposed by other agents. Similarly, a loss in income or even employment can outweigh in importance the possible positive inducements that are offered to voters in exchange for their support, including bribes, meals, and offers of administrative favors provided by the state. Yet despite the substantive importance of intimidation on the political decisions of voters, this phenomenon has remained hitherto understudied in the literature on political clientelism.

As Chapter 4 showed, Imperial Germany exhibited much higher forms of economic intimidation when compared to neighboring countries. Nevertheless, economic intimidation was prevalent in other European countries, such as Britain and France, as well. In Britain, rural employers were reported to have used ample threats toward their tenants to get the latter to vote for particular candidates (O'Malley and Hardcastle 1869: vol. 6). When describing the mixture of electoral influences in North Durham during the 1868 election, Thomas Nossiter notes that "the newer influences of the coal and ironmaster were just as powerful as the older ones of land. Indeed, in some ways the new industrial influences were greater as the industrialist was less circumscribed by customary or economic retaliation. A collier turned 'union man' could be blacklisted without those second thoughts reserved for the eviction of a good tenant farmer turned radical" (Nossiter 1974: 92).

Economic intimidation was also reported to be a pervasive form of electoral irregularity during the Third Republic in France. Consider some examples of economic intimidation that occurred during the Third Republic. In the second district of Alais (Gard), employers at the local mining company were reported to have pressured voters to support a particular candidate, Ramel. On the day of the election, foremen and other employees of the mining company were stationed close to the polling office to pressure voters to support that candidate (*Journal Officiel de la République Française* 1898: 1877). During the 1910 election in Cantal (Saint Fleur), employers were reported to have distributed ballots with visible signs to their employees and to have threatened to lay off those workers whose ballots were not found when the votes were counted (*Journal Officiel de la République Française* 1898: 1910). During the 1914 election in Albertville (Savoie), members of the Socialist Workers' Federation were threatened with layoffs if the candidate supported by the local company was not elected (*Journal Officiel de la République Française* 1914: 466). In another firm located in the same district, workers who supported the opposition candidate were reportedly fired.

Economic intimidation by employers is not only a phenomenon of the past but one that also regrettably occurs in contemporary elections. During a referendum held in Romania in 2012 on a motion to impeach the president, employers in several localities were reported to have seized the identity cards of their employees in an effort to prevent those employees from voting. During the recent 2013 election held in Bulgaria, owners of mines reportedly pressured voters to support a particular candidate (Mares et al. 2014). In recent joint papers with Tsveta Petrova and Aurelian Muntean, I document the existence of systematic economic intimidation in both Romania and Bulgaria using list experiments, a non-obtrusive technique, to obtain answers to sensitive political questions (Mares and Petrova 2014; Mares et al. 2014). We find that the incidence of economic intimidation differs in systematic ways between economically concentrated localities where one single firm controls both employment and output, and localities characterized by high levels of occupational fragmentation. In Sopot, Bulgaria, a locality dominated by one powerful employer, 16 percent of the voters reported having been pressured by that employer to support a particular candidate during the 2014 election. By contrast, we do not find systematic evidence of employer intimidation in Beloslav – a locality that is highly similar to Sopot except in terms of its level of economic concentration. In Petrila, a mining town in Romania where employment is dominated by one single mining firm, we also found evidence of economic intimidation. These recent studies documenting employer intimidation in two postcommunist countries confirm one of the hypotheses of this book by demonstrating that economic heterogeneity can explain some of the variation in economic intimidation.

What factors lower the incidence of economic intimidation during elections? Economic development alone is insufficient to lower the ability of local employers to coerce voters if development goes hand in hand with economic monopolies. Aside from changes in electoral rules, the study of Imperial Germany points to two mechanisms that may lower the incidence of economic intimidation during elections. The first is the diversification of economic activity. As this book demonstrated on repeated occasions, economic diversification increases the costs of electoral repression for employers and lowers the incidence of such repression. The detailed economic data collected from two waves of the German census demonstrate that the concentration of economic activity across Germany declined over time. This general proposition linking economic diversification with the reduction of economic intimidation echoes some of the propositions made by North et al. (2009: 128) about the importance of market competition in generating "open access orders."

In addition to these slow economic transformations, a reduction in the political power of employers can also result from economic reforms that break up monopolies and infuse economic competition in sectors that had benefited from protectionist barriers. Historical examples of such changes include the reforms that broke up the economic power of the *Zaibatsu* in postwar Japan and the antimonopoly reforms adopted by the Allied Powers in postwar Germany. A study by Leonardo Arriola (2012) points to the importance of economic liberalization – more specifically, banking sector liberalization – for political competition across Africa in recent decades. Arriola's study demonstrates that financial liberalization increased the ability of African entrepreneurs to endorse opposition candidates and facilitated the formation of a coordinated opposition. These changes, in turn, eroded the political power of authoritarian incumbents. Yet a related implication that remains unexplored in Arriola's study and in other research on Africa is that economic liberalization reduced the ability of entrepreneurs to coerce voters. By contrast, in settings where incumbents did not break down local monopolies and maintained close political ties to them, economic liberalization failed to bring about political change.

10.2.2. Variation in Opposition Strength in Semicompetitive Regimes

A further implication of my analysis concerns the determinants of opposition strength in semi-democratic regimes (Levitsky and Way 2002; Schedler 2002; Gandhi and Lust-Okar 2009). Existing studies seeking to account for the variation in the strength of the political opposition in electoral authoritarian regimes propose two distinct explanations. The first invokes the ability of political incumbents to manipulate electoral rules (Gandhi and Lust-Okar 2009). Lust-Okar (2005) discusses the electoral strategies that incumbents employ to allow candidates not affiliated with the regime to compete in local and legislative elections in order to divide the opposition (Lust-Okar 2005). According to Lust-Okar, authoritarian leaders create "divided structures of contestation composed of outsiders who are not allowed to compete and insiders who become more invested in the regime, by modifying the electoral rule concerning the eligibility of candidates to compete during elections" (Lust-Okar 2005; see also Gandhi and Lust-Okar 2007).

The second explanation invokes the ability of incumbents to use the patronage resources of the state to preempt the rise of political opposition (Lust-Okar 2005; Magaloni 2006; Greene 2007; Blaydes 2011). The use of patronage induces citizens to vote in favor of incumbents, despite their political preferences. This contributes to what Beatriz Magaloni calls the "tragic brilliance" of electoral authoritarian regimes. As Magaloni explains, "citizens' choices are free, yet they are constrained by a series of strategic dilemmas that compel them to remain loyal to the regime" (Magaloni 2006: 19). The use of patronage by dominant incumbents to preempt opposition support has been invoked as an important political strategy in countries in the Middle East – such as Morocco, Jordan, and Egypt – Latin America – such as Mexico and Argentina – and Africa (Lust-Okar 2005; Bratton and van de Walle 1997; Beck 2008; Blaydes 2011).

Existing explanations of the variation in opposition strength in electoral authoritarian regimes attribute it to the strategies chosen by the political incumbent. This book advances an alternative explanation focusing on the importance of economic conditions in explaining the variation in opposition strength. In Imperial Germany, incumbent elites attempted to deter voters from supporting Social Democratic candidates by relying on the repressive capacity of employees of the state and employers. In deciding whether to take political risks and support such opposition candidates, voters considered the potential economic losses they might incur for political dissent. This cost was affected by a variety of economic conditions in a district, including the likelihood of employment loss, the probability or reemployment, and so on.

In my analysis of the German case, I found that three economic factors enhanced the willingness of voters to take electoral risks and resulted in greater Social Democratic political strength. The first was the occupational hetero-geneity of a district. Voters in districts with higher economic heterogeneity were more likely to take political risks and support opposition candidates than those in districts with low economic heterogeneity, both because firms faced higher costs of economic repression and also because the voters' alternative employment opportunities were higher. Secondly, I found that voters in labor-scarce areas were more likely to support opposition candidates than those in labor-abundant areas. Finally, I found that prior to the adoption of legislation protecting voter secrecy, higher vocational skills translated into higher levels of electoral support for Social Democracy.

These findings open up new avenues of research for the dynamics of oppo-sition support in electoral authoritarian regimes. The weakness of electoral opposition in many authoritarian regimes may not just be a consequence of the strategies of incumbent elites; rather, it is also likely to be the consequence of the low skill levels of voters, high levels of labor abundance, and high levels of economic concentration. The transition from economic environments char-acterized by high levels of labor abundance and high supplies of low-skilled workers to labor scarcity and high skill levels is an economic transition leading to new political opportunities for voters to withstand the electoral pressures of employers and support opposition candidates. These economic changes, which are at the center of my empirical analysis, also facilitate the growth in political strength of opposition parties in semi-democratic regimes.

10.2.3. The Politics of Electoral Reforms in Democratizing Countries

The findings of this book contribute to our understanding of the formation of political coalitions that support electoral reforms to protect the autonomy of voters. My initial conjecture was relatively straightforward. I hypothesized that the adoption of reforms that democratized electoral practices resulted from a distributional conflict between politicians who had the opportunities and the means to engage in electoral intimidation and politicians who lacked such opportunities. However, the types of resources used by politicians during elections and the variety in the types of electoral irregularities differ significantly across countries. It follows that the factors that influence the calculations made by politicians about the advantages and disadvantages of electoral reforms are also likely to vary in systematic ways across countries. Different types of electoral irregularities result in different cleavage lines over electoral reforms.

To illustrate this proposition, in this section, I discuss the implications of the analysis in this book for understanding electoral reforms in other cases that differ in the modal type of irregularity during elections. Drawing on my findings about the determinants of the coalition supporting electoral reforms in Germany, I formulate some conjectures about the determinants of political coalitions likely to support similar electoral reforms in Britain and France. During the nineteenth century, Britain and France displayed different types of electoral irregularities. In Britain, the dominant type of electoral irregularity was bribing, or vote buying. By contrast, the dominant form of electoral irregularity in France was known as *pression gouvernamentale*, or the heavy-handed intervention of the state during elections. This difference in irregularities, I hypothesize, engendered different types of political coalitions advocating electoral reforms.

In contrast to Germany, the dominant type of electoral irregularity present in British elections was bribery. The Corrupt Practices Prevention Act of 1854 (17 & 18 Vict c. 102) provided a very thorough and systematic definition of bribery and identified seven different types of situations that constituted examples of corruption. Consider just one example of bribery identified in the law:

Every person who shall, directly or indirectly, give, procure, agree to give, agree to procure, offer, promise, promise to procure or promise to endeavor to procure any money or valuable consideration to or for any voters, to or for any person on behalf of any voter to induce any voter to vote or refrain from voting shall be deemed guilty of bribery. (17&18 Vict c. 102, in Rogers 1906: 296)

In the British context, I hypothesize that the main line of cleavage over electoral reforms was that between the politicians who could afford to bribe or treat voters and those politicians for whom such practices were too costly. These calculations, in turn, were affected by district-specific conditions that affected the costs of votes, on the one hand, and by the individual resources of politicians, on the other hand. District-level conditions, such as the size of the electorate or its wealth, are likely to affect the costs of votes and, hence, the calculations of politicians about the desirability of electoral reform. In a recent study on electoral clientelism, Susan Stokes and her collaborators argue that both increases in population and increases in wealth have increased the costs of these illicit electoral practices in Britain during the nineteenth century (Stokes et al. 2014). This implies that politicians from more populous and more developed districts support the adoption of electoral reforms that limit vote buying. However, in addition to these district-level variables, the wealth of politicians is likely to affect their available political resources during elections and their preferences about electoral reforms. Poorer politicians are more likely to encounter a greater resource disadvantage and are thus more likely to demand reforms of the political status quo than wealthier politicians.

In a recent joint paper with Kimuli Kasara, I explored this last hypothesis by examining the determinants of political support for electoral reforms that attempted to limit vote buying in nineteenth-century Britain (Kasara and Mares 2014). Our analysis focused on political support for the Corrupt Practices Act, a reform adopted in 1884 and that was successful in limiting election expenses for bribing and treating voters. Our findings lend support to both hypotheses about the economic determinants of support for electoral reforms and to the hypothesis that a salient cleavage about electoral reform results from differences in the resources of politicians. Consistent with the conjectures formulated by Stokes et al. (2014), we found that politicians from more populous and wealthier districts were more likely to support electoral reforms that limited electoral irregularities. However, in addition to these economic factors, we found that the availability of financial resources was an important predictor of support for electoral reforms. We measured these differences in the resources of politicians by using a variable measuring the resources spent by politicians in their respective races as a share of their total wealth relative to the resources spent by their opponents. We found that resource-constrained politicians who were outspent by their rivals were more likely to support electoral reforms. By contrast, politicians with higher financial endowments were more likely to support the political status quo. This example suggests that the sources of political cleavages over electoral reforms that limit vote buying differ from the sources of cleavages over reforms that limit electoral intimidation. One of the salient lines of political cleavage in electoral reforms that limit vote buying is the one between "rich" and "poor" politicians.

Finally, the case of France provides an important comparative contrast to both Germany and Britain (Pilenco 1930). The dominant form of electoral irregularity in France was *pression gouvernamentale*, which involved the reliance by candidates on employees of the state, who deployed both the positive resources of the state – such as patronage and fiscal favors – as well as state-led negative inducements, such as intimidation. Although the apex of *pression gouvernamentale* was reached during the Second Empire, such practices were prevalent and continued into the Third Republic (Pilenco 1930). The most significant electoral reforms aiming to protect voters from the influences of state employees were adopted in 1914.

France shares some similarities to Germany. In both countries, access to the resources of the state was an important political resource deployed by candidates during elections, and this access varied across parties. In contrast to Britain, where the competition was contested between two parties of roughly equal levels of power, electoral competition in France was marked by severe inequality in the political resources between the different parties. The gradual consolidation of the Republican party during the Third Republic went hand in hand with the entrenchment of Radical Party access to the most significant political resources of the French state. By contrast, the main political competitors – who competed both on the left and on the right of the Radicals – lacked political access to the resources of the state. The implications of this book for the coalition that supported electoral reforms to limit the *pression gouvernamentale* would suggest that politicians who lacked access to the resources of the state were the strongest proponents of these reforms. I expect that the likely members of this electoral coalition were the politicians located at the two extremes of the political spectrum – those politicians affiliated with right-wing parties (such as the Royalists, Bonapartists, and Conservatives), and those competing on the left (such as the Socialists). By contrast, I expect that the centrist Radicals, who benefited from the political status quo, were unlikely to support electoral reforms.

Secondly, I expect that politicians who encountered relatively higher political costs of repression – because of district-specific configurations – were also likely to support electoral reforms. Until World War I – and with the exception of a brief interlude between 1885 and 1889 – the French electoral system was also a majoritarian system with runoffs. In this type of electoral system, politicians who were elected in runoffs and who competed under high levels of political fragmentation faced relatively higher costs of electoral repression than did politicians who competed in districts with a unified right. As a result, I expect that the former type of politicians were more constrained in their ability to use the resources of the state during elections and, thus, were more likely to support electoral reforms.

The process of democratization does not end with the adoption of full suffrage; rather, it only begins with the adoption of these reforms. The political experience of nineteenth-century Europe provides countless lessons that are highly relevant for many current imperfect electoral democracies that are contemplating adopting further reforms of electoral practices. Reforms that protect voter autonomy are self-reinforcing and enduring in the long run only if they are sustained by a combination of economic and political factors that increase the costs of electoral repression for economically powerful actors. This book identified the factors that increase these costs of electoral repression and enhance the ability of the electorate to vote unencumbered by a fear of economic and political retaliation for the political choices they make at the ballot box. This study shares with modernization scholarship the premise that economic factors are central for the consolidation of democratic reforms. It suggests, however, that the relevant economic factors contributing to political democratization are economic diversification and labor scarcity.

References

Archival Sources

Bundesarchiv Berlin Lichtenberg

R 1501/343
Betrachtungen über die Einteilung der Reichstagswahlkreise

R 1501/114455
Sitzung des königlichen Staatsministeriums am 17. Januar 1903

R 1501/114456
Das Klosettgesetz
Zur Sicherung des Wahlgeheimnisses
Zentrum und Wahlrecht

R 1501/114696
Die Kruppsche Arbeiterschaft und die Reichstagswahl in Essen
Die verschwiegene Wahlurne

R 1501/114460
Zur Einführung einheitlicher Wahlurnen
Reichswahlreform
Material über die Festsetzung der Stichwahlen
Stichwahlen und Verhältniswahlen
Die Vorschläge über die Abänderung des geltenden Wahlgesetzes für den Reichstag
Betrachtungen über die Einteilung der Reichstagswahlkreise

R 1501/114470
Das Norwegische Wahlgesetz vom 24. Februar 1900
Anschrift des Ministerium des Innern betreffend den Antrag Hompesch für eine Straf-
    bestimmung gegen die Verletzung des Wahlgeheimnisses
Reichsamt des Innern. 8. Januar 1909. Einführung selbsttätiger Wahlurnen
Wahlurnen. Aufzeichnung von Gallenkamp

R 1501/114475
Aufzeichnung über die am 27. Juni 1910 stattgehabte kommissarische Beratung betref-
fend Abänderungen des Wahlreglements
Minister des Innern. Auf die Schreiben vom 5. Marz und vom 21. Dezember betreffend
die Einführung selbsttätiger Wahlurnen
Eingabe wegen amtlicher Wahlurnen
Wahlurnen (Dr. Gallenkamp und Dr. Schulze)
Urteile über Wahlfahlschugen
Äußerung des Ministers des Innern zu der Frage der Beschaffung einheitlicher Wahlur-
nen für die Reichstagswahl
Votum des Staatsministers Dr. Delbruck zur Frage der Einführung von Normativbes-
timmungen über die Beschaffenheit der Wahlurnen bei den Reichstagswahlen

R 1501/114476
Votum zur Frage der Einführung von Normativbestimmungen über die Beschaffenheit
der Wahlurnen bei den Reichstagswahlen
Entwurf einer Bekanntmachung über die Abänderung des Wahlreglements vom 28. Mai
1870
Geheimes Staatsarchiv Berlin. Preussischer Besitz

I HA Rep 90A, no. 112
Kommissarische Beratung betreffend Abänderung des Wahlreglements
Sitzung des Königlichen Staatsministerium vom 21. Oktober 1910. Beratung der
Einführung einheitlicher Wahlurnen
Normativbestimmungen für die Wahlurnen bei der Reichstagswahl

I HA Rep 90A, no. 307

Legislation

Gesetz betreffend die Verfassung des Deutschen Reichs. 1871. Deutsches Reichsgeset-
zblatt. Vol. 16, pages 63–85.
Wahlgesetz für den Reichstag des Norddeutschen Bundes. Bundesgesetzblatt des Norddeutschen Bundes. Vol. 17, pages 145–148.

Statistical Sources

Occupational Censuses

Statistisches Reichsamt. 1884. *Monatshefte zur Statistik des Deutschen Reiches*. Berlin:
von Puttkammer und Mühlbrecht.
———. Statistik des Deutschen Reiches. 1895. *Statistik des Deutschen Reiches*. Berlin:
von Puttkammer und Mühlbrecht. Vol. 112, pages 351–413.
———. Statistik des Deutschen Reiches. 1897. *Berufsstatistik der kleineren Verwaltungsbezirke nach der Zählung vom 14. Juni 1895*. Berlin: von Puttkammer und
Mühlbrecht. Vol. 109, pages 1–724.
———. Statistik des Deutschen Reiches. 1898a. *Gewerbestatistik der kleineren Verwaltungsbezirke Preussens nach der Zählung vom 14. Juni 1895*. Part 1. Kleinere

Verwaltungsbezirke Preussens. Berlin: von Puttkammer und Mühlbrecht. Vol. 117, pages 1–413.

———. Statistik des Deutschen Reiches. 1898b. *Gewerbestatistik der kleineren Verwaltungsbezirke nach der Zählung vom 14. Juni 1895.* Part 2. Berlin: von Puttkammer und Mühlbrecht. Vol. 118, pages 2–480.

———. Statistik des Deutschen Reiches. 1909a. *Berufs- und Betriebszählung vom 12. Juni 1907. Gewerbliche Betriebsstatistik nach der Zählung vom 12. Juni 1907.* Section VI. Kleinere Verwaltungsbezirke Preussen. Berlin: von Puttkammer und Mühlbrecht. Vol. 218, pages 1–554.

———. Statistik des Deutschen Reiches. 1909b. *Berufs- und Betriebszählung vom 12. Juni 1907. Gewerbliche Betriebsstatistik.* Section VII. Kleinere Verwaltungsbezirke ausser Preussen. Berlin: von Puttkammer und Mühlbrecht. Vol. 219, pages 1–504.

———. 1927. *Einzelschriften zur Statistik des Deutschen Reichs.* Berlin: von Puttkammer und Mühlbrecht.

———. Various years. *Vierteljahrshefte zur Statistik des Deutschen Reichs.* Berlin.

Prussian Statistical Sources

Königliches Preussisches Statistisches Landesamt. 1882. *Preussische Statistik.* Vol. 76c. Berlin: Verlag des Königlichen Preussischen Statistischen Landesamts.

———. 1895. *Preussische Statistik.* Vol. 142b. Berlin: Verlag des Königlichen Preussischen Statistischen Landesamts.

———. 1900. *Preussische Statistik.* Vol. 177c. Berlin: Verlag des Königlichen Preussischen Statistischen Landesamts.

———. 1907. *Preussische Statistik.* Vol. 239. Berlin: Verlag des Königlichen Preussischen Statistischen Landesamts.

———. 1914. *Statistisches Jahrbuch für den Preussischen Staat.* Berlin: Verlag des Königlichen Preussischen Statistischen Landesamts.

Primary Sources

Deutscher Reichstag. Various years. *Stenographische Berichte über die Verhandlungen des Deutschen Reichstags.* Berlin: Verlag der Buchdruckerei der Norddeutschen Allgemeinen Zeitung.

Journal Officiel de la République Française. Various years. *Débats parlementaires. Chambre.* Paris: Imprimerie du Journal Officiel.

Preußen Haus der Abgeordneten. 1855. *Stenographische Berichte über die Verhandlungen des Preußischen Hauses der Abgeordneten.* Berlin: Verlag des Preussischen Hauses der Abgeordneten.

———. 1869. *Stenographische Berichte über die Verhandlungen des Preußischen Hauses der Abgeordneten.* Berlin: Verlag des Preussischen Hauses der Abgeordneten.

Secondary Sources

Acemoglu, Daron, and James Robinson. 2000. Why Did the West Extend the Suffrage? Democracy, Inequality and Growth in Historical Perspective. *The Quarterly Journal of Economics* 115: 1167–1199.

_____. 2006. *Economic Origins of Dictatorship and Democracy*. Cambridge and New York: Cambridge University Press.

Ahmed, Amel. 2010. Reading History Forward: The Origins of Electoral Systems in European Democracies. *Comparative Political Studies* 43(8–9): 1059–1088.

Aleman, Eduardo, Ernesto Calvo, Mark Jones, and Noah Kaplan. 2009. Comparing Cosponsorship and Roll-Call Ideal Points. *Legislative Studies Quarterly* 34(1): 87–116.

Alexander, M. 2000. *Die Freikonservative Partei 1890–1918*. Dusseldorf: Droste.

Anderson, M. L. 1981. *Windthorst: A Political Biography*. Oxford and New York: Clarendon Press and Oxford University Press.

_____. 2000. *Practicing Democracy. Elections and Political Culture in Imperial Germany*. Princeton: Princeton University Press.

_____. 2002. Review of *Democracy in the Undemocratic State. The German Reichstag Elections of 1898 and 1903*. *Central European History* 35(1): 109–111.

Ansell, B., and D. Samuels. 2010. Inequality and Democratization: A Contractarian Approach. *Comparative Political Studies* 43(2): 1543–1574.

Ardanaz, Martin, and Isabela Mares. 2014. Labor Shortages, Rural Inequality and Democratization. *Comparative Political Studies* 47(12): 1637–1669.

Arriola, Leonardo. 2012. *Multiethnic Coalitions in Africa: Business Financing of Opposition Election Campaigns*. New York: Cambridge University Press.

Arsenschek, R. 2003. *Der Kampf um die Wahlfreiheit im Kaiserreich: Zur parlamentarischen Wahlprüfung und politischen Realität der Reichstagswahlen 1871–1914*. Dusseldorf: Droste.

Arsenschek, Robert, and Dan Ziblatt. 2008. *A Dataset for the Analysis of German Contested Elections*. Harvard University.

Aurig, Reiner, Steffen Herzog, and Simone Lässig. 1997. *Landesgeschichte in Sachsen: Tradition und Innovation*. Bielefeld: Verlag für Regionalgeschichte.

Bade, K. 1980. Massenwanderung und Arbeitsmarkt im deutschen Nordosten 1880–1914. *Archiv für Sozialgeschichte* 20: 265–323.

Bajohr, F. 1988. *Zwischen Krupp und Kommune: Sozialdemokratie, Arbeiterschaft und Stadtverwaltung in Essen vor dem Ersten Weltkreig*. Essen: Klartext.

Baland, Jean-Marie, and James Robinson. 2008. Land and Power: Theory and Evidence from Chile. *American Economic Review* 98(5): 1737–1765.

Bartolini, S., and P. Mair. 1990. *Identity, Competition, and Electoral Availability: The Stabilisation of European Electorates 1885–1985*. Cambridge: Cambridge University Press.

Beck, L. 2008. *Brokering Democracy in Africa: The Rise of Clientelist Democracy in Senegal*. New York: Palgrave Macmillan.

Bellot, J. 1954. *Hundert Jahre politisches Leben an der Saar unter preussischer Herrschaft, 1815–1918*. Bonn: L. Röhrscheid.

Benoit, Kenneth. 2004. Models of Electoral System Change. *Electoral Studies* 23(3): 363–389.

Berghahn, Volker, and S. Lässig. 2008. *Biography between Structure and Agency: Central European Lives in International Historiography*. New York: Berghahn Books.

Berman, Sheri. 1998. *The Social Democratic Moment*. Cambridge: Harvard University Press.

Bertram, Juergen. 1964. *Die Wahlen zum Deutschen Reichstage vom Jahre 1912: Parteien und Verbaende in der Innenpolitik des Wilhelminischen Reichs.* Dusseldorf: Droste.

Blais, Andre, Agnieszka Dobrzynska, and Indridi Indriadson. 2005. To Adopt or Not Adopt Proportional Representation: The Politics of Institutional Choice. *British Journal of Political Science* 35(1): 182–190.

Blais, Andre, and Indridi Indriadson. 2005. Making Candidates Count: The Logic of Electoral Alliances in Two-Round Legislative Elections. *Journal of Politics* 69(1): 193–205.

Blaydes, L. 2011. *Elections and Redistributive Politics in Mubarak's Egypt.* New York: Cambridge University Press.

Boix, C. 1999. Setting the Rules of the Game: The Choice of Electoral Systems in Advanced Democracies. *American Political Science Review* 93(3): 609–624.

———. 2003. *Democracy and Redistribution.* Cambridge and New York: Cambridge University Press.

———. 2010. Electoral Markets, Party Strategies, and Proportional Representation. *American Political Science Review* 104(2): 404–413.

Boix, Carles, and Susan Stokes. 2003. Endogenous Democratization. *World Politics* 55(4): 517–549.

Brandenburg, Erich. 1917. *50 Jahre Nationalliberale Partei 1867–1917.* Kalkoff: Schriftenstelle der Nationalliberalen Partei Deutschlands.

Bratton, M., and N. van de Walle. 1997. *Democratic Experiments in Africa: Regime Transitions in Comparative Perspective.* New York: Cambridge University Press.

Brösicke, M. 1907. Die Binnenwanderungen im Preussischen Staat. *Zeitschrift des Preussischen Statistischen Landesamts* XLVII: 1–62.

Buchstein, Hubertus. 2000. *Öffentliche und geheime Stimmabgabe: Eine wahlrechtshistorische und ideengeschichtliche Studie.* Frankfurt: Nomos.

Calvo, E. 2009. The Competitive Route to Proportional Representation: Partisan Biases and Electoral Regime Change under Increasing Party Competition. *World Politics* 61(2): 254–295.

Caramani, Daniele. 2004. *The Nationalization of Politics: The Formation of National Electorates and Party Systems in Western Europe.* New York: Cambridge University Press.

Charnay, J. P. 1964. *Société militaire et suffrage politique en France depuis 1789.* Paris: SEVPEN.

———. 1965. *Le suffrage politique en France: Élections parlementaires, élection présidentielle, référendums.* Paris: Mouton.

Colomer, Josep. 2005. It's Parties That Choose Electoral Systems (or Duverger's Law Upside Down). *Political Studies* 53(1): 1–21.

Cook, Chris. 2005. *The Routledge Companion to Britain in the Nineteenth Century 1815–1914.* London and New York: Routledge.

Cusack, Thomas R., Torben Iversen, and David Soskice. 2007. Economic Interests and the Origins of Electoral Systems. *American Political Science Review* 101(3): 373–391.

———. 2010. Coevolution of Capitalism and Political Representation: The Choice of Electoral Systems. *American Political Science Review* 104(2): 393–403.

Davidsohn, G. 1908. Der Kampf ums Wahlrecht. *Die Neue Zeit*: 97–100.

Diamond, Larry. 2002. Thinking about Hybrid Regimes. *Journal of Democracy* 13 (2): 21–35.

Dowe, D., and J. Kocka. 1999. *Parteien im Wandel: Vom Kaiserreich zur Weimarer Republik: Rekrutierung, Qualifizierung, Karrieren.* Munich: R. Oldenbourg.

Duverger, M. 1969. *Political Parties, Their Organization and Activity in the Modern State.* London: Methuen.

Eley, Geoff. 1980. *Reshaping the German Right: Radical Nationalism and Political Change after Bismarck.* New Haven: Yale University Press.

Fairbairn, Geoff. 1990. Authority vs. Democracy: Prussian Officials in the German Elections of 1898 and 1903. *The Historical Journal* 33(4): 811–838.

Fei, J., and G. Ranis. 1964. *Development in the Labor Surplus Economy: Theory and Policy.* Homewood, IL: Richard D. Irwin.

Fenske, H. 1981. *Der liberale Südwesten: Freiheitliche und demokratische Traditionen in Baden und Württemberg 1790–1933.* Stuttgart, Berlin, Cologne, and Mainz: W. Kohlhammer.

Firth, David. 1993. Bias Reduction of Maximum Likelihood Estimates. *Biometrika* 80(1): 27–38.

Flemming, J., and K. Saul. 1988. *Familienleben im Schatten der Krise: Dokumente und Analysen zur Sozialgeschichte der Weimarer Republik.* Dusseldorf: Droste.

Fremdling, Rainer, and Richard Tilly, eds. 1979. *Industrialisierung und Raum. Studien zur regionalen Differenzierung im Deutschland des 19. Jahrhunderts.* Stuttgart: Klett-Cotta.

Freudenthal, Berthold. 1895. *Die Wahlbestechung.* Breslau: Schletter.

Gagel, W. 1958. *Die Wahlrechtsfrage in der Geschichte der deutschen liberalen Parteien, 1848–1918.* Dusseldorf: Droste.

———. 1994. *Geschichte der politischen Bildung in der Bundesrepublik Deutschland 1945–1989: Zwölf Lektionen.* Opladen: Leske and Budrich.

Gandhi, J., and E. Lust-Okar. 2009. Elections under Authoritarianism. *Annual Review of Political Science* 12: 403–422.

Gawatz, Andreas. 2001. *Wahlkämpfe in Württemberg: Landtags- und Reichstagswahlen beim Übergang zum politischen Massenmarkt (1889–1912).* Beiträge zur Geschichte des Parlamentarismus und der politischen Parteien 128. Dusseldorf: Droste.

Gelman, Andrew, and Jennifer Hill. 2007. *Data Analysis Using Regression and Multilevel/Hierarchical Models.* New York: Cambridge University Press.

Gerber, Alan, and Donald Green. 2012. Field Experiments: Design, Analysis, and Interpretation. New York: W. W. Norton.

Gerlach, H. 1904. Die sogenannte Wahlurne. *Die Nation* 22: 692–694.

Gerschenkron, A. 1946. *Bread and Democracy in Germany.* Ithaca: Cornell University Press.

Grant, Oliver. 2002. *Productivity in German Agriculture: Estimates of Agricultural Productivity from Regional Accounts for 21 German Regions. Discussion Papers in Economic and Social History.* Oxford University.

———. 2005. *Migration and Inequality in Germany.* New York: Oxford University Press.

Greene, K. 2007. *Why Dominant Parties Lose: Mexico's Democratization in Comparative Perspective.* New York: Cambridge University Press.

Günther, Wolfgang, Ernst Hinrichs, Klaus Saul, and Heinrich Schmidt. 1993. *Zwischen ständischer Gesellschaft und "Volksgemeinschaft": Beiträge zur norddeutschen Regionalgeschichte seit 1750: Vorträge eines Kolloquiums zu Ehren von Wolfgang Günther am 14. und 15. Februar 1991.* Oldenburg: Bibliotheks- und Informationssystem der Universität Oldenburg.

Gurwitsch, G. 1910. *Der strafrechtliche Schutz des Wahlrechts.* Leipzig: Robert Poske.

Guttsman, W. L. 1981. *The German Social Democratic Party, 1875–1933: From Ghetto to Government.* London and Boston: Allen & Unwin.

Hall, Peter, and David Soskice. 2001. *Varieties of Capitalism: The Institutional Foundations of Comparative Advantage.* New York: Cambridge University Press.

Hanham, H. J. 1959. *Elections and Party Management: Politics in the Time of Disraeli and Gladstone.* London: Longmans.

Hansen, Hal. 1997. Historical Reflections on the Institutions That Shaped Learning for and at Work in Germany and the United States 1800–1945. PhD dissertation, University of Wisconsin, Madison.

Hatschek, J. 1920. *Kommentar zum Wahlgesetz und zur Wahlordnung im deutschen Kaiserreich.* Berlin: W. de Gruyter.

Herrigel, G. 1996. *Industrial Constructions: The Sources of German Industrial Power.* Cambridge and New York: Cambridge University Press.

Hohls, Rüdiger, and Hartmut Kälble. 1989. *Die regionale Erwerbsstruktur im Deutschen Reich und in der Bundesrepublik Deutschland.* St. Katharinen: Scripta Mercaturae Verlag.

Holftreich, Carl Ludwig. 1973. *Quantitative Analysis des Ruhrkohlenbergbaus im 19. Jahrhundert.* Dortmund: Gesellschaft für Westfälische Wirtschaftsgeschichte.

Höppner, S., and S. Lässig. 2004. *Antisemitismus in Sachsen im 19. und 20. Jahrhundert.* Dresden: Goldenbogen.

Huber, E. R. 1957. *Deutsche Verfassungsgeschichte seit 1789.* Stuttgart: W. Kohlhammer.

ICPSR. 1984. *German Reichstag Election Data 1871–1912.* Ann Arbor: University of Michigan Press.

Iversen. Torben. 2010. Two Paths to Democracy. Working Paper. Center for European Studies, Harvard University, Cambridge, MA.

Kalyvas, S. N. 1996. *The Rise of Christian Democracy in Europe.* Ithaca: Cornell University Press.

Kasara, Kimuli, and Isabela Mares. 2014. Unfinished Business: The Democratization of Electoral Practices in Britain. Paper presented at the 4th Annual Conference of the European Political Science Association. Edinburgh. June 18–20, 2014.

Kehr, Eckart. 1965. *Der Primat der Innenpolitik.* Berlin: de Gruyter.

Kehri, J. 1908. *Das Dorf Schalach, Kreis Zauch Belzig und seine landwirtschaftlichen Verhaltnisse.* Leipzig: Mohr.

Keyssar, A. 2009. *The Right to Vote: The Contested History of Democracy in the United States.* New York: Basic Books.

Kitschelt, H., and S. Wilkinson. 2007. *Patrons, Clients, and Policies: Patterns of Democratic Accountability and Political Competition.* Cambridge and New York: Cambridge University Press.

Klein, T. 1989. *Die Hessen als Reichstagswähler. Tabellenwerk zur politischen Landesgeschichte.* Marburg: N. G. Elwert.

_____. 2003. *Gültig – ungültig. Die Wahlprüfungsverfahren des Deutschen Reichstages*, Marburg: N. G. Elwert.

Konservative Partei. 1910. *Die Preussische Wahlrechtsreform und die Konservative Partei.* n.p.

Kranzmann, Gerd. 1981. Die Bielefelder Arbeiterbewegung im Kaiserreich 1890–1914. In Elisabeth Harder-Gersdorff, ed., *Beitrage zur Geschichte der Bielefelder Arbeiterbewegung*, 60–80. Bielefeld: Osten.

Kreuzer, M. 2010. Historical Knowledge and Quantitative Analysis: The Case of the Origins of Proportional Representation. *American Political Science Review* 104(2): 369–392.

Kühne, T. 1994. *Dreiklassenwahlrecht und Wahlkultur in Preussen 1867–1914: Landtagswahlen zwischen korporativer Tradition und politischem Massenmarkt.* Dusseldorf: Droste.

Kuo, Alexander. 2010. The Political Origin of Firms' Strategies. PhD dissertation, Stanford University, Stanford, CA.

Kupfer, Torsten. 2003. *Geheime Zirkel und Parteivereine: Die Organisation der Deutschen Sozialdemokratie zwischen Sozialistengesetz und Jahrhundertwende.* Essen: Klartext.

Kuznets, S. 1955. Economic Growth and Income Inequality. *American Economic Review* 45: 1–28.

Lässig, S. 1996. *Wahlrechtskampf und Wahlreform in Sachsen, 1895–1909.* Weimar: Böhlau.

Lässig, S., and K. Pohl. 1997. *Sachsen im Kaiserreich: Politik, Wirtschaft und Gesellschaft im Umbruch.* Weimar: Böhlau.

Lässig, Simone, Karl Heinrich Pohl, and James Retallack. 1995. *Modernisierung und Region im wilhelminischen Deutschland: Wahlen, Wahlrecht und politische Kultur.* Bielefeld: Verlag für Regionalgeschichte.

Laufs, Adolf. 2006. *Rechtsentwicklungen in Deutschland.* Berlin: de Gruyter Rechtswissenschaften.

Leemann, Lucas, and Isabela Mares. 2014. The Adoption of Proportional Representation. *Journal of Politics* 76(2): 461–478.

Lehoucq, Fabrice. 2003. Electoral Fraud: Causes, Types and Consequences. *Annual Review of Political Science* 6: 233–256.

Lehoucq, Fabrice, and Ivan Molina. 2002. *Stuffing the Ballot Box: Fraud, Electoral Reform and Democratization in Costa Rica.* New York: Cambridge University Press.

Levitsky, Steven, and Lucan Way. 2002. The Rise of Competitive Authoritarianism. *Journal of Democracy* 13(2): 51–65.

_____. 2010. *Competitive Authoritarianism: The Origins and Evolutions of Hybrid Regimes in the Post–Cold War Era.* New York: Cambridge University Press.

Lewis, W. A. 1954. Development with Unlimited Supplies of Labor. *Manchester School of Economics and Social Studies* 201: 139–192.

Lipset, Seymour. 1959. Some Social Requisites of Democracy: Economic Development and Political Legitimacy. *American Political Science Review* 53(1): 69–105.

Luebbert, G. M. 1991. *Liberalism, Fascism, or Social Democracy: Social Classes and the Political Origins of Regimes in Interwar Europe.* New York: Oxford University Press.

Lust-Okar, E. 2005. *Structuring Conflict in the Arab World: Incumbents, Opponents and Institutions.* New York: Cambridge University Press.

Magaloni, Beatriz. 2006. *Voting for Autocracy. Hegemonic Party Survival and Its Demise in Mexico*. New York: Cambridge University Press.

Mahoney, J., and K. A. Thelen. 2010. *Explaining Institutional Change: Ambiguity, Agency, and Power*. Cambridge and New York: Cambridge University Press.

Mann, B. 1988. *Biographisches Handbuch für das preussische Abgeordnetenhaus, 1867–1918*. Dusseldorf: Droste.

Mares, Isabela. 2003. *The Politics of Social Risk: Business and Welfare State Development*. New York: Cambridge University Press.

Mares, Isabela, Aurelian Muntean, and Tsveta Petrova. 2014. Economic Intimidation in Contemporary Perspective: Experimental Evidence from Romania and Bulgaria. Paper presented at the 4th Annual Conference of the European Political Science Association. Edinburgh. June 18–20, 2014.

Mares, Isabela, and Tsveta Petrova. 2014. Disaggregating Clientelism. Paper presented at the Political Economy Seminar. Duke University.

Mares, Isabela, and Didac Queralt. 2014. Autocratic Taxation: Examining the Adoption of Income Taxes in Prussian and German States. Paper presented at the Annual Meeting of the American Political Science Association. Washington, DC.

Mares, Isabela, and Boliang Zhu. Forthcoming. The Determinants of Electoral Irregularities. *Comparative Politics*.

Mayer, Max Ernst. 1910. Bekämpfung der Wahlumtriebe durch das Strafrecht. *Zeitschrift für Politik* 3: 10–29.

Meyer, G. 1901. *Das parlamentarische Wahlrecht*. Berlin: O. Haering.

Mill, James. 1963. *Essays on Politics and Culture*. Garden City: Doubleday.

Moniteur Belge. August 18, 1894. Materiel electoral.

Moore, B. 1966. *Social Origins of Dictatorship and Democracy: Lord and Peasant in the Making of the Modern World*. Boston: Beacon Press.

Müller, K. 1963. Politische Strömungen in den rechtsrheinischen Kreisen des Regierungsbezirkes Köln von 1879 bis 1900. PhD dissertation, University of Bonn.

Naumann, F. 1906. Kann man Liberale organisieren? In T. Barth and F. Naumann, *Die Erneuerung des Liberalismus: Ein politischer Weckruf*, 20–35. Berlin: Hilfe.

Nipperdey, T. 1961. *Die Organisation der deutschen Parteien vor 1918*. Dusseldorf: Droste.

Nohlen, D. 1990. *Wahlrecht und Parteiensystem: Über die politischen Auswirkungen von Wahlsystemen*. Opladen: Leske and Budrich.

North, Douglas, John Wallis, and Barry Weingast. 2009. *Violence and Social Orders*. New York: Cambridge University Press.

Nossiter, T. J. 1974. *Influence, Opinion and Political Idioms in Reformed England: Case Studies from the North-East 1832–74*. New York: Harper Row.

O'Donnell, A. J. 1974. *National Liberalism and the Mass Politics of the German Right, 1890–1907*. Princeton: Princeton University Press.

O'Donnell, Guillermo. 1996. Illusions about Consolidation. *Journal of Democracy* 7(2): 34–51.

O'Malley, Edward, and Henry Hardcastle. 1869. *Reports for the Decisions of Judges for the Trial of Election Petitions in England and Ireland Pursuant to the Parliamentary Election Act 1868*. London: Steven and Haynes.

Patemann, Reinhard. 1964. *Der Kampf um die Preussische Wahlreform im ersten Weltkrieg*. Dusseldorf: Droste.

Paul, J. 1987. *Alfred Krupp und die Arbeiterbewegung*. Dusseldorf: Schwann.

Penades, Alberto. 2008. The Institutional Preferences of Early Socialist Parties: Choosing Rules for Government. In Jose Maria Maravall, ed., *Controlling Governments: Voters, Institutions, and Accountability*, 202–246. New York: Cambridge University Press.

———. 2011. Electoral Reforms in Early Democracies: The Right Wing. Paper presented at the conference on Historical Development in Europe. Juan March Institute for the Study of Societies, Madrid.

Pilenco, A. 1930. *Les moeurs du suffrage universel en France 1848–1928.* Paris: Choisy-le-Roi.

Pollock, J. K. 1934. *German Election Administration.* New York: Columbia University Press.

Prager, E. 1908. Der Kampf um das Wahlrecht. *Die Neue Zeit* 26(1): 803–809.

Prosterman, Roy, and Jeffrey Riedinger. 1987. *Land Reform and Democratic Development.* Baltimore: Johns Hopkins University Press.

Przeworski, Adam, Michael Alvarez, Jose Cheibub, and Fernando Limongi. 2000. *Democracy and Development: Political Institutions and Well-Being in the World.* New York: Cambridge University Press.

Quante, P. 1933. Die Flucht aus der Landwirtschaft. *Zeitschrift des Koniglich Preussischen Statistischen Bureaus* 3: 277–380.

———. 1959. Die Bevölkerungsentwicklung der Preussischen Ostprovinzen im 19. und 20. Jahrhunderts. *Zeitschrift für Ostforschung* 84: 481–499.

Ramcharan, R. 2010. Inequality and Redistribution: Evidence from US Counties and States 1890–1930. *The Review of Economics and Statistics* 92(3): 729–744.

Ranis, Gustav. 2004. Arthur Lewis' Contribution to Development Thinking and Policy. *The Manchester School* 72(6): 712–723.

Rauchhaupt, F. W. 1916. *Handbuch der deutschen Wahlgesetze und Geschäftsordnungen. Nach dem gegenwärtigen Gesetzesstande des Deutschen Reiches und seiner Bundesstaaten.* Munich and Leipzig: Duncker & Humblot.

Rauh, Manfred. 1977. *Die Parlamentarisierung des Deutschen Reichs.* Dusseldorf: Droste.

Reibel, Carl Wilhelm. 2007. *Handbuch der Reichstagswahlen. Bündnisse, Ergebnisse, Kandidaten.* Dusseldorf: Droste.

Retallack, J. 1988. *Notables of the Right: The Conservative Party and Political Mobilization in Germany 1876–1918.* London: Unwyn Hyman.

———. 1990. "What Is to Be Done?": The Red Specter, Franchise Questions, and the Crisis of Conservative Hegemony in Saxony, 1896–1909. *Central European History* 23(4): 271–312.

Rieger, A. 1914. *Die Landflucht und ihre Bekämpfung unter besonderer Berücksichtigung der ländlichen Arbeiterfrage.* Berlin.

Ritter, G. A., and E. Müller-Luckner. 1990. *Der Aufstieg der deutschen Arbeiterbewegung: Sozialdemokratie und Freie Gewerkschaften im Parteiensystem und Sozialmilieu des Kaiserreichs.* Munich: Oldenbourg.

Ritter, Gerhard A., and Merith Niehuss. 1991. *Wahlen in Deutschland, 1946–1991: Ein Handbuch.* Munich: C. H. Beck.

Rogers, Francis. 1906. *Parliamentary Elections and Petitions. Appendices of Statutes, Rules and Forms.* London: Stevens and Sons.

Rokkan, S. 1970. *Citizens, Elections, Parties; Approaches to the Comparative Study of the Processes of Development.* New York: McKay.

Rollwagen, H. 1901. Zur bayerischen Wahlrechtsreform. *Die Neue Zeit*: 522–524.

Rueschemeyer, D., E. Huber, and J. Stephens. 1992. *Capitalist Development and Democracy*. Chicago: University of Chicago Press.

Sabel, Charles, and Jonathan Zeitlin. 1996. *Industrial Constructions: The Sources of German Industrial Power*. New York: Cambridge University Press.

Saul, K. 1974. *Staat, Industrie, Arbeiterbewegung im Kaiserreich: Zur Innen- und Aussenpolitik des Wilhelminischen Deutschland 1903–1914*. Dusseldorf: Bertelsmann Universitäts Verlag.

———. 1975. Der Kampf um das Landproletariat. Sozialistische Landagitation, Grossgrundbesitz und preussische Staatsverwaltung 1890 bis 1913. *Archiv für Sozialgeschichte* 15(1): 163–208.

———. 1982. *Arbeiterfamilien im Kaiserreich: Materialen zur Sozialgeschichte in Deutschland 1871–1914*. Dusseldorf: Droste.

Saul, Klaus, Karl Christian Führer, Karen Hagemann, and Birthe Kundrus. 2004. *Eliten im Wandel: Gesellschaftliche Führungsgruppen im 19. und 20. Jahrhundert: Für Klaus Saul zum 65. Geburtstag*. Münster: Westfälisches Dampfboot.

Schedler, Andreas. 2002. The Menu of Manipulation. *Journal of Democracy* 13(2): 36–50.

———. 2006. *Electoral Authoritarianism. The Dynamics of Unfree Competition*. Boulder: Lynne Rienner.

Schmädeke, Jürgen. 1995. *Wählerbewegung im Wilhelminischen Deutschland: Die Reichstagswahlen von 1890 bis 1912*. Berlin: Akademie Verlag.

Schofer, L. 1975. *The Formation of a Modern Labor Force, Upper Silesia, 1865–1914*. Berkeley: University of California Press.

Schorske, Carl E. 1955. *German Social Democracy 1905–1917: The Development of the Great Schism*. Cambridge, MA: Harvard University Press.

Schultze, Werner. 1973. Öffentliches Vereinigungsrecht im Kaiserreich 1871 bis 1908. PhD dissertation, Frankfurt am Main.

Schulz, A. 1912. Das Vordringen des landwirtschaftlichen Familienbetriebes und des Kleingrundbesitzes in Ostelbien. *Sozialistische Monatshefte* 16(2): 424–439.

Schwarz, M. 1965. *MdR; biographisches Handbuch der Reichstage*. Hannover: Verlag für Literatur und Zeitgeschehen.

Seeber, Gustav. 1965. *Zwischen Bebel und Bismarck: Zur Geschichte des Linksliberalismus in Deutschland 1871–1893*. Berlin: Akademie Verlag.

Seymour, C. 1915. *Electoral Reform in England and Wales: The Development and Operation of the Parliamentary Franchise, 1832–1885*. New Haven: Yale University Press.

Seymour, C., and D. P. Frary. 1918. *How the World Votes: The Story of Democratic Development in Elections*. Springfield, MA: C. A. Nichols.

Sheehan, James. 1978. *German Liberalism in the Nineteenth Century*. Chicago: University of Chicago Press.

Siegfried, R. 1903. *Die verschwiegene Wahlurne*. Annalen des Deutschen Reichs für Gesetzgebung, Verwaltung und Volkswirtschaft.

Simon, K. 1969. *Die württembergischen Demokraten; ihre Stellung und Arbeit im Parteien- und Verfassungssystem in Württemberg und im Deutschen Reich 1890–1920*. Stuttgart: W. Kohlhammer.

Sombart, W. 1927. *Die Deutsche Volkswirtschaft im 19. und Anfang des 20. Jahrhunderts*. Berlin: G. Bondi.

Spencer, E. G. 1984. *Management and Labor in Imperial Germany.* New Brunswick: Rutgers University Press.

———. 1992. *Police and the Social Order in German Cities: The Düsseldorf District, 1848–1914.* DeKalb: Northern Illinois University Press.

Sperber, J. 1997. *The Kaiser's Voters. Electors and Elections in Imperial Germany.* New York: Oxford University Press.

Stalmann, V. 2000. *Die Partei Bismarcks. Die Deutsche Reichs- und Freikonservative Partei.* Dusseldorf: Droste.

Steenbergen, Marko, and Bradford Jones. 2002. Modeling Multilevel Data Structures. *American Journal of Political Science* 46: 218–236.

Stegmann, D. 1970. *Die Erben Bismarcks. Parteien und Verbände in der Spätphase des Wilhelminischen Deutschlands. Sammlungs-politik 1897–1918.* Cologne: Kiepenheuer und Witsch.

———. 1976. Hugenberg contra Stresemann: Die Politik der Industrieverbände am Ende des Kaiserreichs. *Vierteljahrshefte für Zeitgeschichte* 24(October 1976): 329–378.

———. 1984. The Hugenberg-System – The Organization of a Bourgeois Political Front before the Rise of the Nazi Party – Germany. Holzbach, H. *Archiv für Sozialgeschichte* 24: 791–793.

Steinmo, S., K. A. Thelen et al. 1992. *Structuring Politics: Historical Institutionalism in Comparative Analysis.* Cambridge and New York: Cambridge University Press.

Stock, James, and Motohiro Yogo. 2005. *Testing for Weak Instruments in Linear IV Regressions.* New York: Cambridge University Press.

Stokes, Susan. 2011. What Killed Vote Buying in Britain and the United States? Unpublished Manuscript, Yale University.

Stokes, Susan, Thad Dunning, Marcelo Nazareno, and Valeria Brusco. 2013. *Brokers, Voters, and Clientelism: The Puzzle of Distributive Politics.* New York: Cambridge University Press.

Stokes, Susan, Sven Steinmo, Kathleen Thelen, and Frank Longstreth. 2013. *Brokers, Voters and Clientelism.* New York: Cambridge University Press.

Streeck, W., and K. A. Thelen. 2005. *Beyond Continuity: Institutional Change in Advanced Political Economies.* Oxford and New York: Oxford University Press.

Summerhill. W. 2010. Colonial Institutions, Slavery, Inequality and Development: Evidence from São Paulo Brazil. MPRA Paper 22162. University Library, Munich.

Suval, S. 1985. *Electoral Politics in Wilhelmine Germany.* Chapel Hill: University of North Carolina Press.

Teuteberg, H. 1961. *Geschichte der industriellen Mitbestimmung in Deutschland.* Tübingen: Mohr.

Thelen, K. A. 2004. *How Institutions Evolve: The Political Economy of Skills in Germany, Britain, the United States, and Japan.* Cambridge and New York: Cambridge University Press.

Thompson, Alastair. 2000. *Left Liberals, the State, and Popular Politics in Wilhelmine Germany.* Oxford: Oxford University Press.

Tooze, Adam. 2001. *Statistics and the German State, 1900–1945: The Making of Modern Economic Knowledge.* Cambridge Studies in Modern Economic History 9. Cambridge and New York: Cambridge University Press.

Vanhannen, Tatu. 1997. *Prospects of Democracy: A Study of 172 Countries.* London: Routledge.

Warren, D. 1964. *The Red Kingdom of Saxony: Lobbying Grounds for Gustav Strese-mann, 1901–1909.* The Hague: M. Nijhoff.

Weber, M. 1958. *Gesammelte politische Schriften.* Edited by J. Winckelmann. Tübin-gen: Mohr (Paul Siebeck).

White, D. 1976. *The Splintered Party. National Liberalism in Hessen and the Reich.* Cambridge, MA: Harvard University Press.

Wilkinson, S. 2004. *Votes and Violence: Electoral Competition and Ethnic Riots in India.* Cambridge and New York: Cambridge University Press.

Williams, Willoughby. 1906. *Parliamentary Elections and Petitions.* Vol. 2. London: Stevens and Sons.

Wittwer, Walter. 1983. *Vom Sozialistengesetz zur Umsturzvorlage: Zur Politik der preussisch-deutschen Regierung gegen die Arbeiterbewegung 1890 bis 1894.* Berlin: Studien zur Geschichte.

Wulff, Kurt. 1922. Die Deutschkonservativen und die Preussische Wahlrechtsfrage. PhD dissertation, University of Greifswald.

Zakaria, F. 1997. The Rise of Illiberal Democracy. *Foreign Affairs* 76(6): 22–43.

Ziblatt, D. 2008. Does Landholding Inequality Breed Democratization? A Test of the "Bread and Democracy" Thesis and the Case of Prussia. *World Politics* 60(4): 610.

———. 2009. Shaping Democratic Practice and the Causes of Electoral Fraud: The Case of Nineteenth-Century Germany. *American Political Science Review* 103(1): 1–21.

Zorn, Christopher. 2005. A Solution to Separation in Binary Response Models. *Political Analysis* 13(2): 157–170.

Index

Stephen B. Kaplan, *Globalization and Austerity Politics in Latin America*

Junko Kato, *Regressive Taxation and the Welfare State*

Orit Kedar, *Voting for Policy, Not Parties: How Voters Compensate for Power Sharing*

Robert O. Keohane and Helen B. Milner, eds., *Internationalization and Domestic Politics*

Herbert Kitschelt, *The Transformation of European Social Democracy*

Herbert Kitschelt, Kirk A. Hawkins, Juan Pablo Luna, Guillermo Rosas, and Elizabeth J. Zechmeister, *Latin American Party Systems*

Herbert Kitschelt, Peter Lange, Gary Marks, and John D. Stephens, eds., *Continuity and Change in Contemporary Capitalism*

Herbert Kitschelt, Zdenka Mansfeldova, Radek Markowski, and Gabor Toka, *Post-Communist Party Systems*

David Knoke, Franz Urban Pappi, Jeffrey Broadbent, and Yutaka Tsujinaka, eds., *Comparing Policy Networks*

Allan Kornberg and Harold D. Clarke, *Citizens and Community: Political Support in a Representative Democracy*

Amie Kreppel, *The European Parliament and the Supranational Party System*

David D. Laitin, *Language Repertoires and State Construction in Africa*

Fabrice E. Lehoucq and Ivan Molina, *Stuffing the Ballot Box: Fraud, Electoral Reform, and Democratization in Costa Rica*

Mark Irving Lichbach and Alan S. Zuckerman, eds., *Comparative Politics: Rationality, Culture, and Structure*, 2nd edition

Evan Lieberman, *Race and Regionalism in the Politics of Taxation in Brazil and South Africa*

Richard M. Locke, *Promoting Labor Standards in a Global Economy: The Promise and Limits of Private Power*

Pauline Jones Luong, *Institutional Change and Political Continuity in Post-Soviet Central Asia*

Pauline Jones Luong and Erika Weinthal, *Oil Is Not a Curse: Ownership Structure and Institutions in Soviet Successor States*

Julia Lynch, *Age in the Welfare State: The Origins of Social Spending on Pensioners, Workers, and Children*

Lauren M. MacLean, *Informal Institutions and Citizenship in Rural Africa: Risk and Reciprocity in Ghana and Côte d'Ivoire*

Beatriz Magaloni, *Voting for Autocracy: Hegemonic Party Survival and Its Demise in Mexico*

James Mahoney, *Colonialism and Postcolonial Development: Spanish America in Comparative Perspective*

James Mahoney and Dietrich Rueschemeyer, eds., *Comparative Historical Analysis in the Social Sciences*

Scott Mainwaring and Matthew Soberg Shugart, eds., *Presidentialism and Democracy in Latin America*

Joshua Tucker, *Regional Economic Voting: Russia, Poland, Hungary, Slovakia and the Czech Republic, 1990–1999*

Ashutosh Varshney, *Democracy, Development, and the Countryside*

Jeremy M. Weinstein, *Inside Rebellion: The Politics of Insurgent Violence*

Stephen I. Wilkinson, *Votes and Violence: Electoral Competition and Ethnic Riots in India*

Jason Wittenberg, *Crucibles of Political Loyalty: Church Institutions and Electoral Continuity in Hungary*

Elisabeth J. Wood, *Forging Democracy from Below: Insurgent Transitions in South Africa and El Salvador*

Elisabeth J. Wood, *Insurgent Collective Action and Civil War in El Salvador*